Crisis Counseling with Children and Adolescents

William Van Ornum
and John B. Mordock

Crisis Counseling with Children and Adolescents

A GUIDE FOR NONPROFESSIONAL COUNSELORS
New Expanded Edition

Foreword by Eugene Kennedy

CONTINUUM / NEW YORK

1991
The Continuum Publishing Company
370 Lexington Avenue, New York, NY 10017

Copyright © 1983 by William Van Ornum and John B. Mordock
New material Copyright © 1990 by William Van Ornum and John B. Mordock

Printed in the United States of America

Library of Congress Cataloging in Publication Data

Van Ornum, William.
Crisis counseling with children and adolescents.

1. Crisis intervention (Psychiatry) 2. Child
psychotherapy.   3. Adolescent psychotherapy.
1. Mordock, John B., 1938— .   11. Title
[DNLM: 1. Crisis intervention—In infancy and
childhood.   2. Crisis, intervention—In adolescence.
3. Counseling—Methods.   WS 350.2 V217c]
RJ504.4.V36 1983 1991 158'.3   83-7517 ISBN 0-8264-0474-X (pbk)

The quotation from the poem "Silence" by Langston Hughes on page 53
is reprinted from *Fields of Wonder,* by Langston Hughes,
by permission of Alfred A. Knopf, Inc. Copyright 1947 by Langston Hughes.

TO OUR PARENTS

CONTENTS

FOREWORD

The well of human pain is dark and seemingly bottomless. In this century we have come to perceive our experience in a way radically different from that of our not too distant ancestors. What people once put up with as their fate or ascribed to the effects of magic, spells, or bad luck, we now examine and treat psychologically. Human beings have learned to take their emotional pulse in a new way; they have become not only less bedevilled by it but have come to appreciate their feelings, to understand the sources of their anxieties and guilt, and to heal themselves and each other in systematic ways. We have, in fact, lived through the democratization of therapy, the Americanization of psychological health and fulfillment for everyone. We have passed beyond the goal of dealing more satisfactorily with old fears to the enjoyment of therapy as an end in itself.

Despite our progress, the gullet of woe yawns, filled as ever with dread at the center of the human condition. Indeed, our capacity to treat may have, as a condition for relieving pain, brought us closer to it, making us feel it as our own more intensely. Clearly, the airy promises of a therapeutic era when we could put emotional suffering behind us and proceed on the way to our "potential" have not been fulfilled. The human situation, as Lewis Mumford once observed, is "always desperate." We can identify, with Hans Selye, the coexistent elements of *pathos* (suffering) and *ponos* (struggle) in our lives. Perhaps the most significant advance is our deepened understanding of how much we share the same pains, how much we resemble each other in our common hopes and disappointments. One cannot cure without knowing more keenly the anguish of the pain; one cannot confront suffering (pathos) without doing the work (ponos) of dealing with it. Any realistic help that men and women have ever been able to give to each other is rooted in an awareness of separation and loss, in being able to feel with the other because they themselves struggle with the same difficulties. To appreciate the mystery of pain is to understand it a little and to alleviate it a lot. That achievement is within the grasp of everybody who lives or works with other persons.

This book is based on the premise that we long to be of help to the suffering and bewildered individuals around us, and on a special feeling for the way children in particular, who perceive the world and speak of it in ways that transcend adult logic and reason, need to be heard and responded to in the varied emergencies of life. There is nothing romantic about facing the pain of children, pain which runs ahead of the words—ours or theirs—for it. While we have a surfeit of advisors telling people how to raise their children, we have very few with the sensitivity and qualification to offer practical advice on what adults can do to respond to children in the midst of crisis. And we have hardly any who know that therapy is neither romantic self-fulfillment nor the mechanical application of technique.

We can be grateful that the authors of this book have the courage to face up to the many ways in which children taste suffering long before they can give it a proper name. We can be doubly appreciative they do not overromanticize children, espy them as adults, or say, as is heavily the fashion at the moment, that they must always be incorporated into some form of family therapy. They have better sense than that. They offer the distilled wisdom of their training and their abundant common sense, which is here happily applied to situations that require it in large doses. What makes this book unique is that the authors not only know what they are talking about but also speak modestly, economically, and insightfully so that the volume can be used profitably by a wide variety of persons—teachers, nurses, lawyers, clergy, friendly helpers of every kind—who are involved every day in crises such as those outlined here.

The writers also keep their subjects in sharp relief in a book that lives up to its title in a way that very few do these days. It could only have been written by professionals who are adult enough to understand the world of children, its symbols and languages, its shadowy terrors; by sensitive experts who, in short, understand life. It will not, of course, fill in that deep shaft of pain that is at the center of existence, but it will allow those who use it to help others to survive the crises that bubble out of it, and to emerge, in that wonderful phrase, "stronger in the broken places."

EUGENE KENNEDY

PREFACE TO THE
NEW EXPANDED EDITION

Since we wrote *Crisis Counseling with Children and Adolescents* seven years ago, we've been gratified by the comments and ideas passed along to us by teachers, students, parents, and colleagues. We feel that the main theme of this book—learning to be empathic with children—is as applicable today as then, and will continue to be so in the future. In this edition we have added chapters on looking at how alcohol affects children and adolescents, as well as a chapter on understanding children who have been sexually abused.

In the course of our work, we came across a beautiful article on learning to be empathic with psychotic children, particularly psychotic children for whom "whirling and spinning" is a symptom. This article serves as an excellent model concerning being empathic toward all children and the crises they face. "Psychosis in children is rare and whirling in those afflicted is rarer still," writes Paul Pressman, MD. "Why report it at all? It is the author's wish for the reader to recognize something universal in the whirling psychotic. We will see him as a fellow creature—different from us to be sure, but not so different as to be dismissed as freakish and therefore put entirely apart from us.

"But a relentlessly whirling child seems a thing totally alien to us. One cannot touch him psychologically any more than a pebble can avoid being projected off a spinning wheel. A whirler is strange. He is not our kind, like a cretin is not one of us. The word *cretin* is said to be derived from the French word for 'Christian,' *cretien*. The lovely etymology implies that though the cretin is in fact an ugly, retarded dwarf with thick tongue and bulging stomach, he nonetheless is a God-created Christian like the rest of us and deserves the name human."

Pressman goes on to teach us how it feels to be a child saddled by psychosis. His paper, "Whirling, Omnipotence, and Ecstasy" is recommended as a model for sensing how these children think and feel, and what he learned from this extreme and often sorrowful group applies to all children and the crises they face in their lives.

Not only this, but perhaps the whirling psychotic child, as well as the child who has been abused, who is in foster care, or who is born with retardation, teaches us important truths about the universe itself. Pressman writes: "The finger of the Creator may indeed trace spirals. Witness the remarkable spiraling numbers of Fibonacci that describe the growth of living plants, or the double helix of the hereditary material, or even the formation of galaxies in whirling Nebulae."

We hope that this book will help you understand the hearts and minds of the children and adolescents you work with. Their problems may seem relatively commonplace or they may appear as strange and different from your own life experience, but through understanding you will be able to do much good in the world.

WILLIAM VAN ORNUM
Marist College

JOHN B. MORDOCK
The Astor Home for Children

PREFACE

This book is written for all who work with children.

For everyone who works with children is, at some time or another, confronted with a child in crisis.

Teachers, social workers, nurses and doctors, therapists, members of the clergy, guidance counselors, camp counselors, and others in the traditional helping professions; public servants such as police officers and fire fighters; child care workers and day-care center staff; parents, relatives, and neighbors—all who work with, love, and care for children on a day-to-day basis may find the child in crisis to be a frequent visitor in their lives.

Some crises are like an unexpected guest at the door. You quickly gather your wits and put another plate on the table. Other crises cause true panic in the helper. You feel threatened, unsure of the proper course of action. Things are out of control. "What do I say?" "Will the child understand?" "Will my efforts make things worse?" "Who else should be involved?" Working in a crisis situation is bound to create stress for the person whose role is that of a helper.

To intervene in stressful situations, we must first learn how to communicate. While there are numerous books on communicating with children, most are written for beginning psychotherapists or they don't relate to problems encountered in crisis. Even less is written for concerned adults in the child's life.

Crisis Counseling with Children and Adolescents is a practical guide for those who may not have specialized training in child development or counseling. It is intended as a handbook that will provide daily applications to a variety of crisis situations. We have based our work on the scientific understanding of children and hope to present to the reader an integration of the classical theorists, the latest literature in child development and child clinical psychology, and our own experience in working with children.

William Van Ornum is listed as first author because the idea for the book and its original outline came from him. Since that inception stage both authors have worked together as partners to produce the manuscript.

The authors would like to acknowledge the support and encouragement of the administrative staff of the Astor Home and Child Guidance Center. The publication of this book coincides with the 30th anniversary of the Astor Home for Children and the 350th anniversary of the Daughters of Charity of St. Vincent DePaul, who in 1953, under auspices of the Archdiocese of New York Catholic Charities and in cooperation with the New York State Department of Mental Hygiene, opened Astor Home, a residential center, as a pilot project to help determine proper methods of treating emotional disorders in children. From these small beginnings the Daughters now administer a large complex of children's services subsumed under the name Astor Home and Child Guidance Centers. The current executive director is Sister Anne Schneiders. Astor staff have always been involved in developing programs for children and families in crisis. The support of our efforts to disseminate knowledge gained while on the staff of this organization is in keeping with the agency's philosophy of research and training as well as treatment.

More specific acknowledgment goes to those who read and commented on earlier versions of the chapters. David Shaw and Eileen Cardall of Children's Rehabilitation Center in Kingston, New York; Patricia Mahoney of Eugene, Oregon; and Judy Boswell of Pennsylvania State University. Special thanks goes to Barbara Frost, staff psychologist at Astor Day Treatment Center, for assisting us in literature reviews and for compiling a bibliography of children's books. We have also utilized some case material provided by Shelly Kitzman, play therapist at the Family Counseling Center in Green Bay, Wisconsin. The assistance of Barbara Pantridge and William Nichol, librarians at the Dutchess County Mental Health Association and Astor Home libraries is appreciated, as was the help of the library staff at Vassar College in Poughkeepsie, New York, and the University of Southampton in Southampton, England. Our thanks go also to Kayla Chase, Daniel O'Donnell, and Penelope Jaworski for their many kindnesses and good advice.

We are grateful to Eugene Kennedy for providing the inspiration for this book in his series of books on counseling for nonprofessional counselors. Michael Leach of Crossroad/Continuum has been a steady source of encouragement throughout the project. And we thank Patsy Ong, editor, and Verne Moberg, copy editor, for their thoughtful, thorough work.

Surveys and interviews of nonprofessional counselors were completed by June Aquila, Guy Jacobs, and Paul Damin, undergraduate students at Marist College in Poughkeepsie. Thanks for manuscript typing goes to Gerie Crocker, and we would also like to acknowledge Rosemary Sandri and Dianne Terpening, of Astor Day Treatment Center, for their support and encouragement.

Special thanks go to the children, families, and staff of the Astor Home and Child Guidance Centers for providing us with the clinical experiences which made this book possible.

Most of all, our appreciation goes to Mary Wicker Van Ornum, who has worked with us throughout the project and in the final stages devoted several months of continuous labor to helping us meet our deadline. Her professional editing skills and good common sense helped us to keep the book readable and literate, and we convey to her our warmest thanks and gratitude.

·1·

Crisis:
Lost Sense of Self

Too often we give children
answers to remember
rather than problems to solve.   ROGER LEWIN

Working with children means involvement in childhood crises. It comes with the job. Definitions of *crisis* emphasize that a crisis creates a turning point, in this instance a turning point for the child and for you as well. Crises can turn one in different directions. The mediators in a crisis situation can enable children to turn in a positive direction. They can turn them when they know approaches to take and are aware of their own limits.

When a four-year-old's mother dies, the child may feel responsible for her death. Such children brood, ruminate, and remember how they used to make her mad. They woefully conclude: "I made Mom mad, and that's why she died." They feel guilty, and the situation becomes a crucial turning point for them. They can withdraw from peers and adults and stew in guilt feelings; or they can grieve their loss and move on to face the challenges of growing up.

If important adults do not take the time to be with them, to discuss their worries and to correct their misguided thinking, then the crisis can turn them in the wrong direction.

If important adults help them get to the root of their worries, ease their anxieties, and gently but firmly shift their attention toward activities that will involve them with others, then this crisis becomes a positive turning point. The children can grieve and mourn and then progress to involvement with people and activities that provide them with a sense of mastery and self-esteem, qualities essential for growing up adjusted.

Examples of other turning points might be:

• Keith needs heart surgery. Afterward he must restrict his activities for six months. How will he cope?

• Sara is going into foster care again. She always breaks rules and disobeys teachers. Will this new family be able to help her?

• Maria is handicapped. She is a slow learner who needs a special class. In the past, her peers taunted her mercilessly. Will special education contribute to her life?

• Bruce has epilepsy. His seizures occur throughout the school day. Can he lead a normal life?

Some events are a greater crisis for you, the helper, the one faced with the decision, than for the child: "Do I do something about this situation, or not?" "What is the best way to help this child?" A child may be so accustomed to a handicap or chronic disease that it is no longer a crisis for her or him, yet it may be a crisis for you because you do not understand the nature of the child's problem. To the extent that you are unfamiliar, you are anxious and afraid. Throughout this book, we provide information and suggest approaches to help make crises positive turning points for both you and the child.

Adults often need to see children as untouched by suffering, and many try to protect a child from the impact of a grievous event by suppressing information. "What the child doesn't know won't hurt him" or "Let sleeping dogs lie" are old sayings inappropriately applied in times of crisis.

Parents and parent figures display strong temptations to seduce children away from the reality of their feelings or from the harshness of life. When children cry, adults offer distractions. Sometimes they admonish the child for crying or for being afraid. For example, a group of children between the ages of seven and fourteen were playing Monopoly, along with several adults. The youngest child cried when she landed on Boardwalk and had to pay almost all of her money. The parent of this child was annoyed: "If you can't play without crying, don't play." How many times have we all said that? Another adult spoke up: "You can cry and play too." So she did.

As the game progressed, some of the players accumulated property, houses, hotels, and money. Others began to lose and found excuses to quit. But the youngest child—crying each time she lost money, crying each time she landed on Boardwalk—stuck it out until the bitter end, quite proud of herself. Anxious athletes play and scared actors act—why can't crying children play!

That you can cry and carry on with what you are doing at the same time is a profound insight for a child. Let children cry when they play games, and let children cry when they face a crisis. It's a healthy reaction to the sometimes cruel blows of life.

One Halloween the first author of this book rented a gorilla outfit for a costume party at a day treatment center. After the party he paid a visit to the head start center in the same building. Almost all of these young children were initially afraid of the "gorilla"—even after he had removed his headpiece. Several parents were annoyed that their children were afraid; they angrily jerked them away and took them home. Other parents stayed, helped their children master their fears of the gorilla, and thoroughly enjoyed the party.

In addition to their disapproval of the child's being fearful ("Don't be silly! There's nothing to be afraid of."), some parents don't even realize that their children experience fears. A recent study revealed that many adolescents experienced nightmares, restless sleep, and other signs of anxiety after they had watched horror movies on television or in theaters. Many parents don't even restrict their young children from watching such movies. They allow their children to view catastrophe films, such as *Airport, Towering Inferno,* or other movies where people are helpless victims, such as *Jaws.* Children are generally not aware that these are fictional events, and they feel insecure in their environment because of their exposure to violence. Being anxious and misunderstood already, many children are less prepared to deal with real crises when they occur.

Some Background

Originally, crisis intervention services were intended for ordinarily intact, well-adjusted children and families who were in temporary need of help in coping with some hazardous event. Techniques were designed to help clients accomplish a particular series of coping tasks. Crisis intervention teams, composed of emergency service clinicians, were established in community mental health clinics or in hospital emergency rooms to help people deal with crisis situations. These teams were specially trained; most readers of this book are forced to resolve crises with little or no training. You learn as you go and become wiser with experience. And rarely do children experiencing crises—moves, school changes, death, divorce, abuse, handicaps, or hospitalization—receive immediate clinical intervention specifically designed to help them. They are helped (or not helped) by the adults in their daily lives. This network of helpers is often more powerful than any therapist could hope to be, but sometimes adults in a child's life do not know how to respond and lose a valuable opportunity to help the child:

> All the time my patients are teaching me, over and over again, that if only there had been someone at the point of the crisis, to encompass the child, to recognize that the child has feelings about what is going on, to help him through the shattering effect of all that is familiar, then perhaps some of the shock and trauma could have been absorbed and need not have disturbed the individual's development as it did from then on.[1]

Crises can have long-lasting effects; they can render the child less able to deal with future trauma. This belief is based on years of clinical experience and clearly supported by formal research. Many studies have revealed that traumatic life events culminate in disordered behavior and psychopathology. For example, individuals with an excessive number of undesirable life events with undesirable outcomes are especially prone to suicide.[2]

Perhaps the most significant events are separations from loved ones, regardless of the time of life in which they occur. Forty-two percent of children suffering from peptic ulcers experienced separation from a loss of a parent, while only a small number of children with other physical illnesses had experienced similar separations.[3] These and other studies indicate that stressful events are cumulative. Consequently, some children are prone to react more poorly to hazardous events than are others.

The problem child is a child with a problem. Ironically, children who display behavioral problems often are the children who receive the least understanding. Adults usually deal with the problem child instead of trying to understand the child with a problem. Crisis events lurk in the background of troubled children. By learning about these events, you can better understand children and their behavior. We caution against the use of behavioral techniques that deal primarily with surface behaviors or misbehaviors. To understand the child, you need to understand the feelings, conflicts, and crises from which the behavior has evolved.

Many adults command the troubled child to "shape up" or "get your act together." We are firm believers in rules, limit setting, and discipline, but we emphasize that children will be unable to "get their act together" until they can resolve some of the troubling issues that underlie their misbehavior. Similarly, many adults impatiently ship these youngsters off for professional counseling in the hopes of a quick, neat cure. While many children in crisis benefit from professional intervention, they often can be helped just as well by the thoughtful, empathic, and caring adults in their lives. Such people, acting together to help children overcome their crises, can be more effective than weekly visits to a therapist.

How can adults help? How can they learn what to do? The purpose of this book is to help you understand the crises encountered by children and to provide positive approaches for dealing with them.

Elements of Crises

Different Coping Styles

Children's ways of coping are different from adults'—they lack the variety of coping mechanisms available to adults. We must keep this shortcoming in mind.

There are two stages of crisis resolution. First-stage reactions involve the following: The first specific reaction to a crisis is initial shock followed by high anxiety. Most of us have experienced such feelings. Remember when someone significant left you (when you were an adult)? The more you depended on them or your life revolved around them, the greater your loss and anxiety. Both your sense of who you were and your purpose in life were temporarily shaken. You went through the day meeting your main responsibilities, mechanically, with little interest. Minor tasks never got done: the laundry piled up, the checkbook went unbalanced. You slept too much, or not at all. If you had to tackle a new assignment, you felt overwhelmed. Food lost its appeal; often you were nauseous. You took to bed frequently because you had neither the interest nor the energy to deal with anything. (Physiological changes that accompany stress include fatigue.) This was your body's and mind's response to anxiety.

Coupled with these changes were irrational thoughts and less capacity to comprehend reality. You felt compelled to visit old haunts or became obsessed with thoughts you couldn't control. Gradually, you felt a little better. You arrived at this point generally by not doing much of anything, just following long-established routines. Somehow you got by.

But suppose you are a child! Try to get through a school day feeling like this: You are continually bombarded with new challenges, without the energy to face them. You aren't experienced enough to know that the situation will pass or be resolved, *somehow*. In your child's mind, you know only that you feel helpless, caught in the eye of a hurricane. You can't rely on "going through the motions" as an adult can. Your sense of self has not been fully established, and its wobbly beginnings have collapsed. The adult can at least question repeatedly, "Why did this have to happen to me?" or "Why do I have to suffer?" But the child's mind is not well enough developed to problem-solve with these necessary but painful thoughts. Adults fall back on well-established patterns and routines; children fall back on chaos. They lose their sense of who they are—their sense of self.

Second-stage reactions are similar but less intense. The reactions are less debilitating, and some energy is freed to ponder the crisis rather than just respond to it. Adults relive the crisis, time and time again. They daydream about their past life and create some future hopes for a new beginning. All of this is the work of grieving. Eventually, be it a week or years later, they feel stronger, in control again, and pick up their life where they left off.

Children experience difficulty at this stage. They often lack the verbal skills and creative fantasy ability that help adults. This deficit alters their relationship with the world. Inadequate solutions to problems are clung to, rigidly. They need others to communicate their fears and help them sort out fact from fiction. Adults typically seek out friends for advice, comfort, support, and a clearer perspective during a crisis. Children don't realize that such opportunities exist. Talking increases their anxiety; it makes them restless, so they don't talk. Often they are referred for psychological and neurological evaluations because of their restlessness, mislabeled *hyperactivity* or *learning disability*. We seem to forget that fight and flight are the two basic responses to anxiety, and that it is difficult to remember, concentrate, perform, or achieve academically when one is preoccupied with worries.

When children continue to be anxious and not live up to their potential, then they remain in the second stage—they have failed to adequately resolve the crisis. A portion of their energy will be devoted to dealing with the unresolved issues relating to the crisis. This leaves them less energy to deal with life and with future crises. They will be increasingly vulnerable to stress, and they will feel bad about their inability to cope. As we said before, crises are additive.

Experience with uncontrollable events leads to helplessness in subsequent situations.[4] A child's initial reaction to loss of control leads to protest, anger, and defiance. Repeated loss leads to helplessness. This helplessness is most often expressed as passivity or retreat when challenged. Fearfulness, depression, and physical illness are expressions of this helplessness. Helplessness is actually a perception that control can never be regained; children with repeated loss of control become those with lack of control. Children despair at their lack of control. Perceptions of uncontrollability generalize so that eventually children make minimal effort even in minimally challenging situations. Consequently, they feel bad about their inability to cope. Feeling bad leads to decreased self-esteem and increased helplessness so that challenges are avoided as failure is anticipated. Adults cope with crises by restricting their lives, but children are forced to face new challenges, particularly in school, every day. It is asking too much of them. Their protest and despair mount, and they are labeled as misbehaving, defiant, manipulative, or maladjusted. These children soon get the notion that they are "bad!"

Below are the verbalizations accompanying the play of a five-year-old whose parents had been separated for a year and who was referred for professional help because of screaming fits:

> They are together. They are happy. The dad is gone. He was invisible anyway. He got cutted out. We don't have any scissors— need scissors. The dad is not going to come back, never no more—we're ripping him up now. He's gone away. I ripped him up. I don't remember what he looked like. I'm cutting you up. Hey—I cut myself. I'm shooting you. I'm sorry.

This play clearly illustrates the changes accompanying crises. The child is confused as well as angry. His reality testing has deteriorated and he's as angry at himself as he is at others. His anger hurts others and causes him anxiety, which he tries to defend against by hurting himself ("I cut myself") or apologizing ("I'm sorry"). We also see regression in his primitive anger and his screaming behavior.

A less dramatic example is a letter a bright eight-year-old sent to her parents who were separating:

> Dear Mom and Dad,
>   I am sorry for causing so much commotion. I am not getting good grades. I am trying to get good grades though. I will try to do as good as I can. I really want you to stop fighting over little things.

Not only does the child blame herself for the parents' difficulties, she is confused as well. "Much commotion" and "little things" stand in marked contrast to one another. The child hopes her good grades will keep her parents together. Rather than directly verbalizing her worries to her parents, she wrote a note. Somehow it seemed safer, maybe even less painful, to express herself this way. While not as disorganized as "the screamer," she clearly is in a crisis and wrongly sees her own improvement as the solution.

Regressive Acts

When stress becomes too great, children return to more primitive behavior patterns in order to regain their composure. Children who are worried about their parents' impending divorce may display the tantrum behavior of much younger children. Or they may avoid situations that arouse anxiety, thereby restricting their personality development. Sometimes these earlier behaviors can be adaptive. For example, children can master their fear of doctors by pretending to be a doctor and imitating their behavior in playing with dolls or with other children.

What do we mean when we say that children regress to more primitive behaviors? When children operate at their age level, they know how to employ their skills and talents appropriately to relate to people and to master tasks. When they become highly upset—as often occurs in a crisis—they lose their capacity to coordinate all of their abilities to meet the needs of the situation. They become confused and disorganized, and crisis counselors may need to take charge of part of the child's life and guide his or her behavior.

Eleven-year-old Joe would soon be going to the hospital for an operation. He was terrified about this. When his younger brother, Andy, borrowed his video game and didn't tell him, he hit Andy. Joe had regressed—he had lost his ability to talk with Andy about the situation, or go to his mother for help.

In situations of regression, we need to remind children of the things they would normally do if they weren't so upset. Joe's mother made him sit down and talk things out with Andy. The process is like helping children learn to ice-skate: If you can just get them out on the ice, they can do the rest!

Earlier Similars

Crises draw from the child a variety of feelings that were present in past situations.

When you deal with a child in crisis, you are really dealing with two children: the child as he or she stands before you, and the child as a product of previous experience. Some refer to these past experiences as *earlier similars*. A child's inability to handle failing a simple task relates to earlier failures. A young child's fear of the dentist's office may relate to an earlier terror of hospitals. An adolescent's extreme reaction to his or her dog's death may be traced to the much earlier death of a brother or sister. In each instance, the earlier crisis was not fully resolved, contributing to the child's upset.

Upsets and Crises

Upsets—distressing disturbances—are composed of the following three elements: thwarted intentions, unfulfilled expectations, and undelivered communications.[5] While it may seem laborious to dwell on definitions, being clear on meanings opens doors to what crisis resolution is all about. For example, intention is defined as "an aim or purpose, a determination to do a specific thing or act in a certain manner which implies having a particular plan or design in mind." An expectation means "an anticipation, a looking forward to *as due.*"

For example, children whose parents, for whatever reason, feel that whatever they give them is not enough, foster a belief in them that they are owed, a feeling of entitlement that makes no sense to the casual observer. The following vignette illustrates this point.

Frank threatened the physical education teacher with the baseball bat. He and another child had been taking turns at bat while the teacher pitched the ball to them. Each was to take three swings and then relinquish the bat to the other. Frank had taken his third swing and wanted a fourth. He would not return the bat and, when asked for it, threatened to hit the teacher with it.

To successfully intervene with Frank so that the bat is returned and so that he feels somewhat good about himself requires that we understand his intentions and his expectations. He was looking forward to something happening that didn't. In addition, he may have looked forward to it as due him. Frank had a feeling of entitlement.

The crisis, or the crucial part of the situation, was Frank's handling of his upset over being limited to three swings. Perhaps he fantasized that he would hit the ball three times, whereas in reality, he had swung and missed each time. He created a crisis by inappropriately handling his upset and not living up to his self-image.

Frank may feel that the world owes him more than three swings, simply because he feels it does, particularly if his *intention* was to hit the ball out of the park and his *expectation* was that he would be admired by all onlookers. He feels entitled to this admiration. Frank's upset also includes an undelivered communication. The teacher who will get the bat back from Frank and who will improve his ability to deal with future upsets will be the teacher who helps Frank communicate his thwarted intention and unfulfilled expectations in a way that will contribute to his growth. We must also remember that upsets carry with them an unwitting reminder of earlier upsets, "earlier similars." As a young child, Frank experienced humiliation from a father whom he could never please: "You never do anything right!" He became overly sensitive to criticism and responds poorly to the normal peer insults and badgering when he makes mistakes. He limits his horizons and won't try many activities, giving the excuse that they are "dumb games," or he exaggerates his prowess in other games that he thinks no one will ever see him play. Worst of all, he may fantasize that he is better than he actually is and make it your fault ("You didn't pitch it right!") when he strikes out. Let's look at how we might handle Frank's upset.

TEACHER: Brad, you go inside now. Frank, you don't need to hit me with the bat to show me how angry you are.

FRANK: Come on, pitch it again, and I'll give it back.

TEACHER: Frank, I'm sorry you didn't get more hits, but some of my pitches weren't very good. I know you'd like to hit the ball over the fence, but we made an agreement that each would get three swings. If you want to change that, we can do that after Brad gets his three swings.

FRANK: F—— you, I'm keeping the bat.

TEACHER: Sometimes it's hard not to look as good as you think you are. I know you would have liked to have gotten more hits; maybe next time you will.

FRANK: I want to hit now.

TEACHER: Frank, I know you're mad at me for doing what you think made you look bad—I didn't mean to, but baseball's a hard game, and it takes a lot of practice. I liked the way you swung at the ball. If you had connected, it might have gone out of the park!

During this conversation the teacher has kept a safe distance from Frank, trying to discover the elements of Frank's upset. If the teacher senses some relaxed tension, he or she may quickly seize the bat from Frank or choose to talk with him. Usually, the child needs to save face by having the bat taken away.

When interviewing Frank, one must be careful not to point out his thwarted intention or unfulfilled expectation in a manner that will increase his perceived humiliation and increase his upset. For example, the teacher avoided statements like "Frank, I'm sorry you're not as good as you think you are" or "Don't be silly—you're not Reggie Jackson, even if you'd like to be." The teacher tried to word statements to convey an understanding of his intentions and desires without belittling him for having them, as if to say, "It's okay to have such desires, but it's not okay to hit me with the bat because they didn't happen this time." In addition there was admiration for some aspect of his game: "I like how you swung at the ball." Some might question the teacher taking responsibility for his error (the "bad pitches"). Because upset also includes a *state of mind,* a state which becomes more rigid when one is angry, the best course was followed. Later, when Frank is calmer and away from onlookers, he may be able to admit that the pitches weren't all that bad and discuss ways to better handle future upsets. In chapter eleven, "Defiant Children," we will discuss in more detail children who are in crisis states such as Frank.

Enabling Children

Our goal is to help the reader understand the crisis experience from the perspective of children. Such empathy is difficult; there is always more depth to children's thoughts and feelings than is evident from surface behavior.

Children in all crisis states—divorce, death, abuse, handicaps, hospitalization, foster care—have feelings about the crisis that are not evident to the casual observer. Their thwarted intentions, unfulfilled expectations, and undelivered communications go unnoticed. What is noticed are the symptoms of their distress, and too often our concern for these symptoms overshadows our efforts to discover the feelings. Only the severely disturbed mother would hit a child for crying; most would try to discover the reasons for the tears.

Further chapters will emphasize the nature of children's upsets and their elements—efforts to understand how the child feels before we address efforts at changing maladaptive behaviors, the symptoms of distress.

Once you understand children you can begin to assist, to serve as an enabler. Throughout this book we will emphasize approaches to take to enable children in times of crisis. Perhaps what is most important is to *marshal positive forces,* in both the child's life and self. Three ways to do this are to improve the child's relationships with others, to affirm positive relationships, and to look for mature coping efforts.

Improve Children's Relationships

Sometimes the crisis counselor can help important caretakers better understand children. This understanding not only improves their relationship but can also improve children's adjustment to other aspects of their lives.

One four-year-old boy was keeping his foster parents awake at night. He claimed, "Auntie's keeping me awake at night." The foster parents couldn't understand why the boy would lie and were becoming increasingly irritated with his bedtime behavior and ridiculous explanation for it. The social worker was well aware of the universal feelings of young children in foster care. She suggested that the foster parents try to understand and respond to the "lie" from the child's frame of reference—his anxiety in a new home, his uncertainty, his trouble sleeping alone in an unfamiliar room. In a very real sense, his auntie was keeping him awake at night! If we remember that children's maladaptive behavior is an attempt to cope, we will look to their actions as clues to what is troubling them.

Affirm Relationships with Important Caretakers

We will learn that all crises involve lost relationships. A parent dies. A parent leaves. Sickness or handicaps separate children from the mainstream of life. Defiant children are ostracized. When children have suffered such a loss, help them to remember the network of adults who continue to care and to look out for them.

Such reassurance is particularly important when dealing with neglected children or those living in foster care or institutions. The crisis counselor helps children reconstruct early experience to locate some caring relationship. When children feel someone cared for them in the past, it gives them hope and opens the door for positive relationships in the future.

CHILD: Nobody ever loved me.

ADULT: Nobody ever took care of you?

CHILD: I was alone most of the time.

ADULT: I remember how much your grandmother cared for you—all day long while your mother worked.

Neglected children, abused children, and those in foster care or institutions often idealize their relationships with parents, and adolescents sometimes describe their early childhood experiences as wonderful, revealing a longing to return to that state. Children who lose a parent, either through death or divorce, often idealize the departed parent. These fictions serve to lower anxiety, to sustain the child in times of stress. But such idealization is more than just a defense and should not be corrected in the name of reality by the crisis counselor: it is the child's effort at self-definition. "If my childhood was wonderful, then I must be a wonderful person," or "If mother loved me greatly, then I can be loved again." Should the crisis counselor express disbelief, he or she not only robs the child of a helpful coping mechanism but leaves the child feeling dispossessed of self. By undermining the child's "sustaining fiction," the counselor takes away the child's effort to find meaning and worth.

The crisis counselor supports the child, saying to the grieving eight-year-old, "It makes you feel good when you remember your mother," or to the nostalgic adolescent, "Thinking about your childhood reminds you of a lost part of your self."

Look for Mature Coping Efforts

When children tell you about their present crisis or their past life, listen carefully for possible positive experiences in their stories. Helping them to relive positive experiences or memories will lower their anxiety and raise their self-esteem. You're not just after the facts—you're after mobilizing forces. Witness this reaction to a child's dream:

CHILD: I dreamed I ran away from this place and bought lots of food and clothes.

ADULT: It's good that you know how to feed and take care of yourself.

Note how the adult looked at the dream in a positive light. In long-term therapy, a therapist might help the child see that running away doesn't help solve problems. In crisis counseling, when the child's defenses are overwhelmed, the counselor focuses on a positive detail.

CHILD: I dreamed I got into a fight with Wayne and I was cut and bleeding. I had to walk slowly on my way home. I was scared, but I put a Band Aid on it. I woke up feeling awful.

ADULT: What do you think the dream might tell you?

CHILD: Not to get into fights.

ADULT: Yes, but look at how you were careful and fixed yourself up—you can take care of yourself.

Looking for mature coping efforts does not mean sugarcoating the truth or denying serious concerns. It is a way of focusing children's attention on activities and events that they can master, or making them aware of the times in life when they felt strong and competent. More will be said about this later.

A Crisis for the Helpers

We hope that this book will enable the readers not only to deal more effectively with the crises they face in their work with children but to actively seek out and assist children who are in crises. For example, most teachers are aware that a child in their class may just have moved into their district, or that a father has left the household. If not, careful interviews with parents can reveal these events. The teacher can then structure her or his relationship with the child in ways suggested in the chapters to follow.

Families come to mental health professionals because natural helping systems have failed to contribute significantly to conflict resolution. Teachers, child care workers, parole officers, nurses, clergy, and others then look to the trained therapist for help. But often this does not solve the problem because many families do not follow through with treatment. The direct care worker again is left to assist the child who is no better off than he or she was prior to referral.

Or another outcome results. Even when the child is taken regularly for therapy, the clinic staff will often seek out those who work with the child, since direct care workers can assist the child to cope in stressful situations. In either case, direct staff play important roles. Consequently, a collaborative effort is the best approach.

Some Truths About Crisis Counseling

When you decide to help a child in crisis, you should keep in mind some truths that experienced helpers have learned:

• Helping a child resolve a crisis presents a crisis for the counselor.

• Think hard about a child's panic attacks (and your own). Your tendency will be to immediately try to cool them.

• Forego belief in magical solutions. The mental health field has its fads, just like anything else.

• Things can get worse before they get better.

• You will vacillate between feeling confident and feeling uncertain.

• When you have a greater investment in helping the child than the child has in being helped, no useful results will occur.

• You will be influenced by children as much as they are by you. You will be friendly toward friendly children, angry toward hostile children, and irritated by irritating children. Don't think you won't!

• Highly anxious children can agree with most anything you say, and almost any child can be led, simply by the form of the questions, to make false statements.

• Your desire to use what you know will interfere with your development of alternate methods.

• You will experience conflict between your desire to provide follow-up help and acknowledgment of your limitations, and will hope for the best.

In almost every crisis, the helper will experience some if not all of the above feelings. Many times we've gotten angry at children who seem to thrive on resisting our help; other times we thought we *knew* something, but it turned out we didn't. And some children's symptoms have worsened following our intervention, causing self-doubt and worry until we saw that persistence paid off. Keep these truths in mind as you counsel children. Your awareness of them can spare you turmoil.

Our Theoretical View

Some readers will be interested in the theories of human behavior upon which we base this book. We have taken predominantly a psychodynamic/phenomenological perspective because we are concerned with the subjective experience of children in crisis, how they perceive the event, feel about it, and distort it. Throughout we emphasize inserting yourself into the frame of reference of the children as-they-see-the-world. Building upon Carl Rogers and other phenomenological psychologists, we believe that constructive change in helping relationships occurs when two persons communicate understanding in the context of an "I-Thou" relationship. In each of the topical chapters, we present a phenomenology of the crisis including factors of the crisis and universal feelings evoked in children. Following most chapters we have listed selected books for children that capture the universal feelings evoked by the particular crisis.

Children are more than their behavior. The following example emphasizes the attention given to the subjective experience of those who have a problem.

A child was asked to bring her sick foster mother a cloth napkin. After doing so, the child asked for candy from a bowl on the bedside table. The foster mother denied her this request, and the child snatched back the cloth napkin and cut it into pieces. This behavior may be explained by understanding the importance of food to the deprived child and the precariousness of a relationship with a sick foster mother. The child feels she has "given" to the foster mother, and when not given in return, she becomes a victim of her own infantile feelings of "an eye for an eye, a tooth for a tooth." Rather than punishing the child or thinking her crazy, the foster parents can understand how past deprivations can make even mild losses seem like total rejection.[6]

Knowing how children feel is essential. Also essential is understanding cognitive ability: knowing the way they think. Children of different ages think differently, and their thoughts color their perceptions of a crisis. Consequently, we make use of the findings of cognitive developmentalists, most notably Jean Piaget, and adapt their views to crisis counseling. How children *perceive* crisis events such as death, divorce, foster care, and hospitalization is important. We believe that knowing how children *feel* and *think* and helping them to clarify their own thinking will enable crises to be resolved constructively, not traumatically. We believe that a child's misperceptions can influence behavior many years later.

Much of the recent literature and research on helping children has emphasized behavioral approaches. These involve monitoring and directing the actual behaviors the counselor believes are likely to result in the child overcoming the problem. Shy, withdrawn children are shown how to behave more assertively and are rewarded for doing so. Defiant children can earn a trip by cooperating for a week. And so on. More recently, this approach has been called *social skills training*.

The behavioral approach carries two assumptions. First, that children's acts themselves are the problem and not the manifestation of a deeper concern. Second, that behavior can be changed directly by arranging circumstances to support a new behavior or teaching an alternative behavior and then assuming that it pays off. Following the behavior change, whatever attitudes, feelings, or beliefs that are going on inside will come to match this. For example, a behaviorist might treat a foster child with bedtime fears in this way: He or she would discuss the bedtime routine with the child and the parents, find a suitable reward that the child would work for, and draw up a contract—one in which the child agrees to the parents' bedtime routine and they agree to a reward. The child repeats the details of the contract and is made responsible for charting success and collecting the reward. Failures to keep the routine are ignored and successes are rewarded.[7]

A key tenet of the behavioral approach is that you can control an environment thoroughly. Unfortunately, crises are often out of everyone's control. The best we can do is change maladaptive feelings and perceptions. Therefore, we suggest employing behavioral approaches after the child's legitimate worries and fears are recognized.

Although we emphasize a personal relationship approach to crisis counseling, we acknowledge the usefulness of behavioral strategies. We use them every day ourselves. The second author was trained in behavioral therapy under Joseph Wolpe and has helped to develop behavioral strategies with children.[8] Such strategies are particularly helpful in building self-esteem and marshaling positive forces, qualities essential to surviving any crisis.

Note to Professionals

Crisis situations create a crisis for the professional. Many psychologists, social workers, or psychiatrists work as part of a team which includes line staff workers who spend the greatest amount of time with the child each day. When crisis strikes, the professionals are besieged by requests: "Jill's dad died. What do I say to her?" "Rob's parents used to beat him. Tomorrow I have a parent-teacher conference with them. How do I talk with them?" "Alice is going into foster care—again. She's so young. What can I do about it?" Every professional is called to translate and apply the tools of the trade for these workers. Yet often jargon and heavy theoretical views obscure this task. We have tried to explain the approaches of crisis counseling in a readable and practical way. We hope that professionals will find this book helpful in their consultative work with nonprofessional counselors.

In chapters to follow we present notions about communication with children and adolescents, review some basic relationship principles, suggest interview goals, and discuss how to structure the relationship to foster change in children. We then define the types of counseling that are helpful to children in crisis and contrast them with psychotherapy. We will do this in chapter four, "Empathic Focusing." We turn now to a discussion of talking with and listening to children—the place to begin the counseling process.

·2·

Talking and Listening to Children

When I was a child, I spoke like a child, I thought like a child, I reasoned like a child; when I became a man, I gave up childish ways.

ST. PAUL (*1 Corinthians 13:11*)

Communicating with children—talking with them, understanding what they mean, and feeling that they understand you—can be immensely satisfying or thoroughly frustrating. It is a special experience. It is also a special skill.

Children rarely talk directly about their worries because they rarely understand their role in their problems. Not only are they incapable of seeing that their present behavior is an incorrect effort to solve a problem, but they also are incapable of identifying the problem, the kind of help they need, or the kinds of relevant questions they should ask to get help. Hence, they have considerable difficulty involving themselves in adequate interchange with a helper about the task of coping with their problem.

Adults need not only to create an environment in which children want to express their feelings, but also to teach children to communicate effectively.

We have culled from the literature and from our own experience those principles and practices we believe are useful to adults to help counsel children in crisis. This particular chapter outlines unique characteristics of children at various ages, basic communication skills, and ways children tell you they have a problem.

Children Think Differently from Adults

How does one communicate with a child? Certainly talking in a softer tone of voice, in simple phrases, and in short, clear sentences helps. Playfulness and a sense of humor are common bridges that will connect you with most children. A pat on the back or a hug often says more than a host of words. Nevertheless, our conversation with children requires more effort than these approaches because children's thinking differs from ours.

An adult who is able to truly understand a child may often feel like a visitor to an exciting foreign land: We are treated to new sights, new ideas, and new ways of looking at things. Each day is brimming with new experiences to be interpreted and catalogued from a child's original perspective. Children create their own connections and assign unique meaning to common daily events. Every child is a poet and a dreamer. A child's outlook on life is refreshing, filled with awe, enthusiasm, and a sense of wonder. But there is another side to all of this. A child's imagination creates huge fears from small ones and magnifies anger into monsters of rage and devastation. When we talk with children, we must participate in the world from their frame of reference if we are to understand them.

Jean Piaget recognized the unique perspective of childhood. As a loving parent and eminent psychologist, he watched his own children grow and described the different ways in which they viewed the world at different ages. Piaget chronicled a detailed description of the thinking ability of children at different ages. At each stage there is a limit to the quality of logic that is present. Or perhaps it is more accurate to say that children have their own particular logic.

Toddlers have a cognition different from adolescents. Four-year-olds may believe they can control the moon and the planets, or that these celestial bodies are alive. Grade schoolers immerse themselves in hobbies and pastimes and avoid serious discussions. Adolescents hope that they can transform the world with their ideals.

Adults listening to and talking with a child in crisis have to remember that the child's thought may follow a logic all its own. An event may make sense to us, but after relating it we find it makes no sense to the child at all. We have chosen to divide childhood into three general stages: *the magic years, the middle years,* and *adolescence.* The first two are discussed in this chapter; adolescence is treated in the next.

The Magic Years

The magic years (ages three to six), as Selma Fraiberg[1] refers to them, are the years of early childhood, of nursery school and kindergarten. Children at this age are learning to be part of the world which is greater than their own family unit. These years are years of discovery, of wonder and awe at the largeness of the world, a time of play, reckless abandon, and fantasy. Yet the magic that colors young children's thought does not simply refer to their belief in demons, fairies, or Santa Claus. Magical thinking refers to children's belief that their own thought processes can influence objects and events in the world outside of themselves. This kind of thinking reflects children's inability to understand the concepts of chance, fate, random events, and all of the unpredictable developments that we adults come to accept as part of daily life. Young children from three to six years of age lack the conceptual thinking ability to realize that events which occur together with a thought are not caused by that thought. Magical thinking reflects children's omnipotence, their belief that they are the center of the universe and are big enough and powerful enough to influence all of the events in the world around them.

"The boy who destroyed the circus tent" provides an example of magical thinking. David, age seven, was enrolled in a residential treatment center for children with learning problems as well as emotional difficulties. At this center great preparation was being made for an upcoming professional conference. David's therapist would be attending this conference for several days, and David knew that he would be missing his regular sessions. The night before the conference, David was fascinated by the work going on around the tent. He pulled at several of the ropes, just to see how strong they were. That evening there was a torrential rain, and the circus tent collapsed!

David felt he caused this disaster. Not only had he tugged at the ropes, he had been angry and had secretly wished that his therapist would not attend the conference. David's inner logic proceeded in this manner: "I didn't want Dr. M. to go to the meeting; I pulled the tent ropes; the tent fell down. Therefore, I pulled the tent down." David was very upset over this, and it took a skilled interviewer to convince him that he was not the cause of the tent's collapse.

Furthermore, children in the magic years do not understand why they become sick and don't feel well and are disturbed by the unfamiliar body changes that accompany illness. They often feel responsible for having become ill. They brought the illness about because they were bad or did something they should not have done. They see the sickness as their punishment. Adults inadvertently reinforce these attitudes with admonitions: "Wear your jacket or you'll catch cold," or "Don't run in the street or you'll fall and hurt yourself." Statements like these serve to underscore children's belief that they caused their illness.

How do you respond with understanding to the child who displays magical thinking? First, recognize that sometimes it is impossible to completely change young children's patterns of thought. Second, help children to *fully express* what it is they think they did. You can patiently repeat the questions, "What else did you do?" or "That thought there, the one that just popped into your head, tell me about that." Third, help them to discover for themselves the real, or most probable, cause for the event. Do not tell them the reason; help them find it. Remember that their *active search* for the reason is important. Fourth, focus on possible guilt the child may feel as a result of a perceived power and control over an unfortunate occurrence: "You know, Bobby, I'll bet that you sometimes wished that your daddy was gone. And now he's gone. Tell me about those wishes." When they are fully expressed, you can say, "Your daddy had many reasons for leaving. His reasons had nothing to do with you. Could you find out what they were? Who could you ask?"

Helping young children to fully express themselves assists them in developing greater self-control in crisis situations. For these youngsters, speech serves a self-directive function. Witness this four-year-old who started talking to himself as he sat down at a table alone: "I want to do that drawing there. . . . I want to draw something, I do. I shall need a big piece of paper to do that."[2]

By talking their thoughts aloud, children move themselves, lead themselves. They follow their oral instructions into action. Piaget's six-year-old daughter summed up the guiding role of speech beautifully after she had misplaced one of her favorite dolls. When queried by her father, "You've no idea where you put it?" she replied, "No, I've no more ideas. . . . My mouth will have to give me a new idea." "How?" her father asked. *"It's when I talk my mouth helps me to think."*[3]

The unique magical thinking of children is often evident with the addition of a new member to the family. Overwhelming feelings of resentment, anger, and jealousy are aroused toward the new brother or sister. Sometimes they wish the baby had never been born. "If Mommy really loved me, she wouldn't have had this new baby."

Such children are in a bind. They cannot express their negative feelings too directly or act them out too strongly. If they do, they run the risk of provoking their mother. So the anger and jealousy seep out in small ways: teasing, bickering, or hiding toys or candy.

A problem can arise if the sibling becomes ill or dies. Often the surviving child believes that his or her anger at the sibling and some of the things he or she may have done—poking the sibling, calling names, taking the child's cover off at night—may have caused the tragedy. This makes the survivor feel powerful, but in a terrible and negative way: "My desires can cause great harm in the world!" Such mistaken beliefs can generate immense guilt and confusion in the child and may cause inhibition and withdrawal, and a reluctance to socialize or participate in former activities.

In talking with children who wonder if they have brought misfortune to someone they love, explore with them the ramifications of their thinking. Talk with them about what they think they did, what "bad" feelings they had which led to misfortune. Give them ample opportunity to explain themselves. Then gently emphasize, again and again, that happenings in the world are not always the result of anger or "bad" feelings. A sensitive approach, stressing that no one is to blame, may alleviate the child's guilt and self-blame.

Egocentrism

Young children are egocentric, not in the sense of being selfish, self-serving, or conceited, but in being *centered* on themselves and failing to take into account the viewpoints of others.

Children attribute to you, simply because you are there, the same feelings and wishes that they have. How many times have we heard young children ask: "Is your mommy making turkey too?" or "Are you going to visit your daddy this weekend?" Angry children expect you to be just as angry with them as they are with you, and sad children believe that you are equally sad. Consequently, when dealing with angry children, for example, take a passive stance. Openly express that while they are angry at you, you're not mad and will not hurt them even though they're so mad they'd like to hurt you. Since most of us regress when we are angry, this approach can be used at all age levels.

"You made me do that!" is a frequent expression of young or developmentally immature children. Adults rarely take these words seriously. Sometimes they should! Many young children attribute their misbehavior to the influence of others. This is projection—a classic defense mechanism described in psychology textbooks. Children become angrier when we counter "Don't be silly—I didn't make you bump your head" because they truly believe otherwise. Getting them to accept responsibility for their behavior is very difficult. Adlerian psychologists call this getting them *to own the problem*. Young children defend against anxiety by denial, repression, projection, or displacement—all defense mechanisms which prevent their feeling anxious or self-accusatory. To get them to *own* a problem requires that they face their anxiety; not an easy task, but one we hope will become easier as you gain more experience in talking with children.

Young children often talk past one another. Watch any nursery school class at recess and you will see youngsters speaking at great length to no one in particular. Young children often speak in a nonsocial manner, to themselves, a phenomenon that Piaget called *private speech* or *egocentric speech*. Private speech indicates children's failure to distinguish between themselves as speaker and the other person as listener. They don't realize that things taken for granted by themselves must first be clarified to others. They assume that words carry more meaning than they do and are not concerned whether the listener understands them or not. Not until around the age of seven do children learn to distinguish between their own viewpoint and that of others.

Sometimes we have to talk in the children's language to communicate with them. When we use our language, it may appear as if they are communicating when, in fact, they aren't. Contrast the following interchanges between an adult and a child:[4]

(Interchange One)

ADULT: You never been in a fight?

CHILD: Nope.

ADULT: Nobody ever picked on you?

CHILD: Nope.

ADULT: Nobody ever hit you?

CHILD: Nope.

ADULT: How come?

CHILD: I dunno.

ADULT: Didn't you ever hit somebody?

CHILD: Nope.
ADULT: (incredulously) You never hit nobody?
CHILD: Mhm.
(Interchange Two)
ADULT: Is there anybody who says your momma drink pee?
CHILD: (rapidly and breathlessly) Yee-ah!
ADULT: Yup!
CHILD: And your father eats doo-doo for breakfast!
ADULT: Ohh! (Laughs.)
CHILD: And they say your father eats doo-doo for dinner!

When the adult uses the *child's language* to phrase questions, the child's response reveals that much playground teasing and probably fighting takes place among his peers. Why the child responded as he did to the first set of questions is a mystery. Perhaps he says *nope* to all adult initiated and phrased questions regardless of content, or perhaps the words *You never been in* or *Nobody ever* were foreign to his communication pattern. While we're not suggesting that you talk *baby talk* or try to be like a child, we are saying to remain flexible. Occasionally, humor, physical contact, and child language will facilitate communication.

Unless we actively guide our conversations with young children, we can expect considerable failure in communication. They won't say what they mean, and we won't hear what they say.

They Take Things Literally

Young children often take things literally. When, in exasperation, you exclaim, "I'm getting sick and tired of your behavior!" you have communicated poorly. The child may take you literally—you are getting *sick* and *tired.* An older child may catch your drift, but your true feelings remain unexpressed. Only your anger is communicated. Nor have you allowed the child to respond. If you say, "I'm really disappointed and angry that you ripped up your work," you clearly convey the reason for your anger. You have also left the child an opening, a chance to respond and explain. And you have established a model of clear communication for the future.

Many common adult phrases are so abstract that young children will be unable to grasp them. For example, if a child tells you an obvious lie and you say, "That's a lot of baloney!" he or she will look for the baloney. "Don't give me that" or "Don't pull my leg" will earn you a quizzical gaze from a puzzled child. Or if the child is about to lose his or her temper, you might be inclined to say, "Keep your shirt on" or "Hold your horses," but realize that these expressions are too abstract. "Keep your cool," "Don't give up the ship," "Hang in there," "Don't throw in the towel".... There are many other expressions that children, even those well beyond the magic years, will take literally. Even the most mundane language can be misinterpreted. A six-year-old boy in foster care whose father wasn't showing up regularly for visits was told by a counselor: "I'll bet you get mad when your father doesn't keep his promises." The boy said, "He gives them away?"

They Make Unique Connections

Children in the magic years often make their own unique connections between events, objects, and people. Their creations are like some works of modern art, which make sense to their creator but to no one else. They group together things or events that seem totally unrelated to an adult observer. Children fail to see the "real" (adult) connection because they are unable to consider several aspects of a situation simultaneously. Piaget called this *syncretic thought*.

Let's look at how a child can make subjective connections between the simple materials of daily life. A group of young children are shown a thimble, a spoon, and a bicycle bell and asked to tell how they are all alike. One child, handling only the spoon, says they are all painful objects. Our knowledge that her mother force-fed her enables us to guess that she saw the spoon as painful, perhaps the thimble as also related to pain (actually to pain avoidance), and it's anyone's guess how the bicycle bell fits in. The child couldn't express why she saw them as painful objects—she just did. Older children see them as "all made of metal."

Even when children have some rudimentary understanding of how something works, they often cannot explain it. Witness one child's account of how a faucet works: "The handle is turned on, and then the water runs. There, there is no water running, there the handle is turned off, and here the water is running. There, there is no water running, and here there is no water running."[5]

Since young children have great difficulty organizing and communicating their thoughts, imagine the confusion a crisis stirs in a young child.

For example, a young child may see illness and going to the movies

as related because Grandpa was at the movies when he had a heart attack. The child now becomes anxious whenever he's near a theater, yet
few adults would ever guess that such an association existed. The child
has made a subjective connection between going to the movies and experiencing a heart attack. The adult may learn about these connections
by careful questioning about an event:

ADULT: What was Grandpa doing when he had his heart attack?
CHILD: Coming home.
ADULT: Coming home from where?
CHILD: I don't remember.
ADULT: Home from work, shopping, the movies, the gas station . . . ?
CHILD: The movies, I think. (Child gets nervous and tense, fidgets in
    chair, kicks seat.)
ADULT: Do you think that going to the movies may have caused
    Grandpa's heart attack?

Careful interviewing will help you discern false connections and
educate the child about the real cause of events.

Helping the Child Decenter

Recognize that young children often—but not always—focus their
attention on a single striking detail of an experience to the neglect of
others. Quite literally, they cannot see the forest for the trees.

Piaget used the word *egocentricity* to describe how young children
are unable to distinguish between their own point of view and those of
others. The overcoming of egocentricity involves the ability to shift
one's point of view rapidly, to decenter one's attention from one's
momentary perspective to consider simultaneously other possible perspectives. Since the development of interpersonal communication
skills are fundamentally dependent on the development of role-taking
skills (ability to take different points of view simultaneously), we can
expect considerable communication failures in conversations with
young children unless we take some steps to avoid them.

Given the fast demands and the level of their information-handling
abilities, centering is often the best children can do. Centering is a focusing of their efforts on only one area. The child can do otherwise
under other circumstances.

Young children can recognize and coordinate different viewpoints
but are susceptible to lapses in performance, dependent upon the conditions they meet. When children's patterns of thought are relatively

unsystematized, their awareness of other perspectives is perhaps more quickly swept aside by the currents of their own immediate experience and actions.[6] They dwell on a single detail of an experience to the neglect of others.

For example, young children encouraged to state what they didn't like about the story "Little Red Riding Hood" might only be able to reply, "He ate grandma."[7] They might have difficulty remembering the other important details of the story. Or when asked about "Jack and the Beanstalk," these children might say, "I hate string beans. I hope we don't have them for dinner." Likewise, the four-year-old accidentally pushed in line might respond with aggression. The child devotes her attention to being pushed and neglects to perceive that it was an accident. Another child who was timed-out after hitting the gym teacher could only say, "I picked the tape off the floor and hit Mrs. Coles." No amount of prompting elicited more detail. After talking with Mrs. Coles, the adult learned that she had asked the boy to stop taking the tape off the floor that marked sitting places for each child. He continued, and she asked him to remove himself to the time-out chair. He refused and hit her when she escorted him to the chair. With this knowledge the adult could lead the boy to fill in the gaps in his report.

Piaget emphasized that most children under seven *center* on one aspect of a situation and have trouble *decentering* on the whole picture. For example, in one study of children's understanding of cause and effect, children were shown a set of drawings in which a boy asks his mother for a drink.[8] She gives him an orange drink when he really wanted a green drink. The children were then asked, "Whose fault was it that Steven did not get the drink he wanted?" Children under age seven typically blamed the mother and indeed judged Steven's message to be adequate. When asked, "How could we make sure she got it right the next time?" the young children under age seven did not mention improving the message but would repeat "got it right" or "try harder." Young children typically communicate in ignorance of the role of ambiguous messages in communication failure. Consequently, the adult's job is to guide them to see the issues more clearly. One might also wonder if "fault" is a clearly understood word for children under seven. If a counselor was talking with a child who was mad at his mother for giving him the wrong drink, he or she might say: "Was there more than one thing to drink in the refrigerator . . . ? Maybe you need to make sure Mommy knew which drink you wanted?"

The crisis counselor's job is to help children see the whole picture: to recognize the different facets of their experience, to organize their thoughts, and to overcome their tendency to center on a single striking detail. It's like helping a child assemble a jigsaw puzzle, pointing out the different pieces and helping to find where they go.

Later in this chapter we will discuss asking specific questions, asking for comparisons between things, and asking leading questions. All these tactics enable the child to look at other perspectives, to shift the center of attention to other areas, to decenter. The following conversation illustrates an attempt at decentering:

CHILD: You hate me!

ADULT: Why?

CHILD: Because you yelled at me.

ADULT: You could get hurt if I let you fight with Robin. Do you remember the times I don't yell at you?

CHILD: No.

ADULT: How about yesterday. I praised you for all your good work at school.

CHILD: Oh yeah, I forgot.

ADULT: Somehow you remember when I scold you, but forget when I praise you.

The magic years: feeling responsible, assigning unique connections, being egocentric, taking things literally, and centering. Keep these characteristics in mind and you will communicate more effectively with children ages three to six.

The Middle Years

Dramatic changes occur in the thinking ability of middle years children (ages seven to twelve). Their conceptual thought is more advanced, and they can work out many problems in their head rather than through trial and error. Middle years children apply their new ability to learning important skills that will help them throughout life, such as reading and mathematics. These youngsters decenter—they can see the viewpoints and recognize the feelings of others—the foundation for cooperation and later, mature behavior.

The fantasy life of middle years children illustrates their shift in focus. They dwell on people and events from the real world, not from the world of fantasy and make-believe. The night fears of magic years children concern beasts and animallike creatures such as monsters, goblins, gremlins, and spooks, whereas middle years children's night fears feature humanlike pursuers: robbers, kidnappers, giants, witches, or "the bogeyman."

Emotionally, children in the middle years are often viewed as uncomplicated and enjoyable. They are seen as "calm, pliable, and educable," and some refer to ages seven and twelve as the "latency years." Freud originally used this term because he felt that the strong feelings present in early childhood are dormant. Children in the middle years are interested in applying their newly discovered reasoning ability to the world around them. They spend energy developing hobbies, learning to play games, and attempting to master the environment. They repress the range of emotions, some wonderful, some terrifying, that they experienced in the magic years.

Of course, not all children in the middle years follow this pattern. And even those who do, break out of it from time to time. Note the excited, zoolike behavior of children at school recess. Or ask one of these children what his or her life is like:

ADULT: Is it really so tough being eight years old?

CHILD: How would you like to be half the size of everybody else and not have a dime to your name?[9]

These youngsters must follow the rules of their parents and teachers because outbursts of rebellion are doomed. "All that is possible is surrender and an attempt to please the masters, by learning well what there is to be learned."[10]

Avoiders of Issues

Children in the middle years experience difficulty dealing with the emotionally charged themes that characterize crisis situations. They fear their own regression to the fears of the magic years. Note how panicked they get after hearing ghost tales from an older sibling. Often they're afraid to enter their own bedroom unless it is first checked out by an adult. Adults need to continually focus on the subject to keep them from avoiding the issue:

ADULT: Maybe you were mad after Jennifer stole your glove?

CHILD: Are we going to the movies tonight?

or

ADULT: Next Tuesday is when you'll be going into the hospital for your operation.

CHILD: Can I have my allowance now?

Child therapists often employ games or structured activities with children of this age group either to focus their thoughts or to provide an activity to siphon some of the anxiety these youngsters feel at discussing painful issues. These methods can be employed by nonprofessional counselors as well.

Simple games like checkers, jacks, tick-tack-toe, or playing cards provide outlets for the child's energies while not demanding excessive mental concentration. As the two of you play, you can bring up whatever the child needs to talk about.

Sometimes the discussion becomes a monologue, with the counselor doing most of the talking. One such monologue occurred during a session with an eight-year-old girl who was noisily pushing a truck along the floor while her counselor tried to discuss suspected incestuous relations with a much older brother. The counselor monologued what he suspected had happened and his speculations about her reactions. As he did, the "truck noises" got louder and louder. They soon drowned out the sound of his voice, whereupon he stopped and said, "I guess you're not ready to talk about these things." To his surprise the girl responded, "Keep talking—I wondered when you'd get to this." The truck noises helped her to listen to the counselor and to avoid being embarrassed, and she continued to make noises throughout the interview. Others have held their hands over their ears, but they still hear.

Another way to structure communication with middle years children is through *communication toys* such as tape recorders, play telephones, puppets, costumes, and drawing materials. Actively play with the toys to stimulate the child's involvement. You might draw a picture, call a child on the phone, or have one puppet talk to another about a problem similar to the child's: "This is a picture of a girl, and this is a picture of a hospital. The girl will be going to the hospital soon. What does she think her visit to the hospital will be like?" Or, "This boy will soon be getting a new daddy and two new sisters. Draw me a picture of some of the things they will do together."

Storytelling is an effective and enjoyable way to guide a child's thinking. We have devoted a section to this approach in chapter four, "Empathic Focusing."

Many times adults will feel they have grasped what a child is feeling or trying to say only to be met with "You don't understand." Often it is because we are too analytical; we have understood the general while the child wants us to understand the specific. "I've got it. You feel bad because you think your mommy loved your sister best." The child retorts, "No! No! No! It's because I want her dress." "That's what I said," the adult insists. "I just said it differently." "You still don't understand," the child sighs in frustration.

When you guess wrong, and "wrong" can be simply how the child perceives your guess rather than what actually may be so, the reluctant child will not correct you. He or she will say, "I want to go back to class," or "I don't care."

Jumping to Conclusions

Despite their increasing cognitive abilities, jumping to conclusions from false premises is a characteristic of the child in the middle years. "There goes Grandma!" a child may say any time a yellow Volkswagen goes by because Grandma has a yellow Volkswagen. Or these children may cry and scream hysterically when they cut themselves because they silently conclude that the bleeding will never stop. One nine-year-old girl, upon inspecting a newly constructed rabbit pen, instantly exclaimed, "The foxes will kill the rabbit!" She was asked to carefully examine the size of the mesh in the new fence, and to see that it would be impossible for a fox to get through the tiny holes. In crisis counseling with these youngsters, unmasking false premises is often a key task:

CHILD WITH BROKEN ARM: I'll never be able to go to school again!
ADULT: I guess you feel having a broken arm changes your whole life.

Blind to Inconsistencies

Talking to children in the middle years can present other problems. These youngsters may seem quite bright, with a wisdom that goes beyond their years. But one problem we face in talking with middle years children is that sometimes they don't understand us and sometimes *we fail to appreciate that they don't understand us.* In particular, they may not understand what is a common characteristic of many crises: seeing the inconsistencies of a given situation.

For the crisis counselor, verbalization of inconsistencies is often an important job: "Daddy is moving away, but he still loves you," or "Your new friend has problems in learning, but he's just like you in so many other ways." These statements may be insightful to the adult, but do they make sense to the young child? Some fascinating research reveals that children often don't truly understand what they hear. The following story was read to a group of children to see how adept they were at picking up the inconsistencies within:

> Many different kinds of fish live in the ocean. Some fish have heads that make them look like alligators, and some fish have heads that make them look like cats. Fish live in different parts of the ocean. Some fish live near the surface of the water, but some fish live way down near the bottom of the ocean. Fish must have light to see. There is absolutely no light at the bottom of the ocean. It is pitch black down there. When it is that dark, the fish cannot see anything. They cannot even see colors. Some fish that live at the bottom of the ocean can see the color of their food; that is how they know what to eat.[11]

One would think that a child could immediately grasp that fish that can't see cannot choose to eat their food by its color! This is not what occurred. When children were asked general questions about the story, most of them—in fact, 96 percent of the children in the third through sixth grades—missed the inconsistency in the story. Only after very direct, probing questions were the children able to say that fish who live in the dark part of the ocean obviously can't see colors.

The knowledge that eleven- and twelve-year-old children can listen to contradictory material and not see the inconsistency is disconcerting. Ordinarily, when inconsistencies occur in life, they will not be explicitly stated, reiterated, or rephrased. If children fail to notice inconsistencies when they are stated so obviously, they are unlikely to notice them when doing academic work or considering everyday occurrences. It is also unlikely that they will be attuned to them in discussions about personal crises.

Keep this in mind when talking with children. Make things very clear to them, repeat statements, and rephrase the message in different ways.

Middle years children: uncomplicated and enjoyable, avoiders of issues, jumpers to conclusions, and blind to inconsistencies. Remember these qualities when you talk with children in this age group.

General Approaches

From our discussion of the magic years and the middle years, it should be clear that effective counselors shift gears when talking with children of different ages. Acknowledge the limits of children's thinking and reasoning, and do not force adult "logic" on them. Remember that all children are unique and tell a story all their own. To truly understand, we must carefully listen and then be able to communicate our understanding. Let us now look at some effective approaches for talking and listening to children.

Children Ask Questions

Childhood and curiosity go hand in hand. To be a child means to ask questions: "How do birds fly?" "Who made God?" "When will we get there?" "How come?"

Many questions children ask reflect an insatiable thirst for knowledge, information, facts—the whys and wherefores of the world. Others are not so innocent. They are designed to see if it is safe to express feelings. A foster child who asks his social worker whether she likes his foster mother is actually asking for permission to speak his own feelings about her.

One common, indirect way in which children hint that they have a problem is by approaching an adult and asking a broad, general question. The motive behind this might be sheer curiosity, or it might be the children's roundabout way of indicating that something is troubling them. Sometimes a child might ask a teacher, "Do you ever hit your own kids at home?" Granted, the child might be trying to ascertain whether the teacher is a firm disciplinarian or a "soft touch." But such children may be trying to communicate that they are being hit by their own parents and that they have some important concerns about it. Likewise, the query, "Do you drink?" might be designed to elicit value differences, or it could be the first step toward revealing an alcoholic problem within their own family.

Keep in mind that any question children ask an adult may convey a covert message. It may be a veiled cry for help, may suggest an area of difficulty for the child, or be a test of your reactions should they wish to confide in you. Questions can be the children's way of exploring if their feelings are "stupid" or if their concerns are legitimate.

Many times direct answers to a child's questions result in no communication taking place. Queries such as, "Who broke this toy?" really mean "What happened to the boy who broke this toy?" Children interview you to check out if you're safe. Sometimes they'll pick up something on your desk and ask what it is. They may go over to a blackboard and deliberately misspell a word to see your reaction. They may volunteer something like "My mother spanked me." Don't ask for details at this stage. Just reflect what it must feel like to get spanked. The child may ask if you hit your kids, smoke, drink, are divorced, or other personal questions. Simply answer these questions truthfully without elaboration and add that it is all right for the child to get to know you better. Children ask questions in order to trust adults, and they continue to ask them of adults they trust.

Adults Ask Questions

The use of questions in talking with children is an art in itself. Some questions facilitate communication; others kill it.

Many times we ask children questions like "What's the matter?" "Did your sister hit you?" or "Do you understand the assignment?" These questions typically result in yes or no answers. Avoid them. They can impede communication and are usually unproductive. For example, a child tells an adult how her brother hit her with a stick, and the adult asks, "Does it hurt?" The child's reply of no makes it difficult for the adult to help the child explore her feelings of anger toward her brother. Better to ask no questions, or at least a more natural one, such as, "How do you feel?"

Adults are often too general or abstract when talking with children: "What kind of person is your new friend?" "What changes do you think will happen when the new baby comes?" "What choice do you have?" or "Why did you do that?" are questions that will usually elicit a flat reply: "She's okay," or "I don't know."

Comparisons help. Asking children to describe how two people or two events differ from each other is more productive than asking a general question such as "What is your school like?" or "Why don't you like gym?" Here is an example in which communication did not take place between adult and child when the adult was trying to help a young girl express feelings that her mother may have liked her sister best:

ADULT: Linda, what kind of person was your sister?

CHILD: She was okay.

ADULT: What was she like, what did she mean to you?

CHILD: She was nice.

Notice how communication improved when the adult began to ask for specifics or comparisons:

ADULT: How did your sister act when you took one of her toys?

CHILD: Mad.

ADULT: What did she do when she got mad at you?

CHILD: Yell at me!

ADULT: If you were playing with toys that belonged to your sister or brother, and you broke some of their toys—would they both get mad at you in the same way, or would they be different?

CHILD: Betty would yell and then tell my mother. Tom would punch me and maybe go into my room and break a toy.

ADULT: What would your mother do when Betty went to her?

CHILD: Send me to my room and make me pay for it out of my allowance.

Often when you ask children questions, they are afraid that giving the "wrong" answer will get them into trouble. Make the purpose of your meeting clear. Explain that questions are not a test, but a way for you to get to know them better. Indirect questions or statements, those referring to "the child's problem" rather than "the problem with the child" are more effective.

> *Direct Statement:* I understand you have problems going to bed at night.
>
> *Indirect Question:* What do you think is a good bedtime for a child?
>
> (Then) What time do you go to bed?

When You Don't Understand

Don't be afraid to tell children that you do not understand their intended message. Adults often pride themselves on guessing what the child means rather than informing children directly that they don't understand. If you don't understand, let them know: "Nate, I think you're trying to tell me something, but I'm not sure what it is. Maybe you could say it again in different words?" Many times this helps children communicate what they are trying to say. If your comments elicit discouragement, view this as an opportunity to reflect the underlying feelings:

ADULT: Nate, you look hurt and discouraged because I didn't understand what you were trying to say. It's frustrating when people don't understand each other. Let's try again. . . .

Be direct and honest with the child, even if you have learned otherwise. While leading educators list numerous modeling strategies to extend a child's communication skills and never seem to mention focusing directly on the child's utterances,[11] others who explicitly inform their young children when they do not understand them have children who are more effective communicators.[12]

Clarify Your Intentions

Many adults—teachers, coaches, scout leaders, camp counselors—are responsible for working with groups of children at a time. When a child needs individual attention, the adult pulls him or her aside privately after school or after the game. Children often see an interview as a prelude to reprimands or punishment, so that even the most innocent question seems ominous. Since many children in crisis display "misbehavior," they fear discussion because it may somehow get them into further trouble!

The crisis counselor needs to make clear his or her purpose in talking with the child: "Kathy, you haven't been yourself lately. You don't seem to have your usual energy. Maybe we could talk and see if there's something on your mind. You're usually not late for practice and usually don't miss the ball so much. Maybe I can help you figure out what's going on?" When children see the meeting in a positive light, they are more likely to open up.

Since many crisis interviews will occur in a principal's office, classroom after school, camp cabin or tent, parole officer's car, hospital bed, or a child's bedroom in a group home, we need to remember that these are settings in which the child is in a clearly subordinate position. In such situations shift gears. Your role now is as counselor, helper, friend—not authority figure. Avoid:
- sounding didactic and professional
- overwhelming the child with authority and wisdom
- joining forces with the child in criticizing other authority figures in his life
- ending statements with "Isn't that so?" "Get what I mean?" or "That's right"; also, nodding or shaking your head in response or producing an inflection in the tone of your voice at the end of a sentence. These *cues* set up children's responses—they'll say what they think you expect from them.
- leaving the door open or talking within earshot of others (This limits privacy.)
- being "nice" in a saccharine manner

• approaching the child with misconceptions gleaned from others or from file records
• defending feelings, ideas, or friends that are attacked or denied by the child
• becoming so confused during the interview that you can only ask, "What else is on your mind?"
• feeling inferior in the presence of a gifted child, or superior in the presence of an average one.

Whose Problem?

Problem children are children with a problem, and interview efforts should be directed at getting the children to talk about their problem rather than the problem with them. Defiant children are a problem to adults, but their problem can be fears of rejection and failure. We suggested that indirect questions help overcome the child's resistance to talking about the problem with you. Other approaches are more direct:

ADULT: I've talked with your Mom, and she's concerned about your school work. She thinks you didn't try hard enough, but I've known many children whose parents have separated who think a lot about that at school, and their work suffers. What about you?

If the child's been a discipline problem, a poor opener would be, "Your mother tells me you hit other boys at school." Better to say, "I gather that things are not going too well at school."

Allow the Child Some Freedom

Adults frequently instruct children to sit still and stop fiddling when they are talking to them. Let the child fiddle. In fact, encourage it—provide something to fiddle with. Good fiddlers can make good talkers. Let the child stand, move around, or whatever else, as long as it helps the child feel in control. Few people truly communicate with those who are trying to control them, so let children use their own physical movement to give them a sense of control.

Observe Nonverbal Cues

Because of the child's inability to correctly answer questions, or the adult's inability to correctly formulate them, the adult should closely observe the child's nonverbal cues. Listen closely to what the child's words and tone of voice, gestures, and facial expressions reveal. Learn to listen with "the third ear."[13] Pick up those aspects of the presentation to which the child is personally deaf. Then you can consider how to communicate what you "heard." This skill is empathy and is discussed in more detail in chapter four.

Reluctant Children

Some children will not respond, no matter how skillfully an adult encourages discussion. And if you push for information, these children will defend themselves: "It may be possible to make children talk, but words dragged from a reluctant, defensive child will not lead to meaningful communication."[14]

With reluctant children indirect approaches work best. You might simply sit down and draw something that will capture the child's attention. Take the posture of getting alongside of, rather than squarely facing, the child. Your first statement to a terrified child might be, "How nice you came to see me in your new blue running shoes!" Establish a natural line of shared experiences about a game played, a program watched, or a book read. Or get a third thing going that can be a focal point to relieve tension, such as drawing, painting, or games: "Here is a family of dolls to play with, and here's a dollhouse. Perhaps you'd like to talk to me by playing while I watch." Or "Here are some crayons and paper. Maybe you would like to draw some pictures."

Since many troubled children fail to talk to themselves, you can make what are called running comments as they play. These are simply statements made to help children "see" what they are doing or what they might be doing.

(The child is busy playing with fire truck, but saying nothing.)

ADULT: The firemen are getting the truck ready to go!

(The child drives truck to a house.)

ADULT: The firemen are going to rescue the people.

Children often respond to such comments by elaborating on their play or correcting the adult: "No, the people are already dead. The firemen were too late."

Sometimes children are not sure what they are playing. Play often is an attempt to master an anxiety-arousing experience not fully understood or incompletely experienced. The adult's running comments can help the child fill in the missing pieces.

Avoid Overidentifying

Many adults who work with children experiencing ongoing crises can easily overidentify with them. Such an attitude is understandable when we appreciate the youngster's helplessness and vulnerability. As a result, the child is seen as the victim of bad parents or bad situations. Added to this are unconscious feelings about our own parents or crisis situations we have faced. Overidentification frequently can be seen in remarks or behaviors designed to make up for the bad in children's lives. These take the form of excessive compliments to children, gratification of their demands, and affectionate comments and gestures. While these actions can be soothing to the children, they will not always help them find ways to cope with the realities of the crisis they face. For additional discussion of overidentification, see chapter nine, "Child Abuse."

The ideas and approaches we have outlined equip you to communicate better with children. Next we look at some of the concerns of adolescents, then discuss the importance of empathy and structure in crisis counseling.

Suggested Reading

Fraiberg, S. *The Magic Years—Understanding and Handling the Problems of Early Childhood.* New York: Charles Scribners, 1959.

Gardner, R. A. *Therapeutic Communication with Children.* New York: Science House, 1972.

Gardner, R. A. *Psychotherapeutic Approaches to the Resistant Child.* New York: Jason Aronson, 1975.

Ginott, H. G. *Between Parent and Child; New Solutions to Old Problems.* New York: Macmillan, 1965.

Looff, D. H. *Getting to Know the Troubled Child.* Knoxville: University of Tennessee Press, 1976.

Sarnoff, C. *Latency.* New York: Jason Aronson, 1976.

·3·

Adolescence

I think what is happening to me is so wonderful and not only what can be seen on my body, but all that is taking place inside me. I never discuss myself or any of these things with anybody; that is why I have to talk to myself about them.

ANNE FRANK
The Diary of a Young Girl

A dolescents often are absorbed in a world within themselves. They withdraw from contact with others, and are limited by self-centeredness. "Are you deaf?" is a common plea from parents and teachers in response to their silence or sulking.

Adolescents react to an imaginary audience. When they feel self-critical, they assume others are equally critical of them. They feel particularly sensitive to shame. Because adolescents are more concerned with being observed than observing, with being interesting rather than interested, old friendships sustain them through this time as new friends are difficult to come by. Moves can be especially traumatic for this age group.

Adolescents regard themselves as unique and special—only they "can suffer such agonized intensity or exquisite rapture."[1] They develop *personal fables,* stories they assume about themselves which aren't true. Learning to appreciate others' viewpoints helps adolescents see beyond their personal fables; they learn to integrate their own emotions with the feelings of others.

Because their social role is unclear, adolescents are inclined to shyness, sensitivity, and aggressiveness to mask their insecurity. Social fears are common, such as feeling rejected, being ignored, feeling disapproved of, looking foolish, losing control, speaking in public, being watched working. Because of their unstable sense of self, they fear unpleasant or peculiar people. They particularly fear those in authority. Some have described adolescence as a period of prolonged "sensitivity training."

Over two-thirds of adolescents express a desire to change their physical appearance. Girls think of themselves as too heavy or too tall, while boys feel they are too thin, particularly in their upper arms and chest.[2] And God forbid if the girl should be small-breasted or the boy have any breast tissue! Acne brings humiliation. Because their bodies are changing, adolescents display fears of body injury, and fears of medical and dental treatment.[3]

Adolescents' thinking is radically different from that of children. They are able to recognize possibilities as well as actualities. They can think conceptually in abstract and universal terms and tend to over-idealize. Their new cognitive ability combined with a search for identity—the search for meaning in life is, after all, a search for identity—perhaps explains their preoccupation with issues of social justice, religion, morals, and values. Adolescents' powerful and almost nagging sense of idealism means that they *know* the way things should be; they expend a great deal of energy through anger and frustration when things are not working out the way they "should." By adulthood many of our views on sex, work, religion, and social values have crystallized into a lasting part of our personality. But for adolescents each day serves up new feelings and attitudes. One day they are attracted to traditional church worship and the next day to the scientific determinism of Bertrand Russell or the existential despair of Sartre.

Adolescents' impressions of themselves—their identity—comes from the feedback they get about themselves from others. They believe, and behave, differently in the company of different people. Sometimes adolescents even try to keep their different sets of friends apart and get nervous when they meet. The structure of adolescent identity is conceived as a group of characters. It includes all the people a youngster is with in different social situations. Adolescents copy people's speech unconsciously and surprise themselves by the way they behave. They play out roles expected of them, and much of what they play feels false, feels "not me." Some parts of the adolescent which feel true may be hidden or barely sensed. For example, should an American adolescent spend time in England, her speech will suddenly take on a British accent; should she strike up a close friendship in England, her English friend will want to be like her and begin to speak "American."

Adolescents tend to place people in categories. Peers are "jocks," "druggies," "intellectuals," "nerds," "preps," or "vals." Adults are judged by the way they dress or by their professions, rather than by who they are. Such categorizations allow adolescents to ignore powerful issues or confrontations: "You people always ask questions like that."

Sexuality adds a new dimension to adolescents' thoughts and feelings. Happy, outgoing children become isolated and sad adolescents who doubt their sexuality. In early adolescence heterosexual relationships are conflictual, and in middle adolescence they are idealized. Adolescents judge their behavior in the context of sexual normalcy and abnormalcy.

Interviews with urban adolescents reveal that they show no resemblance to their popular stereotype. They are not mindless consumers, practitioners of violence and sensuality, or rebels against all authority. Most are seriously interested in being effective interpreters and performers in the social environments that are presently significant to them.[4] So when they temporarily regress in the face of a crisis, have faith in them and they will resolve their difficulties.

Adolescents are idealists who tend to have unrealistic expectations for themselves and others. A crisis (divorce of parents, death of a loved one, broken romance, school failure) can lead to the subsequent loss of the ability to find value in things as they really are: "My parents split up; you can't count on anyone anymore."

Unlike depression, in which self-hate exists, disillusionment involves self-aggrandizement and degradation of others, interwoven with cynicism. The result is a powerful resistance to change, which can make a counselor feel hopeless.

Crisis Counseling with Adolescents

Formal counselors are viewed by adolescents as people who will tell them they are not okay. They categorize counselors as shrinks who are weird themselves. They are definitely *not* glamorous adults. Weird people—and those who work with weird people—are to be avoided: "Psychologists are all nosy people." Or, "You shrinks are all the same.

Same stupid couch ... same stupid diplomas on the walls ... same damn pictures of your family on the desk."[5] Adolescents with problems are worried about being stigmatized, and referral to a counselor can intensify this feeling and add to their sense of alienation. The counselor is not only viewed as "one who deals with weirdos" but also as an authority figure—and so is doubly feared. An authority figure will discover their thoughts or private actions, intimate details about themselves that they feel are too horrid to mention. It is no wonder that adolescents reveal themselves to everyone but counselors!

Teachers, athletic coaches, supervisors of afterschool jobs, neighbors, church youth group coordinators are the people adolescents turn to as a first line of defense against the crises they face as part of growing up. Let's look at some of the approaches these adults (and formal counselors as well) can employ.

Confidentiality

It is best to discuss at the outset any limits to confidentiality so that you will not be setting the stage for a later accusation of betrayal. Richard Gardner, a noted therapist, talks about how he handles the confidentiality issue. Early in treatment adolescents frequently ask him, "Are you going to inform my parents about what I tell you?" Gardner responds by saying that he won't divulge the things that are talked about in the sessions.

> However, I will also tell him that if he is involving himself in some kind of behavior that is extremely destructive *and* that he cannot stop after discussions with me and members of the treatment group, *then* I may very well have to resort to divulging what he tells me, even though he may not wish me to do so.[6]

Gardner does not specify the kinds of things that will or will not cause him to break confidentiality, believing that this gives the adolescent food for thought.

Marshal Positive Forces

Remember that adolescents are attuned to negative reactions from others. If they are depressed, they will recall unpleasant memories more readily than pleasant ones. They will underestimate the positive feedback they receive and overestimate the negative. You need to focus on the positive, mirroring their hopeful feelings rather than their depressive ones. Use supportive approaches.

ADOLESCENT: I feel like I can't do anything right.
ADULT: Nothing seems to be working for you lately.
ADOLESCENT: Yeah, I'm really down in the dumps.
ADULT: I feel like that sometimes, a really lousy feeling.
ADOLESCENT: (silence)
ADULT: I usually go visit a friend when I feel depressed. What do you do?
ADOLESCENT: Nothing. Maybe go to sleep.
ADULT: Maybe you could try talking to a friend. You have some interesting ideas. I enjoy talking with you. So would others.

Remember, too, that you are an *enabler,* facilitating the development of strengths and making the young person feel *more able.* Crisis states disrupt adolescents' problem-solving ability. They've solved difficult problems before. Help them to remember how they did it—get them in touch with their prior successes. Share with them your own personal thoughts and feelings in an effort to help them understand theirs. Reveal what has worked for you but be careful that your comments don't come across as advice or moralizing.

Adolescents often have what appear to others as silly ideas. Confronting them about these delusions only increases their intensity:

ADULT: That's why you got into trouble—because you have those ridiculous ideas.

or

ADULT: I can't follow your story. That idea is foolish.

Confrontations like these will alienate you from the youngster. Avoid disagreeing. Start with the least strongly held beliefs and offer other possible reasons why things are the way they are.

ADULT: You could be right, but I would like to discuss this with you in more detail. Why do you believe this?
ADOLESCENT: (Gives explanation.)
ADULT: Do you think there might be other reasons? Might they not talk to you because . . .

Outline other possible explanations and encourage the young person to express alternative ideas.

Self-Disclosure

One of the most effective ways of facilitating discussion with adolescents may be to share some in-depth background about yourself, either presently or from a time when you were younger. This is not to be done in the preachy fashion of "when I was your age," but rather as a sincere attempt to bridge the gap between two people through honest sharing.

Self-disclosure may be used to help show that you understand a particular situation which may be painful to discuss. Tentatively phrased, it can be a starting point for further discussion on how the adolescent experiences the world:

ADULT: When I was in college, my parents split up—right before my graduation! You'd think they could have waited just a bit. I felt devastated, alone, and angry, even though I was an adult. You and your dad always seemed close to me. How has his leaving affected you?

or

ADULT: Next week I have been invited to a party where I know only the host. It really makes me nervous to talk to a group of complete strangers. Do situations like that ever make you nervous?

or

ADULT: When I was young, I never felt I could please my dad. Whatever I did never seemed good enough. Do you ever feel that way about yourself?

Some sources caution against becoming too "personally involved" with youth. Yet in the authors' experience, it is often the staff who are willing to share personal material who are the most effective. Self-disclosure, when done appropriately, provides positive role modeling as well as an invitation to discuss things further.[7]

Encourage Written Expression

Many adolescents experience difficulty in directly relating their feelings, especially positive ones, in a face-to-face manner. Encourage them to write. The private nature of writing helps them uncover feelings they have denied or avoided, which they can then openly express to others, or reread to themselves from time to time, unobserved and without interruption. Writing helps adolescents pay more attention to the situations they find themselves in, and to differentiate among their various feelings. They can ponder their revelations in solitude, become actively involved without embarrassment, and can review their positive qualities and problem-solve to meet challenges.

One activity that helps adolescents express themselves is keeping daily logs organized into two categories—*situations* and *myself*. Under situations adolescents write accounts of at least two things that happened to them that they had not initiated. They describe their reactions and how they feel about their reactions. Under *myself* they write actions or behaviors they had chosen to initiate, to involve themselves in, giving the reasons, reactions, and feelings. Following the successful completion of these logs and appreciation of their value, they can then make a "Feelings Workbook." The goal is to help youth learn how their feelings make them behave. They ask simple but reflective questions of themselves, such as "Why am I doing this?" and write their answers in the workbook.[8]

Writing letters—which are never sent—helps adolescents become more aware of themselves. A young person could write a letter to someone he or she has difficulty with or strong feelings about. The process allows the writer to rehearse and prepare a script for a future conversation and reflect on what he or she is going to say. Writing letters that are never sent helps one to fully express feelings. Even writing to lost ones assists in the grieving process following a death, divorce, or romantic breakup.

Suggest Alternatives

When told what to do, most adolescents do the opposite. However, when their choices are respected and encouraged, they will often try to make a mature and intelligent decision. Providing alternatives for them helps clarify their thinking.

ADULT: You're very upset and don't know what to do. Some things you might want to consider are talking with your dad, going for a walk, or maybe going over to the gym to work out.

or

ADULT: You sure seem angry at Betty. You could tell her off, in front of everybody, let her know what you really think of her. Or you could go for a run and consider what to do later. Or you could write her a long letter about how you feel. You can think about these options and decide the best thing to do.

Explaining the consequences of a threatened action while withholding judgment can help an adolescent make a more informed decision.

ADOLESCENT: I'm going to run away to New York City. I don't have much money, but I can hitch a ride there.

ADULT: Be careful if you hitchhike. A lot of people take advantage of kids who hitchhike—they use them sexually.

When you talk with adolescents, concentrate on helping them see how they themselves may be the cause of their troubles. As long as they blame others, they can persist in inadequate problem-solving efforts. Steps toward constructive change come about once they see themselves as the "problem maker" and begin to accept responsibility for their actions. Even abused children can initiate their abuse. To break this pattern, they can learn to stop complaining when they know their father has been drinking. When individuals can admit that they bring about their own troubles (see their role in the matter), they realize they can bring about their own successes.

PRINCIPAL: Jan, you say that European History is so ancient, so boring and so useless—that's why you failed it. I think something else is going on. You don't even try to do the work. Remember how you didn't like computer programming but kept trying? You got a "B" and now you're in the advanced class. You know that you're the one in charge of doing well or doing poorly. Is something else troubling you?

Stay Empathic

Adolescents in crisis often behave in ways that elicit punishment from others. We strongly believe that firm and clear limits with consequences for going past them are crucial to any setting involving adolescents, be it a school dance, football game, or the home environment. However, when these sanctions are applied, it is equally important to be able to communicate to the youngster that you understand the feelings and experiences that his or her misbehavior is camouflaging.

Control by itself is of little influence in curbing nonconformist behavior. Nor is permissiveness effective. What matters is *support*—communicating to adolescents that you understand their feelings, are willing to listen to them time and time again to hear their point of view, that you care about them—and that your rules stand precisely because you care. Most nonconformist behavior results from strict, rigid, high-control parents who fail to convey support.

Adolescents need a firm but flexible set of standards and rules against which to define themselves. The controlling yet supportive family provides such standards. Control is most effective when it is accompanied by communication.

For example, adolescents undergoing stress often run away. To them, running away is a logical recourse in resolving problems. They not only are fleeing from a stressful situation, but they also are running toward something—usually toward less alienated feelings and more control of their lives. Alienated adolescents, disillusioned by a crisis, need to reestablish commitment bonds, to increase self-esteem, to find meaning and purpose in life. But before they can do this, they need to get over the shock state that blocks their motivation to find solutions. Further punishment by adults clearly does not contribute to this process. Exploration of feelings is a more effective approach.

ADULT: Last week you ran away. . . . Things were getting so difficult that you wanted out of the situation. How has being away made things different for you? Has anything improved?

A hidden message often underlies the more extreme forms of adolescent behavior. Self-mutilating adolescents, through their deliberate behavior, express independence, autonomy, and personal freedom. It is their way of controlling their social environment. Self-mutilation can be an effort at control over fears of violence, aggressive impulses, sexual thoughts, as well as feelings of powerlessness and helplessness.[9] One such girl, Melinda, put it succinctly: "It's my body, and I can do anything I want with it. It's mine—it's the only thing I can control completely. I'm the boss."[10] Adult-inspired programs that attempt to control behavior without dealing with the reality of these feelings inevitably fail.

Staying empathic means being able to apply sanctions and still be concerned about the feelings and experiences of the adolescent:

PRINCIPAL: Over the weekend you were caught by the police breaking windows and spray-painting the gym. You are going to have to make restitution for this, and there is a mandatory suspension, besides.

STUDENT: (long silence)

PRINCIPAL: Sometimes kids destroy things for fun. It's their way of having a good time. Other times they just go along with the group. Still other times they may be mad—really mad—about something, like maybe their parents aren't getting along, and it's tough to live at home with all the fighting and arguing.

STUDENT: (Starts to cry. Talks about divorce of his parents.)

Successful interviews with adolescents hinge on playing down differences in status. Both the interviewer and the adolescent should have similar chairs, perhaps pointed to each other at a forty-five-degree angle and without desk or table in between. This arrangement avoids making your meeting a face-to-face confrontation and conveys the impression of a *we* rather than a *me-you* relationship. The atmosphere should be that of two people working together, engaged in the discussion of a subject that concerns them both. Do not take notes. It may make the adolescent uncomfortable or suspicious.

You need to do most of the talking initially. Explain the reason for your meeting and talk about the counseling process as it relates to the young person's problem. You want the youth to develop a comfortable impression about you, about the person to whom he or she might reveal themselves. Remember that adolescents' initial fears, regardless of how they present themselves, are a major hurdle.

Some adolescents will be so reluctant to talk that indirect procedures will need to be employed. First, always reflect the youngster's silence, paying close attention to his or her movements.

ADULT: It's hard to know where to start—you're feeling particularly uneasy and feeling foolish just sitting there saying nothing, but you don't know who I am and what I'll think of you—lots of kids feel that way. We don't have to begin by discussing troubles. If you'd rather, you can tell me anything that interests you, or what you're good at.

Most quiet and reluctant adolescents are scared—scared of being overwhelmed by their own vulnerability, scared of being dominated in the interview, of revealing their unworthiness, of not being able to find words adequate to the task of self-description, of your being in collusion with their parents, or of others finding out what they have said.

Some adolescents respond angrily at being sent to counselors. Passive-aggressive ones refuse to take off their coats: "I'm here because I was told to see you, but I'm not going to say or do anything." Their anger is an attempt to distance themselves from the adult so that they will not become dependent. Counselors need to define the counseling process, to communicate their interest in helping youngsters but also their inability to do so for those who truly want no assistance.

ADULT: Some students refuse to talk to me, or to anyone else, for that matter. They feel they can solve their own problems—and they can. But most of us, when we're upset and angry, don't always think clearly. My job is to help you think about ways you can deal with your concerns. I can't tell you what to do. I know you don't want to be here—and being forced to do something I don't want to do would make me angry too! But you're here, so let's work together to discover how we can make something positive out of this situation.

If the adolescent does talk initially, talk primarily when you are addressed. This gives the youngster the feeling that he or she can control the degree of your participation, which reduces anxiety. However, don't let silences between verbalizations become too long as silence creates pressure to talk, and you will need to reduce the pressure by talking yourself.

If the adolescent talks abstractly or intellectually, keep your comments in the same vein rather than looking for feelings or miscommunications. Again, this gives the adolescent the feeling that he or she can control the closeness of the relationship and that you respect his or her defenses. This helps them feel accepted.

ADULT: I guess you think I'm going to give you advice on how to handle your worries. Lots of people think we do that, or look for hidden motives and things. Actually, I try to help people look at things more clearly. I may tell you what I've learned from other adolescents who have helped me to learn about their problems, and if any of that fits your situation, then that's great. At other times you will be bouncing ideas off me that I will help you become clearer about. Sometimes counselors are like coaches. You study the videotapes of the games with your coach, and he helps you see your actions in such a way that you can improve next time. You may need to figure out how to present yourself better, or to make your ideas clearer to others, or to decide what strengths you have that will enable you to solve this thing.

Sometimes adolescents talk a lot but say nothing significant. They tell stories rather than describe genuine feelings. They try to fool you with the impression that they're okay. They comply in order to gain some other end; they respond with empty, practiced answers, or in a bored and unauthentic manner, slouched in their seat. Or they pursue every question with great interest. You need to address the student's evasiveness in a direct and nonjudgmental manner:

ADULT: I get the feeling that what you say doesn't match up with how you really feel. It seems you're hiding the fact that you really don't want to be here. I can understand that, but how does it feel having to hide your real feelings?

If these efforts fail, you may need to be even more direct:

ADULT: Look, you can see me regularly and fool me if you want to. I'm no mind reader, but who are you really fooling? You've come to see me because people who care about you feel you're troubled. They could be wrong, but how would I know if you don't tell me?

Not to deal with their concerns about you isn't helping—they'll just send you to someone else if I tell them you aren't working with me. Maybe you could tell me your side, at least, or just how you feel about having to hide that you don't want to be here.

Counselors as Advocates

Working with adolescents requires doing something practical for them. This can be a positive starting point in earning their trust, especially if they are being sent to see you. Help them to negotiate the family, school, the courts, or other social systems. They need concrete assistance in managing disputes between themselves and adults in their environment. Consider also the need to make strategic changes for students, temporary efforts to reduce stress. Lessons can be changed, tests postponed, and even disciplinary measures can be altered to help the adolescent through the crisis.

Formal counselors need to become familiar with the student's family and its circumstances. Successful counselors of adolescents are those who clearly have the adolescents' permission to see their family and who explain the reasons for the contact.

> GUIDANCE COUNSELOR: In order for me to continue seeing you, I need your parents' permission. Education law gives them the right to refuse counseling for you, even if you want it. How do you think I could approach them on this, or do you want to talk to them yourself?

Since counselors frequently need to communicate with parents about their son's or daughter's difficulties, or help teachers or principals better understand a student, discussing this possibility with the youngster beforehand lessens the chances of later accusations of betrayal.

In formal counseling adolescents will frequently miss appointments. Because they are action oriented, they can become quickly disillusioned when the sessions do not immediately relieve their distress. A letter or phone call to the adolescent is helpful. Convey your concerns about any possible disillusionment. Explore the dissatisfactions and be prepared to modify your procedures to suit his or her needs.

·4·

Empathic Focusing

I catch the pattern
Of your silence
Before you speak.

I do not need
To hear a word.

In your silence
Every tone I seek
Is heard.

LANGSTON HUGHES
"Silence"

Children express themselves best to people they trust. Children will trust you when they feel they are not being evaluated or controlled, when ideas are put to them tentatively rather than with absolute certainty, and when there is spontaneity. Children are quick to catch discrepancies in adults: "He doesn't really mean it," or "My parents say they love me, but they don't act like it." *Acting like it* usually boils down to being empathic, and empathy is conveyed when children realize we truly understand them. To be empathic, we must first *learn to listen.*

As a parent, teacher, or nurse on a pediatric ward, you may find that listening often takes a backseat to the briskly efficient kind of talking that channels or controls. Our responsibility at the moment may cloud our ability to listen to what children wish to say to us. Our barrage of words and instructions interfere with understanding what the child is feeling and experiencing. With all the tasks that need completion, the adult risks being perceived more as a drill sergeant than as an understanding companion.

Or, many adults confuse empathy with sympathy. Although these two qualities are similar, they are not the same. Sympathy is feeling *about* someone else's plight: "I'm sorry that your mom left your dad," or "I'm sorry Bobby hit you," or "I kinda know how you feel." In each of the instances the adult offering the sympathy has made a statement about how the children feel—without really understanding the children's feelings. To sympathize is to give words of concern, unfortunately all too often dictated by social custom. To empathize is to truly understand the experience of the child and to communicate this understanding back to him or her. Empathy is difficult; there are many obstacles in the way of achieving it. Many adults find it nearly impossible to empathize with some children—particularly when their defiant behavior acts as a smokescreen. When this occurs, a valuable opportunity is lost. Empathy, a simple tool of magnificent power, is one of the most effective means of helping children in crisis. In this chapter we are indebted to Carl Rogers, who throughout his career has practiced empathy skillfully and has described it clearly:

• Empathy means entering the private world of the child and becoming thoroughly at home in it, realizing that children's thinking differs from adults'.

• Empathy means temporarily living in the child's life, moving about in it delicately without making judgments.

• Empathy means putting your understanding into words that the child can understand.

• Empathy means sensing meanings of which the child is scarcely aware.

• Empathy means not trying to uncover totally unconscious feelings, since that would be too threatening.[1]

Although it sounds simple and looks easy, empathy is difficult to practice. It was a highly skilled adult who was able to understand the child below:

CHILD: Roberta and Ed both fell in a ditch on the way to school today.

ADULT: Oh.

CHILD: I saw a snake on the road yesterday.
ADULT: You did, huh?
CHILD: Sally had her shoe taken by two boys at lunch.
ADULT: Sometimes it doesn't seem safe to leave home.

In crisis resolution empathy may turn out to be the most significant element: When people are hurting, confused, troubled, anxious, alienated, terrified, or when they doubt their self-worth or are uncertain of their identity, empathy will help them feel understood, and this in turn activates strong and healthy forces.[2]

Empathy brings closeness. Since all crises involve separations, children in crisis who receive empathy find themselves once again connected to the human race. The experience goes something like this:

> I have been talking about hidden things, partly veiled from myself, feelings that are strange—possibly abnormal feelings I have never communicated to another, or even clearly to myself. And yet, another person has understood, understood my feelings even more clearly than I do. If someone else knows what I am talking about, what I mean, then to this degree I am not so strange, or alien, or set apart. I make sense to another human being. So I am in touch with, even in relationship with, others. I am no longer an isolate.[3]

Empathy clarifies jumbled feelings. Children in a crisis often feel combinations of distressful feelings. The weight of these feelings presses down, and they become more confused. Their efforts at problem solving or task mastery, such as schoolwork, are blocked. They gain greater control over their lives when they can label painful feelings.

Empathy increases participation. Children who feel understood can transcend their crisis and become involved once again with their life. Empathy can improve school performance. Children's reading scores improve significantly when teachers exhibit a high degree of understanding in their classroom, in contrast to when such understanding is not apparent.[4]

Even sophisticated psychotherapists find that empathy is at the core of their effectiveness. When eighty-three practicing psychotherapists from eight different schools of therapy defined their concept of the ideal therapist—the therapist they would like to become—they ranked empathy highest out of twelve variables. While they regarded empathy as their ideal, in actual practice they often fell short of this themselves.[5] Empathy is like any carefully honed artistic talent or athletic skill— easy to recognize and define but difficult to practice. It is simply not as easy as it looks. Fortunately, we *can learn* to be more empathic.

When we are empathic, we help children put their thoughts and feelings into words. This approach differs from the guiding, leading, commanding, cajoling that are often employed when assisting a child with a project, or keeping a group of children working together cooperatively. Let's look at a classroom situation, in which the focus is on completing an assignment and the teacher's statements are geared accordingly.

A child is having difficulty completing a picture he was assigned to draw. His teacher tries to spur him on, saying, "Yes, Freddie, you can draw. You are really good at drawing, and I'm proud of you," or "Freddie, you can draw if you try harder."

Statements like these might prod the child to finish his work, but they fail to contribute to an understanding between child and adult, leaving little time and energy to focus on solving the child's problem. When you say to a child whose parents are divorcing, "It's a difficult time, but you're a strong boy," or "You're a smart girl, and you'll make it," you do not convey empathy. You present the adult's preachy world view that things will turn out all right if everyone tries hard enough.

Going back to young Freddie, our struggling artist, empathic statements to a child who can't draw might be, "You must feel bad that you can't draw as well as you'd like," or "You must really feel kinda hopeless now about finishing this picture," or "Sometimes I'll bet you feel like you just can't do *anything* right!" These comments communicate understanding of the child's struggle.

Empathy can be blocked. Many times we use strategies that close the door to true communication.[6] Some of these include

• ordering ("Don't shut that door!")

• admonishing ("Please try to be more quiet when playing downstairs.")

• moralizing ("The right thing to do is to try your best and finish your work.")

• advising ("If Clara hits you next time, tell the teacher.")

• praising ("I was so proud of you when you made that hit in the baseball game.")

• reassuring ("It's tough now, but I know you are going to feel better in the morning.")

• probing ("Why did you have to do that?")

In Parent Effectiveness Training workshops, adults were asked to remember a time when they shared deep personal feelings with a friend. Then they were asked how they would feel if some of the above responses were given in return for their shared feelings. Most participants said such responses inhibited communication: "They make me stop talking," or "They shut me off," or "They make me feel frustrated."[7]

There are some simple ways of responding that set a tone of empathy in your conversation with children, that stress that you are a listener, receptive to what the children have to say.[8] These *door openers* include: "I see." "Oh." "Mm hmm." "How about that!" "You did, huh?" "Is that so?" Door openers tell children that you accept them and what they have to say, that you will be nonjudgmental and receptive—in other words, empathic.

One caution: Empathy is *not* merely parroting back what has been said. Empathy represents a true understanding, an emotional rather than intellectual understanding, and verbalization of a person's experience—listened to by one and retold by the other.

Sometimes adults wonder if empathy can make a situation worse. Will mentioning anger to children cause them to act on it? Will talking about problems provoke anxiety? Adults may fear that acknowledging or giving attention to a difficulty reinforces it, but this fear is not unlike a young child's magical notion that thinking about an event causes it to happen. This is an unfortunate attitude because the *avoidance* of dealing with children's strong feelings can sometimes make them worse. If done in the appropriate manner, reflecting children's feelings back to them can help both them and you to sort things out.

ADULT: Artie, it looks to me like you're really upset about something. You storm around, slam doors, and mumble to yourself.

CHILD: I am not. Leave me alone.

ADULT: I get really uncomfortable when you look angry and say you're not. I get upset with the stomping around and slamming of things. I think maybe I did something to get you angry.

CHILD: Well, you didn't. I'm mad at Jim . . . and don't know how to deal with him about it.

ADULT: Would you like to tell me about it?

When you talk with children, avoid labeling their feelings too early. This is not true empathy, and you may even put words in their mouths. For example:

TEACHER: (during recess) So you were mad this morning when Jake spilled your milk.

CHILD: (Nods.)

TEACHER: That would really make me mad. I'll bet you even want to hit him.

CHILD: (Nods.)

TEACHER: You must want to get back at Jake.

CHILD: (Nods.)

TEACHER: All right. Now you can join the others.

(Child rejoins group, seeks out Jake, his best friend. Shows no sign of anger, because he was never angry to start with. It was the teacher who was angry at the spilled milk, not the child! The child nodded his assent simply to be released and go to recess.)

Premature labeling of feelings removes the responsibility for disclosure from the child. Sometimes, especially when working with younger children, you first need to know if they possess the capacity to identify their feelings so that you can accurately reflect them back.

Responding empathically to children in crisis is a key theme of this book. In our experience we find that empathy is hard work, requiring us to focus children and guide their thinking.

Focusing Children: "Universal" Feelings

When you counsel children in crisis, you need to be empathic, but this may not occur spontaneously as a by-product of your relationship. You need to work at being empathic—by leading, guiding, and focusing the child in certain ways. We presented a variety of approaches in the previous chapter that are helpful in communicating effectively and empathically with children.

Focus children: Children in crisis will try to impose a particular relationship upon you. The defiant child will look for scolding, the withdrawn child for consolation and coaxing, the passive-aggressive child for aggravation, the omnipotent child for power struggles. The child's behavior is an overt communication, and if you respond in a similar way, you will not be able to understand the hidden, covert message. When you decline to provide the expected feedback to the child, you are one step closer to addressing the child's deeper communication, and can help him or her become aware of the hidden message.

ADULT: You look real mad today.

CHILD: I'm not mad.

ADULT: Well, your body sure looks like it to me. Perhaps you're wondering what I'll do or think if you're mad.

Statements such as the above break the typical pattern of adult responses to children's communication, and create a possibility for change.

Knowing What to Look for

Unlike adults, children do not possess a facile verbal ability to express themselves. Crisis counselors need to know what to look for, to be aware of feeling-themes that surface during crises. They must suggest to children some possible feelings underlying their confusion. They must strike a balance between letting children express themselves and helping them to do so. Piaget noted how difficult this is, especially for beginners:

> It is so hard not to talk too much when questioning a child. . . . They either suggest to a child all they hope to find, or they suggest nothing at all, because they are not on the lookout for anything, in which case, to be sure, they will never find anything.[9]

Keep children focused on their crises and feelings, but don't fill in all the details for them. Knowing children and their crises can help you guide their thoughts so that they can convey their worries to you. Moving from expressions which first look unrelated to the child's problem, to actual expression of the child's worries is often effective, as seen in this example in which the nine-year-old boy's father had recently died:

CHILD: When I grow up, I'm going to work with animals.

ADULT: You'd like to take care of them, to be nice to them?

CHILD: Yes.

ADULT: Everyone needs to be taken care of. We all need other people to look after us. Since your dad died, I'll bet your mom has a lot to do, taking care of you and your sister.

The crisis counselor needs to be on the lookout for universal feelings that occur during crises:

- Young children often feel responsible for a sibling's death.
- Abused children often feel that they are "bad."
- Foster children miss their parents tremendously.

• Children preparing for an operation misperceive many simple medical procedures.

These universals are based on our understanding of the feelings of other children who have undergone similar crises. By pointing out that many boys and girls in a certain situation feel the same way, you can open the door to discussion of the crisis with the child.

Adults working with children need to learn about these universal themes. How can this be accomplished? Three important ways to do this are by recalling your own experience in working with children, reading children's literature, and reviewing the writings of dynamic psychology.

Ricky, eight years old, was scheduled for a tonsillectomy. An active and outgoing youngster, he was well liked by his teachers and admired by his classmates. Two weeks before his surgery, Ricky's model behavior dramatically changed. He became cranky and irritable and resisted attempts by adults to find out what was wrong. One teacher commented to him that many boys and girls whom she knew were scared before operations. When Ricky heard this, he felt reassured and exclaimed, "I'm sure scared, too!" Then he and his teacher discussed his fears and how they were common feelings that others have experienced and a normal reaction before going to the hospital.

Storytelling may be particularly helpful with young children. A child experiencing an acute crisis may be crying, throwing a temper tantrum, or refusing to talk. Place the child in your lap and initiate a story with your most dramatic voice: "There once was a roaring lion. She roared so loud she scared the other animals away. She kept roaring. She must have been very, very mad. I wonder what she was so angry at?" In this approach, the crisis counselor begins the story in metaphor, parallel to what the child is experiencing. Sad, scared children are coaxed to talk with stories about kittens or bunnies; children reaching out for love and acceptance respond to tales about lonely puppy dogs.

Children's literature provides the crisis counselor with a wealth of information about universal feelings. Reading or being read to about a child who moved to a strange new town, or a girl who was sad and angry when her mother died, helps children realize they are not alone in facing difficult times and puts them in touch with how others have dealt with their problem. An excellent guide to the expression of universal feelings in children's literature is Sharon Dreyer's *The Book-*

finder (Circle Pines, Minn.: American Guidance Service, 1977). Written for everyone who works with children, *The Bookfinder* describes over 1,000 children's books according to more than 450 universal feelings and themes, including:
- Grief: Joan Fassler's *My Grandpa Died Today*
- Guilt over Divorce: Peggy Mann's *My Dad Lives in a Downtown Hotel*
- Entering School: Rebecca Caudill's *A Pocketful of Cricket.*

Stories can be read to children individually or in groups. For example, several youngsters in a class or child care group may be undergoing similar crises. It may be appropriate to assign readings about other youngsters who handled these universal difficulties, an approach that not only helps the individuals but heightens the awareness and sensitivity of the entire group.

A third source of information about universal feelings comes from dynamic psychology. Dynamic psychology helps the crisis counselor know what to look for, as illustrated by the examples of the two different foster children presented in chapter one. Although their overt behavior was one of defiance, their covert feelings were fear of rejection and loss of love. Acknowledging this covert message helped the children to adjust better. Dynamic psychologists have learned how children think and feel about the developmental challenges and crises they face—their universal reactions to life situations.

Some of the emotions stirred up by crisis situations are of such overwhelming intensity and power that children may view them with repugnance and withdraw from reaching out to someone for support or help. They simply do not want to talk with anyone. Rage, guilt, and the fear of losing control are frightening emotions even for an adult. However, if children discover that other children have feelings similar to their own and that these feelings are normal, their discomfort may lessen, and they will open up to you.

Focusing Children: Supportive Counseling

We have presented a number of counseling principles and techniques, yet we have failed to distinguish between crisis counseling as suggested in this book and psychotherapy as delivered by a trained professional. We deliberately did not make this distinction earlier because we feel the reader needs some exposure to basic counseling practices before being asked to distinguish between types.[10] Teachers, pastors, child care workers, nurses, and others need to know where to draw the line between providing appropriate help and attempting in-depth therapy.

First, we are suggesting that *all adults,* whether they are trained therapists or not, should counsel children in the manner suggested in this book. Crisis counseling is an approach unique unto itself that can be used by any sensitive adult. Crisis counseling can be considered *supportive counseling*—counseling that helps children label certain feelings evoked by crises, that marshals positive forces both within children and within their environment to assist them in coping with high anxiety. We've said repeatedly that unmanageable anxiety causes helpless feelings and regression. The supportive counselor helps children to reestablish or to develop defenses against anxiety. At times psychotherapists wrongly apply techniques to children whose defenses have been overwhelmed or are poorly developed.

The child's personality is already massively disorganized by the crisis being faced. Crisis counseling does not try to change the child's personality; it tries to restore lost function and develop coping skill. Children need their sense of self restored, their confidence increased, and their relationships reaffirmed. Children need support, not personality alteration. Their defenses need to be bolstered, not attacked.

Psychotherapy designed to alter personality is one in which children's defenses against anxiety and the unconscious wishes which contribute to this anxiety are interpreted to them in an effort to give them insight into why they feel and behave as they do. Yet pointing out children's defenses will often raise their anxiety. The underlying assumption is that children can manage this anxiety and choose other, more appropriate defenses against it until they are no longer anxious. In reality children in crisis usually respond by rigidly increasing their defenses—the only way they know that works in the situation. Teachers and child care workers often unknowingly interpret the defenses when they say to a child:

ADULT: Every time you think you're going to look bad you leave the game. (escape)

or

ADULT: Every time you're scolded by me, you hit Louise later. (displacement)

or

ADULT: Every time you think no one loves you, you claim you don't care. (denial)

If these interpretations worked, children would no longer handle their anxieties in the ways pointed out to them, and we could simply interpret maladaptive behavior away. This is not to say that well-trained therapists who carefully time their interpretations cannot help children. What we are saying is that *children in crisis* are not amenable to such an approach, no matter how skillfully applied.

Insight-oriented psychotherapy, therapy designed to change personality, is appropriate for children who are not in a crisis and who are capable of managing anxiety without undue regression. They can tolerate the anxiety raised by interpretations of their defenses, drives, or unique unconscious wishes.

Crisis Counselors Support Defenses

The counselor's statements below demonstrate support of coping efforts—more specifically, the support of a defense rather than an interpretation of it. The child had been discussing his dead mother when he abruptly stopped.

CHILD: I don't want to talk about it anymore.

ADULT: You feel real nervous talking about her right now.

CHILD: Yes.

ADULT: So not talking, pulling back, helps you not to feel so anxious. Is there anything else you are doing right now to prevent you from feeling anxious?

CHILD: I don't know.

ADULT: Think about it. Do you use a fantasy or memory to feel less anxious? What might it be?

CHILD: I thought about playing a game.

ADULT: Good, it's good to do that.

A therapist doing insight-oriented work might respond to the child's refusal to talk by interpreting rather than encouraging the use of defenses. Such a therapist might say, "I notice that whenever you talk about your mother, you get nervous and stop talking." He or she also might encourage the child to look at painful aspects of his relationship with his mother. The therapist might literally want to stir things up and respond to the child accordingly.

Interpretation of defenses can be perceived by very anxious children as admonishments, as efforts to get them to behave better. Consequently, interpretations often raise children's anxiety and heighten the crisis. Another example of a supportive approach follows.

CHILD: Can I call my mommy on your phone?

ADULT: I realize that when you see me, you often think of your mom. We can't call her from here but we can talk about her.

CHILD: Can we play checkers?

ADULT: That's great! Now when I say no to you, you ask me for something that I can do for you. Remember how you used to get real mad and demand that I call?

Again, the insight-oriented therapist might have responded: "You know, every time I won't let you call your mother, you change the subject and ask for something else." Contrast this comment with that of the crisis counselor, who supported the child's wish to play checkers as a way of alleviating anxiety.

When the crisis counselor feels that a particular defense must not be actively encouraged, he or she responds empathically whenever the child becomes defensive. To the child who leaves the game when frustrated he might say:

ADULT: Sometimes it's real hard to stick with something you're not doing well at.

To the child who displaces:

ADULT: I can't let you hit Louis when you're mad.

To the child who denies:

ADULT: You feel hurt when you think no one likes you.

Don't Play Detective

Trained therapists will interpret children's unconscious wishes only after the children are clear about the use of defenses and are ready to look at some of the wishes that raise their anxiety and bring their defenses into play. These wishes are not universal ones experienced by most children in crisis, but rather are the particular ongoing maladaptive responses of a child to a past situation. For example, the crisis counselor would tentatively suggest to a child whose parents are separating:

ADULT: Lots of kids I know think they caused their parents to split up. What do you think you did?

or

ADULT: Lots of kids get angry at their parents when they split up.

Now consider how a therapist examines in detail the unique relationship of a ten-year-old girl to her mother following a divorce and referral for psychotherapy after excessive fighting at school:

THERAPIST: You've been upset for some time since your dad left.

You really get scared at night, sometimes even wanting to sleep in your mother's room.

CHILD: (Denies vigorously.)

THERAPIST: It makes you upset to even think about such a wish . . . maybe you think you're a baby to want such things. Maybe that's why you act so tough on the playground—to hide that you have baby wishes and fears. What do you think?

Don't go probing for unique wishes in crisis counseling. If children tell you their fears and worries, fine. But don't play detective. To do this, even for trained therapists, is inappropriate in most crisis situations. Interpretations of defenses and underlying wishes are activities for insight-oriented therapists who apply these techniques when children are *ready* to utilize them. Crisis counselors should focus on supporting or developing appropriate defenses, identifying positive feelings, encouraging verbalization, reestablishing relationships, and affirming the child's identity.

Identifying Positive Feelings

Developing positive feelings can help calm children in crisis.[11] The following "dialogue" is an example of such an effort with a boy who lost his mother:

CHILD: I was so nervous in class today.

ADULT: You must have been real upset. Do you still feel that way?

CHILD: A little bit. . . .

ADULT: When did you begin to feel less upset?

CHILD: When I left the class.

ADULT: What did you do?

CHILD: Thought about watching TV with my grandma.

ADULT: That's good that you were able to do that. Perhaps you could do that in class.

Insight-oriented therapists would focus on interpreting the defense, and well-meaning teachers might try to keep these children in class or not allow them to sit in the hallway. They would both focus on what got these children upset rather than on *what gets them less upset*. Crisis counseling focuses on the latter and goes one step further to teach anxious children to use positive feelings for another person to calm themselves:

ADULT: Are there any times here when you feel less anxious?

CHILD: When I'm with Bill.

ADULT: Describe what that feels like.
CHILD: I feel protected.
ADULT: You feel safe and secure with Bill.
CHILD: Yeah, but when I'm not with him I feel horrible.
ADULT: Perhaps you could think about Bill when you start to feel
    anxious—imagine what it would feel like to be with Bill, think
    about the things that you and Bill do together.

Encouraging Verbalization

While we have discussed asking questions to elicit information, actually this also engages the child in thinking. Questions are asked to
encourage verbalization and not to reinforce inappropriate action, and
are an ego-supportive technique. The inappropriate action in this case
was the girl's refusal to talk. Other children may break things or refuse
to cooperate with others.

CHILD: I haven't spoken to my mother in a week.
ADULT: When you get really angry, sometimes you stop talking.
CHILD: Yes.
ADULT: Does that help you feel better?
CHILD: Not really.
ADULT: What do you think you actually want from your mom?
CHILD: I guess to stop saying hurtful things about my father, because
    I love him and it hurts me, too.
ADULT: By not talking, you showed her how much she hurt you so
    she wouldn't do it again?
CHILD: Yes.
ADULT: Do you think she got the message?

Reestablishing Relationships

In chapter one we mentioned that successful crisis resolution involves helping the child reestablish relationships with caretakers. As
we will learn in later chapters, when one parent dies children temporarily lose their relationship with the surviving parent. This can happen with children of divorce. Abused and neglected children need to
feel something positive about their parents. Handicapped and ill children have troubled relationships with parents, and children in foster
care and institutions have even more troubled relationships. Counselors need to find ways to get children to relate more appropriately to
their caretakers since improved relationships would increase their coping skills.

Helping Children with Their Identity

Most of us are aware that children adopt the fears of their parents or of other adults who are close to them. When parents face a crisis, children also face one. The parents' anxiety can become the children's anxiety. When this occurs, help children to see themselves as separate and distinct persons, different from their parents:

MOTHER: You've probably heard me talk about not being able to afford this big house now that Dad's gone. But that's for me to worry about. You'll be able to keep all your things if we need to move into a smaller house.

Another instance when a child's emotions are likely to merge with an adult's is during a time of defiance. The angry young child expects you to be mad at him because he is mad at you.

ADULT: I'm sorry you couldn't clean your room. I'm not mad at you, though. We'll be playing baseball outside, and when you're done you can join us.

In summary, crisis counseling is supportive counseling. Supportive counseling is utilized when children are or are about to be overwhelmed; it is concerned with marshaling forces for crisis resolution. Children are helped to recognize and identify issues and see them in perspective. The goal is to develop or expand children's organizing capacities—to foster their use of effective coping strategies, and to enable them to identify the obstacles to and the progressive forces for crisis resolution. Through development of trust in others, children come to cope more effectively with the crisis they face. When distressed, most of us think poorly. The focus should be on tracking children's unreasonable beliefs, scrutinizing them together, helping them to replace these beliefs with reasonable ones, explaining self-defeating behavior, and encouraging and developing effective problem-solving behavior. Throughout this process, remember Sigmund Freud's counsel: "I advise you to lay aside your therapeutic ambitions and try rather to understand. When you understand, therapeutics will follow."

We now turn to actual crisis situations—death, divorce, illness, handicaps, abuse, and foster care. Keep in mind the attitude, the developmental age of the child, and the techniques that have been discussed in these first four chapters. You will probably refer to them from time to time for ideas to apply in each crisis situation.

·5·

Death

I was very young when my mother died,
and I found the funeral and everything
very comforting. I found the worst
part was after the funeral was over.
The cruelty of everyone going back to
their life as it used to be and mine
would never be the same.

AUDIENCE MEMBER,
The Phil Donahue Show

Who can really understand the impact that the death of a loved one has upon a child? In sudden deaths, such as the loss of a parent in a fire or car accident, the grief may seem insurmountable. Or consider the death of a sibling: that special bond of shared secrets, quiet understandings, and deep companionship will forever be an aching void.

Death is difficult to deal with. The subject makes us anxious. Because it is ultimately a mystery, it is beyond our understanding and out of our control. Death, particularly childhood bereavement, reawakens painful and repressed emotions of separation and loss experienced in our own early development, feelings from which we withdraw.

Adults are able to reflect upon and describe their responses to the death of a loved one. Do children, who cannot verbalize their experiences so easily, respond similarly?

Adult Bereavement

Grief—keen mental suffering or distress over loss, sharp sorrow—involves strong irrational feelings, frightening in intensity, such as anger at the departed for desertion, typically expressed indirectly through displacement. Emotions felt for the person who has died are aimed instead at family, friends, and coworkers. There is guilt about hurtful things said to the lost one. There are searching thoughts and behaviors—yearnings that result at the sound of footsteps on the stairs or keys in doors or the sight of a face in the crowd. There are trips to places where fun was shared. There is anger at survivors for letting it happen, vacillating with solicitous behavior should they die also.

The pain of the loss makes recall of pleasant memories difficult because the recall is accompanied by pain. We shut out the good to block out the bad. Yet we fear that we will forget what the dead one looks like. The aftermath of death crystallizes all the hurts we may have felt in a poor relationship. Empty days stretch on forever; sleepless nights. We feel the lost one's presence and gather his or her things around for comfort. We push toward closeness with survivors, yet often blame them for the death of the loved one. All of this is grief.

Grieving takes time. Grieving is grief multiplied by the days and the months after the loss. It is a process implying deep mental suffering, often endured in silence. If a lost person is to remain a good and loving memory, the survivors have to let themselves be reminded of him or her continually in their daily life, to remain open to recollection. The closer the relationship with the departed, the more frequent and painful the reminders until the very pain becomes cherished as part of the precious object. Witness the number of "lost love" songs and our desire to hear them. When we can finally accept that we shall never see the lost person again and our omnipotent possessiveness relinquishes, we turn inward and use our experiences with him or her to enrich our lives. The dead one lives on in us as an internalized part of ourselves, as an inspiration and source of strength. We then transfer some of our feelings to living substitutes. Grieving is healthy and necessary. Failure to grieve has been associated with later psychopathology.

Much of grieving has to be done privately, but part of it can be and should be done with others who have suffered the same loss. Sharing decreases the intensity of the pain and makes it more acceptable. It helps the survivors to accept their loss and new status as those without. This is the role of mourning, the outward signs of grieving, the open expression of the sorrow accompanying the death of a loved one. Cultures assist mourning through wakes, funerals, religious ceremonies, memorials, and other rituals.

Grieving and mourning help us to admit that a death has occurred and recognize its final imprint on our life. They shore us up as we say good-bye to the lost one, and prepare us for beginning a new phase in life.

In many ways children grieve and mourn as do adults, but with essential differences and characteristics depending on their level of development.

The Magic Years

Generally children under age three are incapable of understanding death. Yet while they may not understand it, they most definitely react to its effects, particularly if it is a parent who has died. These children must be reassured that their needs for love and safety will continue to be met. Affirming the caretaking relationship with the surviving parent and other family members is particularly important. Discipline is also important because young children control their impulses in an effort to please the adult to whom they are attached; they develop proper behaviors because they fear the parent will withdraw his or her love. When that parent dies, the child's controls break down. The surviving parent should be helped to understand children's need for clear and firm external controls. Often these parents will be less inclined to provide discipline because of their own grief. However, easing up expectations on young children is not what they need.

Children in the magic years (ages three to six) play games and answer questions about death that indicate that they see it as reversible. When queried about whether dead things can be brought back to life, they respond, "Take them to the hospital," or "Let them rest up and sleep."

During the magic years symbolism abounds. Anything can stand for anything. Children may resist certain activities because they symbolize loss. For example, number games may be avoided because they stimulate thoughts about changes in the number of people in the family now that a parent is gone.

Because children think in concrete terms, they give concrete responses to places the lost one might have been. They may chase red sports cars calling, "Daddy! Daddy!" because their father drove one. Although grieving adults make similar associations, to them it's just a reminder; to a young child, it's the real thing.

If a parent dies, surviving adults in young children's lives often bear the brunt of displaced anger. While adults are conscious of their anger toward a lost one and can separate this from their other relationships, children cannot control their grief and direct it toward whoever is in their life at the moment. Stepparents are easy targets and are often bewildered by the anger they weather from a young stepchild, seldom realizing that the anger is meant for the lost one—anger at being deserted. Feelings for the lost one, whatever their nature, are expressed toward the desired replacement, causing both the child and the stepparent much suffering and confusion. "I like this person, so why do I give him so much trouble?" the child will wonder in more rational moments.

Being egocentric, magic years children worry about whether they will get enough to eat and who will feed them when their mother dies. If their father dies, they are concerned about who will buy the food. They are openly sad and angry and worry about their own, and the remaining parent's, survival. If the parent they are closer to dies, they go through the stages of protest and despair associated with separation from parents (see chapter seven, "Health Crises"). If they are more attached to the surviving parent, they do not go into the detached state.

Children can lose both parents—one to death, and the other to grief—if the surviving parent experiences a severe grief reaction. This can have a marked impact on preschoolers, who need to form an attachment with another adult. Children need to feel protected, cared for, and loved, and when unable to attach themselves to a new adult, they feel helpless, lose interest in things, and frequently become sick or prone to illness.

If the mother dies, young children wish that their father will remarry so they can have a new mother: "I want a mommy!" They desire a person to fill the caretaking void. Often fathers become angry at the child for desiring an adult to fill a role and neglecting to remember the mother who has died. If the father dies, the desire for a new father is less obvious but is nevertheless there in most cases. When a parent dies, the surviving spouse must transcend personal grief to explain to the child that he or she was not abandoned. Help parents to reassure children that the parent who died loved them very much and did not want to leave them.[1]

Because children in the magic years often believe their specific thoughts or misbehavior caused their parent's death, their wishes for replacement are more conflictual than those of toddlers. Fantasies about death and its cause or meaning characterize their play. Those who have developed good controls will try to hold their bad wishes in check to prevent bad happenings, but they may become aggressive toward those whom they feel are not in good control, such as young siblings whose careless thinking could cause trouble again. Or they may openly express desires for cruel revenge against murderers and criminals.

Since magic years children condemn themselves severely, they are equally harsh on others. And because they see parents as omnipotent and all-powerful, they blame the surviving parent for not preventing the death of the other. But perhaps the worst blow of all is to their own illusion of power and control—mother doesn't reappear when they wish it! They feel helpless, depleted, empty, cheated. They feel bitter and angry but have difficulty knowing why. Helplessness can lead to unhealthy dependency upon others and hatred of those upon whom they most depend.

With preschoolers it is important to understand children's conception of events. Let them talk and let them cry.[2] By making yourself available, you will learn what they think they did: "I yelled at Mommy too much, and she died," or "I wish I never hid Tommy's bike. Now he died." Explore with them why they think they caused the death, and provide them with the real explanation. Be prepared to repeat this process many times. For example:

ADULT: Peter, you yelled at Bobby. Then he died. You feel that your yelling made him die. Remember how sick Bobby was? Remember how we took him to the hospital every week? Sometimes people are very, very sick, and then they die. They die because they were very sick. Bobby did not die because you yelled at him, but because he was sick. You could have been nice to Bobby all the time, and he still would have died.

Because they are naturally egocentric, young children often become afraid that they will die when someone close to them dies. If an illness caused the death, emphasize to children that the person was very, very sick. If an accident killed the parent, stress that accidents are extremely rare. If an older person has died, reassure children that most people die when they become very old. Make every effort to explain the circumstances surrounding the death: "Grandpa was sick, and finally he had to go to the hospital. The doctors tried as hard as they could try, but he was so sick that he died."[3]

Bedtime kindles anxiety in children who are grieving for someone who has died. Because death is often compared to sleep, many youngsters take this literally. They equate sleeping with dying and are afraid to go to sleep.

We are uncomfortable with young children's queries: "Why did Kitty die?" "Will we ever see Grandpa again?" "Will I get sick like Bobby and die?" We are tempted to answer their questions quickly and move on. Although facile sidestepping of the issue may put us at ease, it does little to appease children's very real concerns. Children's games, stories, and fantasies all reveal that they think a great deal about death. Avoiding the issue may magnify their fears: "Never think you're protecting your children by keeping things from them. Always assume that what they imagine is 150 times worse than any reality."[4]

While adults fear that explanations stimulate needless worry, the opposite actually occurs. Children react to unexplained and hidden stress in their environment with greater anxiety than they do to comprehensible stress. Here are some effective ways to speak to young children about death:

ADULT: Daddy is gone and doesn't come home to sleep and eat and take Julie to the park to swing on the swings, and Julie doesn't know where Daddy is and thinks maybe she did something to upset him.

ADULT: Kirk isn't sure what it means that Daddy is dead, and he will never see him again. Kirk is angry that Daddy died and won't ever take him out in the yard again to play catch.

ADULT: Mommy is very sad that she'll never see Daddy again. We don't know why people die, they just do. No matter how hard we wish Daddy wasn't dead, he is. And we'll never see him again. But we'll keep his pictures and things to remember that he loved us and we loved him.

One of grief's tasks is to remember the lost one as an inspiration. One father encouraged his twin daughters to remember their mother in this way: "I'd ask them, 'What was one of the funniest things you remember about Mommy? What's one of the best things Mommy cooked?' I wanted them to remember good things about their mother, to remember that she loved them, and not to feel guilty about her going away."[5]

The Middle Years

Because they cannot think abstractly, children in the middle years are specific and detailed in their reflections about death. Adults might view their preoccupations as gory, macabre, or morbid, but they are normal responses for children ages seven to twelve. References to what the undertaker does, or what happens to the body after it is buried, are expressions of children's curiosity. Such questions help children master their own fears about dying and separation.[6]

For these children, explain as many facets as possible of the circumstances of death. They will want to know the details, and in the absence of information they will fantasize about gruesome particulars. For example, when a child who attended a residential school died suddenly, some of the boys in his dorm formed a group with the goal of collecting accounts of his death. The child care workers decided to allow this activity because it helped the group to mourn together as well as gave them the information needed to understand the death.

When a parent dies, many middle years children show denial: "My daddy is coming back to see me," or "Uh, uh. My daddy's not dead." These children do not comprehend the finality of death, even though they are aware of their loss.

If the cause of the parent's death was illness, children may develop excessive bodily concerns. If an accident, they may have specific or general fears about similar situations. If a suicide, they may develop guilt.

Many middle years children regress, especially when the day's distracting activities are over. In families these children may want to sleep with or near their parents during mourning. Even otherwise mature ten-year-olds may seek the company of a favorite teddy bear.

Boys between the ages of nine and fourteen often want to assume the role of the dead father. Playing the father role is one way of maintaining the father's presence, but it is also an effort to overcome helplessness and dependent longings.

Other losses become extremely painful because they rekindle the memory of the lost parent. Children display exaggerated reactions to other losses—be it a lost opportunity, lost pet, or even a lost baseball game. Extreme temper tantrums and tears can follow the cancellation of a planned trip or activity.

The recollection of the lost one, memories so crucial in grieving, is often blocked in middle years children. Recollection also includes memories of bad times and can stimulate the child's guilt for past misbehaviors. If guilt becomes too strong, children may misbehave to elicit punishment they feel they deserve. The poorer the relationship with the dead parent, the less active the grieving will be. In such instances professional counseling may be needed.

Children who are grieving withdraw their investment in outside activities, just as grieving adults do. One cannot grieve and master new challenges simultaneously. This resistance is often misinterpreted as laziness or defiance. Sniffed one insensitive relative about a grieving child: "If her father were alive, he'd make her work!" While middle years children need to experience the satisfaction that mastery of activities brings, encouraging task accomplishment before the expression of feelings can hinder the grieving process. Nevertheless, children should be helped to maintain their daily routines and hobbies so that they will have something to fall back on when they're feeling sad. Help children to recognize their loss and how they feel about it, but also show them how to compensate for it with new interests and activities.

As a result of the trauma of death, children's ability to distinguish fantasy from reality is partially impaired. Temporary delusions, such as thinking the dead parent has returned, are not uncommon. Reassure children that these delusions are experienced by many boys and girls who have suffered a death in the family. Explain that these scary hallucinations will diminish as time goes on.

Allowing children to verbalize their loss helps them grieve. Putting feelings into words assists in overcoming the disorganization that accompanies grief. Adults can take the initiative by describing their reactions to a loss through *I-messages.* Since death often provokes a confusing onslaught of negative emotions such as guilt, rage, and depression, I-messages give children permission to grieve and lets them know their feelings are normal. I-messages can contain elements from the four grief stages related by Elisabeth Kübler-Ross:[7]

DENIAL: Jeff's gone. I just don't want to believe it. I can't believe that he won't be with us anymore.

ANGER: It just doesn't seem fair to me. I'm angry. I keep wondering, "Why did this have to happen?"

GUILT: Why was I so irritated with Jeff when he didn't do the dishes? I sure wish that I had told him more often how much I liked him.

ACCEPTANCE: It's been almost six months. I still think of Jeff. But I know that he'd want me to keep up with new things around here.

Adults are frequently confused by the variety and intensity of emotions stirred up in them by a death. How much more difficult this is for children!

Adolescence

Surveys of high school students reveal that almost 90 percent have had some exposure to death. For adolescents, the death of an important person in their life can create numerous stresses, particularly if it is the death of a parent.

Adolescence is a time of separation from parents. When this happens abruptly, the gradual process required for healthy identification with a parent cannot take place. Adolescents first develop their own ideas by resisting the ideas of others. Through rebellion they discover who they are. When a parent dies, the process of resisting, developing independent ideas, and then rediscovering the parent's viewpoint has not been allowed to come full circle. Death of a parent can throw an adolescent into a tailspin.

Adolescents are preoccupied with themselves, which can soften the blow of a death since energy is not so much focused on the dead one but can be redirected toward the self. But self-preoccupation has drawbacks—it renders the young vulnerable to worries. If a death was due to illness, the adolescent can develop excessive fears of disfigurement, pain, or sickness. In addition, the sleep loss, early morning awakening, and weight loss that accompany normal grieving can threaten the adolescents' self-image and increase their worries.

During adolescence the sense of self is fragile. Often accompanying the grieving process is an other-worldly experience in which the presence of the dead person is seen or felt—an hallucination. While most adults view these visions as helpful, adolescents may respond with fears of going crazy. Reassure the youth that this is a natural aspect of bereavement. Similarly, adolescents are frightened by intense ambivalent dreams in which they save or destroy the deceased. Again, an explanation of the grieving process reassures them.

Particularly when a parent has died, adolescents need encouragement to express their anger. They doubt the rationality of such feelings: "I'm grown up and can take care of myself. Why would I be angry because my father died?" They need coaxing to expand on worries that they see as selfish or heartless: "How can I go to college now? I'll never earn enough money by myself," or "I don't want to have to take care of my little brothers and sisters."

When a parent dies, the role of other adults in the adolescent's life is especially significant. Because two parents help dilute the intensity of an adolescent's feelings as he or she matures, both the surviving parent and the adolescent will need support to keep the proper distance from one another. Athletic coaches, church group leaders, or favorite teachers can play an especially meaningful role in the lives of grieving adolescents.

Grieving and Life Tasks

Keeping in mind the unique characteristics of children's grief in the magic years, the middle years, and adolescence, let us look at the grieving process that we must help the child through. The problem-solving tasks of bereavement include

• accepting the pain of the loss
• remembering and reviewing the relationship with the dead one
• becoming familiar with the jumble of feelings that are part of grief—anger, sadness, despair
• expressing sorrow and sense of loss
• finding an acceptable formulation for a future relationship with the deceased
• verbalizing feelings of guilt
• and finding a network of caretakers.[8]

Where do you draw the line between letting children grieve and making realistic daily demands of them? First, realize that you can't cheer suffering children out of their grief. Reflect grief feelings and encourage their expression. Children will be visibly more upset as they talk things out, but their preoccupation with their grief will lessen.

Daily tasks are important for children. If not completed, they will fall behind their peers. But if pressured to do them, they will not be able to grieve. If they totally withdraw from their tasks, they will be robbed of the satisfactions that will help them build their sense of self and self-esteem.

If your role is to teach or guide, continue to offer instructions and give assignments, but modify your requests and talk with the children so they know you are alongside them throughout this trying time. An example of a modified classwork assignment might be:

TEACHER: I understand, Peggy, that it's really hard for you to concentrate because your mommy died. You're thinking about your mommy, what you used to do with her, and that brings tears to your eyes. I can see little tears right now as we talk. And yet you come to school just like always, like your mommy is still at home. I know how much you're struggling and I commend you for coming to school and trying to do your work. How much energy do you think you have today to do some math? Is there anything I can do to help you find some energy, because I know that you are struggling with some painful things?

We need to be sensitive to what children are going through, to communicate this to them, and enter into a contract with them about how much they can achieve. A routine of moderate work helps children mourn. It prevents them from being preoccupied to the point of becoming morose; it is nonproductive to sit around feeling sorry for oneself. A routine that is manageable is helpful, since feelings of accomplishment, mastery, and success remind children that they have positive opportunities in their life. If the routine is too difficult, children will resist it and give in to their preoccupations.

Our society's attitude toward death does little to help the grieving process. Euphemisms abound, which only intensify the survivors' feelings of loneliness, isolation, and frustration. Modern life separates life from death; people go to hospitals to die, and many children and adults have never shared the experience of dying. Elisabeth Kübler-Ross commented: "This is perhaps the first generation of American youngsters who have never been close by during the birth of a baby and have never experienced the death of a beloved family member."[9]

Even trained therapists avoid death. One experienced psychiatrist wrote that a discussion on death with dying friends provoked two sets of bothersome feelings: "one having to do with the death of loved ones, the other having to do with my own death."[10]

Perhaps in past times, people were able to grieve more naturally. In ancient Greece the wife's role was to prepare the family for the father's death. The classic tale of Penelope weaving the shroud with which to bury her father-in-law Laertes indicates that death was a significant part of life. Children watched their mothers weave these shrouds and heard their mothers and fathers, like Achilles and Helen of Troy, discuss both the kind of life and the kind of death they wanted.

It was children's responsibility to see to it that their parents received a proper burial and that proper funeral games were held; if not, their spirits were doomed to wander aimlessly forever. Perhaps our children would grieve more naturally if we did not try to shield them from death.

Quiet and withdrawn behavior delays the mourning process. When John F. Kennedy died, a number of youths displayed exaggerated reactions. When their backgrounds were examined, many of the mourning youngsters were found to have lost a significant person early in life. People around them at the time noted their failure to show distress at the death. They never grieved. But years later the death of this popular president triggered an intense delayed grief period. Similar reactions, particularly among young people, occurred when John Lennon died.

What can we do for children struggling with grief? We need to be available. We need to listen. We need to recognize, understand, and make allowances for the grieving process.

We will not be stronger than the grief, but we can help children do what they must do.

Special Types of Grieving

The Dying Parent

When a parent is dying of a terminal illness, children have an opportunity to work through some of their feelings over a period of time, rather than being thrown into the shock following a sudden death. Children should be told that the parent is dying and what will happen to the family upon that death. Young children should be told close to the time of death.

Being able to think and talk about what it will be like without the parent facilitates coping and attachment to the surviving parent. Children can be given simple responsibilities both prior to and following the parent's death. It is best if the sick parent tells the child about the future.

> ADULT: Mommy has no control over death. I am receiving the best care possible and will stay alive as long as I can. You and Daddy will have to plan how you're going to get along without me when the time comes. I'd like to hear about your plans.

When the parent dies, the child should be told quickly and in a straightforward manner.

Death of a Sibling

While reactions to the death of a sibling can be similar to reactions to the death of a parent, there are essential differences. Children rarely are as attached to and dependent upon their siblings. Consequently, loss of self and regression are seldom involved. Denial and indirect expression of grief, however, still appear. Unique responses may include children's sense of smallness and undervalue compared to the sibling who died and the nagging feeling that they should have died instead. If-only-I-hadn't doubts occur alongside their magical notions of causation and guilt over transgressions against the sibling.

Parents often relate differently to surviving children. They overprotect them or reject them and sometimes even adopt another child to replace their sibling. Because children are more like their sibling who died than an adult, fears of their own death are strong: "If Mommy let Lewis die, she might let me die, too."

Children and Suicide

When a parent or sibling commits suicide, children have considerable difficulty grieving. Our society tries to hush up suicides and has decreed that suicide is an unjustifiable act—the ultimate sin—and that people who commit suicide are "bad" people. Generally, suicides do not evoke great sympathy. People don't know how to respond to the family members of a suicide victim. Their doubts and condemnation are silently conveyed to children: "Your daddy was a bad person. He killed himself, and that's a terrible thing to do." Our uncertainty clouds any compassionate message we might hope to send.

When a suicide occurs, help children to deal with this loss as they would with any loss. You need not go beyond reflecting how sad they feel about the death. Dealing with issues of guilt and ambivalence is best left to a professional therapist or worked out with family members.

Funerals

Funerals provide a valuable opportunity for children to learn more about death. Initially, the proceedings and rituals will be confusing to them, and they will ask questions and expect realistic answers. If we are reluctant to talk about a death, or death in general, children will sense that the subject is taboo and follow our tight-lipped example. Their questions will remain unanswered, their fears will grow, and they will develop misconceptions.

One aspect of funerals which often puzzles children is when the minister says words over the casket as it is being lowered into the ground. It looks to them as if he is talking to the dead person. The child may ask: "If Grandma's really dead, why is the priest talking to her?" or "Will Grandma be cold in the ground?" These questions help you discover the child's concerns so that you can address them as matter-of-factly as possible. Your answers, of course, will be based on whatever religious orientation or philosophy of life the child's family follows.

One particularly touching funeral was that of a young man who was retarded. He was in his early twenties when he died, and he had two younger brothers, ages eight and ten. These boys had never met him because his retardation was so severe that he had to live in a hospital for much of his life. The young boys caused a stir at the wake because they touched their brother's body in the casket and began to ask numerous questions: Why was his body so cold? Could he see them? Why were his legs deformed? Their mother took them aside and carefully answered each of their questions. When they left the funeral home, they were more at peace with their brother's death and with his handicaps in life.

Perhaps most important is that funerals allow children to witness the grief of others. Not only does this help them to express their own grief, it confirms that others valued the dead person and thereby value their life as well—a reassurance children seek.

Religion and Death

Religion can help children grieve and mourn. Besides the comfort that belief in a loving and protective God provides, ideas about life after death, resurrection, and other religious concepts keep children's feelings about death conscious and contribute to their grieving process.

Questions about death should always be answered within the framework of the children's own religion or belief. It is not your role to expand the child's awareness of religious options during a time of grief. Be careful to discuss your intentions with the children's parents, and let them know that your interest in what their children make of their religion or philosophy is purely supportive. Ask for their assistance if the children seem to have religious misconceptions that distort their view of death. This reassures parents that you are not intruding into an area in which you don't belong.

To a religious child it might be comforting to say: "Grandma is dead now. She has left us and has gone to be with God. God is taking care of Grandma, just as He takes care of all of us. We all miss Grandma. Maybe if you like, you can pray for her sometime."

Elisabeth Kübler-Ross presents a talk she had with one three-year-old girl whose mother was dying:

> "Dr. Ross, do you think it is all right if I go to bed tonight and pray to God that He takes my Mommy now?"
>
> "Yes, you can ask him anything you want."
>
> "Do you think it is all right with him if I ask him to send her back again to me?"
>
> "Yes, you can ask that, as long as you understand that where Mommy goes this time is very different from here, and it may be quite a long time until you see her again."
>
> "Well, as long as I know that I will see her again and she is all right."
>
> "That much I can promise you."[11]

It is important to strike a balance between offering consoling words of a religious nature and acknowledging children's painful experiences. Overemphasizing or smothering children with comforting words does not comfort. It confuses. It prevents them from going through the grieving process and the negative feelings that need to surface.

Encourage children and family members to express their anger—even at God.

> Many chaplains are very good as long as the patient displaces his anger onto the hospital administration, nurses, or other members of the helping profession. But as soon as the patient expresses anger at God, they have the need to put the brakes on. I think it is very important that patients are allowed to express their anger at God, and my answer to chaplain students is always, "Do you really think that you have to come to God's defense? I think God can take it. He is bigger than that!"[12]

Children frequently misunderstand some of the religious ideas they are instructed to adopt. Questions such as, "Why does God want Daddy to live with Him instead of us?" are difficult to answer. Saying that "God needed another angel" may cause children to fear that they might be needed also. Clarifying misconceptions of religious beliefs can benefit children.

Death and the Classroom

"What do you say when the hamster dies?"

The death of a classroom pet, discovered by a devastated six-year-old, unnerves many experienced grade school teachers: "How should I answer their questions?" "Will their parents approve of my explanation?" "How much can the children handle?" "Why spoil a nice day by talking about a sad event?"[13]

The classroom can be a forum for helping children understand death. Mourning the death of a pet can be a constructive experience. "A small dose of painful experience can be mastered by even a small child."[14] The death of a pet may be children's first close experience with death and may help them get used to the reality. "You probably feel pretty bad that Hector has died. I'll bet you miss him. . . ."

You can help children understand death better by talking to them when someone they knew only slightly dies: the mailman, an actor, their second cousin, an acquaintance.

If Gary comes to class and announces that his brother was killed in an accident the previous week, it would be unwise and inappropriate to focus on him by asking, "How does this make you feel, Gary?" Such a question is likely to leave Gary feeling anxious, isolated, and awkward in front of the group. A universal approach focusing on how everyone might feel in a similar situation could do more to support Gary and help him clarify some of his jumbled feelings. Express how sad we feel when people die and how we miss them. Explain that people are remembered even after they have died, and a part of them is kept alive inside our hearts.[15] Through universal statements you can help both grieving children and other youngsters in the class to better understand and accept death.

However, before embarking on any intensive "death education" effort, consult with a professional clinician to help determine the needs of the group, and also the unique needs of any child in the group. If individual children have experienced the recent death of a parent or significant other person and are beginning to come to terms with the loss, it may or may not be appropriate to involve them in a group discussion on death.

Some schools offer courses on death, in which students are exposed through literature to the many thoughts and feelings that death evokes. You might want to devise a similar curriculum. Appropriate materials might include *Death Be Not Proud, Go Ask Alice, Sunshine, Dreamland Lake,* and *Wild in the World.* To see how other societies deal with death, students can research their burial customs. Guest speakers, including a doctor, minister, psychologist, and lawyer might visit the class to discuss various aspects of death and dying. Student comments after such courses reveal a greater sense of comfort about death: "I always thought of death as being dark and sinister. Now I realize that death is something that comes to every living creature. There is no escaping it," or "After discussing it with others, I don't think death seems like such a terrible happening."[16]

When a child in your classroom or other group setting dies, you can use I-messages in your daily conversations with children and share your own feelings about the death of the child. In later phases of grief, ritual can play an important part in helping everyone accept their loss and return to normal routines. Displaying a picture of the deceased reminds everyone that he or she is present in spirit. Symbolic group rituals that honor the deceased include dedication of the yearbook or baseball field, planting a tree in remembrance, or attending a memorial service together. Through these activities you convey this positive message: "They live on in us, and now our lives must go on, too."[17]

Referral to a Professional Counselor

Nonprofessional counselors should examine their own attitudes before referring children who have suffered a loss through death. Is it the children's crisis, or the helpers' crisis? Certain signs in children might suggest that professional counseling is in order.

A serious decline in the way that the children relate to their world—their school, their family, their friends—continuing for several months suggests that a referral to a professional counselor would be helpful.

Children who feel extremely responsible for a death can benefit from being seen by a professional. These youngsters often show a preoccupation with death long after the death has occurred. Time by itself does not heal these wounds.

One nine-year-old girl was left at home to babysit for her five-year-old brother while her parents went to a movie. They were watching TV together until the boy said he would be going downstairs to get a toy. Instead of that, he walked outside and was struck by a car. The last words of her parents as they left had been, "Now don't let Michael out of your sight." The girl felt responsible for her brother's death. At one level she was responsible—she had disobeyed her parents. Yet on a moral level she was clearly not responsible for her brother's death: a nine-year-old should never have been given this responsibility in the first place. It would take intensive professional help to alleviate the child's guilt and feelings of accountability.

Another signal of trouble is if death-related play continues extensively for long periods of time after the death. It is normal for children to work through their feelings about a death through playing with ambulances, hospital scenes, mock burials, or similar activities. But if these scenarios do not disappear, or if they are accompanied by a severe impairment in the child's daily functioning, professional therapy may be required.

Suggested Reading for Children

Miles, M. *Annie and the Old One.* Atlantic Monthly Press, 1971. (Ages 6–9)

Morris, J. *Brian Piccolo: A Short Season.* Rand McNally and Company, 1971. (Ages 13+)

Rabin, G. *Changes.* Harper & Row, 1973. (Ages 12+; death of his grandfather)

Shotwell, L. R. *Adam Bookout.* The Viking Press, 1967. (Ages 11–13; death of his parents)

Smith, D. B. *A Taste of Blackberries.* Thomas Y. Crowell, 1973. (Ages 8–11; death of a friend)

Stein, S. B. *About Dying: An Open Family Book for Parents and Children Together.* Walker and Company, 1974. (Ages 3–8)

Stolz, M. S. *The Edge of Next Year.* Harper & Row, 1974. (Ages 12+; death of his mother)

White, E. B. *Charlotte's Webb.* Harper & Row, 1952. (Ages 8–12; death of a friend)

·6·

Divorce

If a small boy is sitting in the classroom
dreaming of being a pirate, his world is not
the classroom but the high seas.

JOHN RICH

Divorce threatens to destroy our cultural image of the perfect family. It also signifies the collapse of the support and protection a child needs. In other crises the parents offer support, but in divorce they themselves are the cause of the crisis. Parents see divorce as a remedy for their conflict. Children do not share this view—it collides with their desire to keep the family whole, and drives them and their parents apart when togetherness is needed most.

Many children are unprepared for divorce—they awake one morning to find one parent gone. One study reported that approximately 80 percent of young children *were not provided* with either an adequate explanation for the divorce or assurance of continued care.

> No single family in our study was able to provide the children with an adequate opportunity to express their concerns, to recognize with them that the divorce was indeed a family crisis, and that while things were likely to be difficult for a while, the expectation was that life would improve.[1]

What is remarkable is that none of these relatively well-educated suburban families studied (59 percent of the fathers and 33 percent of the mothers had college degrees) realized that telling their children about divorce is not a *pronouncement* but a process that requires thoughtful explanation, one in which children need to feel the love, attention, and support of their parents. Obviously, the stress on parents prevented them from fulfilling this function, typifying the diminished capacity to parent during this period. Others will have to help them assume this role, or take over some of the responsibility for communicating to children both what they need to hear and what they need to express.

Children's Initial Response

Children initially respond with shock, apprehension, and anger. Knowledge of parental discord does not reduce the impact. Most experience the mental and physical symptoms outlined in chapter one. In addition, fears, pleading, placation, and panic are present. Some run screaming through the house. Three-fourths strongly oppose the separation. Those numb and initially unchanged can show delayed reactions. Because of the "single pronouncement," many younger children disbelieve and postpone their responses. Furthermore, not only does divorce separate parents from each other, it separates parents from their children. Over one-half see their fathers as insensitive during this period, and one-third feel their mothers are unaware of their distress.[2]

Their Lives Change

In school, children of divorce can be roughly subdivided into two categories: those whose aggressive, immature needling of the teacher and teasing of peers win them a certain popularity at the expense of adult disapproval and those whose overly mature, depressed, isolationist and adult-pleasing behavior wins approval and attention from adults but disapproval from peers who see them as teacher's pets. Both the immaturity and hypermaturity are responses to the new responsibilities thrust upon them.

Children of divorce experience abrupt changes in their lives. Their mothers take jobs, both parents actively search for a new social life, and they sleep in two homes. Many "latchkey" children come home to an empty house, are left with babysitters, eat alone, put themselves to bed, make their own lunches, etc. And it all happens quickly with no transition period. Because children of divorced parents may spend long hours alone, in empty houses, other children are forbidden to play with them owing to their lack of supervision.

Their parents are no longer predictable. Children become worried by their parents' distress, particularly when they show this after the children show theirs, and they learn to suppress their feelings. Parents' confessions to thoughts of suicide give credibility to the children's already existing fears that the custodial parent will die. They become particularly distressed at the bitterness between the people they love and become preoccupied with details in their parents' arguments. Fairness and loyalty to both parents become central issues.

Their parents' crying is particularly upsetting. They feel constrained from questioning and wait for their parents to initiate any discussion of the divorce. Great awkwardness in communication results.

While school can provide a refuge from family troubles, almost no help was provided by the schools attended by children in the study. Evidently teachers and other school personnel hesitate to intrude in family matters, or are themselves unsure or uncomfortable in responding to a child whose parents are divorcing. Consequently, few children receive help from school counselors to cope with their crisis.

How Children Feel

Divorce shatters the picture of family life, causes pain and confusion, and creates challenges that children's usual coping strategies are not equipped to meet. They fantasize about what will happen to their parents. Divorce means loss. (Because divorce and death are both losses and generate many similar reactions, consult also chapter five, "Death."). When one parent leaves and the other is mourning the lost partner, he or she has very little attention to give to the children. Consequently, they feel they have lost both parents. Abandonment fears crystallize. These fears intrude into other situations in the children's lives. If they have to go into the hospital, they become afraid that their parents will not visit them. They are preoccupied with fears—fears they rarely volunteer to express.

For younger children there are thoughts that "I caused the divorce. Mom and Dad were arguing over me, and that's why Dad left." This leads to the additional thought: "If I caused the divorce, I can uncause it." These children make efforts to get their parents back together, diverting energies from playing, making friends, and doing homework.

They feel angry, caught in a situation over which they have no control. Since their anger cannot be expressed directly, it is aimed at other people or situations. Remember the young child's scissor story in chapter one?

The world is seen as less reliable. Their sense of future is in jeopardy. Since the marital tie can dissolve, so can the parent-child tie. Each visit to the noncustodial parent is feared to be the last. (Some of the fears and worries foster children experience when visiting natural parents, discussed in chapter ten, are also experienced by children of divorce.) They worry about the stability and survival of each parent. Their identification with the parting parent results in every criticism of the parent becoming a criticism of themselves.

Many younger children fear awakening to find the custodial parent gone, creating sleep disturbances. Older children are preoccupied with loss of the family's ongoing presence. Younger children yearn for the lost parent while older children fantasize about more nourishing and fulfilling relationships with the parent. Younger children are unwilling to let the custodial parent out of their sight, while older children are touchy, cranky, and unruly in the parent's presence. Many are angry at the custodial parent for driving the other parent away. Let's look more specifically at the feelings of children in our three different age groupings.

Children in the Magic Years

For young children, the routine separations of daily life become filled with dread. Any departure results in anxiety. The mother going shopping or a child going to school can be stressful. Children fear getting lost on the way home, or that they will find their house empty. Some young children scurry after their mother when she walks to another part of the house.

Bewilderment appears. They return to "what's that?" questions that characterized their earlier behavior, seemingly an effort to overcome the disorganization that accompanies crisis—what belongs to what and who belongs to whom.[3]

Possessiveness occurs. Children claim dominion over things in their environment as if to compensate for their loss: this is mine! Security blankets are returned to, self-stimulatory activity increases, or lapses in toilet training occur. They regress.

Elaborate, macabre fantasies are spun. The less explanation their parents give about the divorce and their new way of life, the greater the children's fantasy. They fear being hungry, which is obviously connected with abandonment fears. But other fears make less sense. One child feared his absent mother burned in a fire. This fear was traced to a minor house fire that had occurred earlier. Fantasy is especially prevalent in girls, who daydream that the departed parent loves them best and hopes for a restored family. Often children believe that the parent left to be with another family. This belief and denial exist simultaneously: "I don't care that he left—do you think he'll get another boy?"

These children play less with peers, show more emotional neediness, get angry easily, mostly at the custodial parent, but inhibit their aggression on other occasions, particularly toward the noncustodial parent, and feel guilty that they caused the breakup.

Children in the Middle Years

Six- to eight-year-old children show pervasive sadness. They express their sorrow directly. Fantasy is conspicuously absent, although their fears are exaggerated. One such fear is that of going to live with strangers: "I'll have to live in a foster home." Their yearning for the noncustodial parent is similar to grief over the death of a loved one. Such yearning is particularly strong in children of the same sex as the noncustodial parent. Boys want their mothers to remarry, and they wear their father's clothes. Like younger children, they feel deprived, and food becomes important.

When the parents begin to get along as parents rather than as partners, children's fantasies of reconciliation reappear (sometimes rekindled by the parents' fantasies). Loyalty conflicts are more obvious at this age level and can be quite intense.

Nine- to twelve-year-olds, who have stronger egos than the six- to eight-year-olds, show more soberness and clarity. They actively struggle to master conflictual feelings and reach out to others. They respond well to counseling. Denial and distress coexist. The shame and difficulty they feel is not diminished by the high incidence of divorce they see around them.

Vigorous activity, bravado, and courage mark their behavior. Involvement in constructive activity helps them to forget their powerlessness. For example, one girl wrote a newspaper article about her parents' divorce.[4]

Their anger is fully conscious, intense, and directly expressed at the parent they blame. Some adopt a dictatorial posture, ordering their parent about in unforgiving tones.

Their disenchantment with their parents' behavior shakes their own identity, leading to minor delinquent acts. They are more vulnerable to stress-related illnesses. Fears of being excluded and the need to demonstrate usefulness to a parent results in their being coopted into battle as an ally of one parent. Only children are particularly vulnerable to alliances, as are racially or ethnically mixed children who are pressured by their extended families.[5]

Adolescents

The normal advance and retreat of adolescence is temporarily hampered by divorce. Adolescents feel like their parents are leaving them instead of vice versa. The adolescents' need for periodic refueling from their family in order to advance out into the world is disrupted. Accelerated autonomy is foisted upon them—they are simply asked to grow up too quickly. When the discipline, order, and controls provided by two parents disappear, misbehavior results.

Disillusionment about relationships and commitments appears. They doubt their own ability as sexual partners and their ability to succeed in marriage even long after the divorce:

ADOLESCENT: I'm not ever going to have a long-term relationship. I'll have short ones like my mother (noncustodial parent) and live alone.

Emptiness, fearfulness, chronic fatigue, troublesome dreams, and difficulty in concentration hamper their effective functioning. They grieve the loss of the family of their childhood. Already well-functioning adolescents are less disrupted and less lonely, but like younger children, they, too, have irrational ideas about divorce. Boys are particularly upset when they think their father has been thrown out.

When their parents become more socially active and date others, adolescents can no longer view them as asexual, causing concerns about their own sexuality. They show intolerance for the "immaturity" of their parents, whom they think shouldn't act like adolescents. They feel personally betrayed; they can no longer view their parents in an idealized way. Intellectually, they know they were not responsible for the parental split, but they fear that talking about their pain, sense of betrayal, and embarrassment will reveal them as failures to the world. To defend against their vulnerability, they express great anger and rage.[6]

There is another emotion that may be felt, but which may be very difficult to express: relief. It is hard to admit that one is glad there won't be so many fights. Young children prefer the fighting over the separation. This is usually not the case with adolescents, who are embarrassed by their parents' fighting: "At least now I can bring friends home."

Developmental Factors

Remember that how children feel is more a function of their developmental age than of their chronological age. Emotionally troubled and immature children can regress considerably and respond more intensely. Very mature children will show less regression and more adultlike grieving. Remember, too, that abused children or physically ill or handicapped children will respond in a way in keeping with their own unique experiences: "Dad left home because he didn't want a boy who couldn't walk," or "Dad beat me, so Mom took me to Grandma's and we never went back."

It's Never the Same

After the divorce, children (and adults) often expect that their next family will be like the first—only better. They don't realize that the nuclear family is gone forever. Blended families are not the same, and they shouldn't try to be.

In all families, parent-child relationships are ambivalent ones, and to expect continuous caring from individuals who find themselves together after remarriage leads to disappointment and anger. While roles and rules can be worked out relatively quickly, feelings between people are not so easily handled. Stepparents are targets of displaced anger toward natural parents and are blamed for making Mommy or Daddy unavailable for reunion. Young children who believe they caused the marriage to fail feel they have the power to break up the new relationship. Children often wish stepparents would die so that natural parents can reunite. This wish persists for years. Teenagers have a particularly difficult time: "I already got two parents. I don't need any more to tell me what to do!" Younger children have difficulty feeling love for the stepparents because they fear they might leave too. "I can't take it. I lost one mommy, now I'm going to lose two," cried one child every time his father and stepmother fought.

Parents who remain unattached for a long period prior to remarriage typically develop close, confiding relationships with their children. When a new love enters their life, he or she usurps this relationship. Jealousy of the new mate characterizes children's relationships with the stepparent. Loyalty to the other parent may prevent attachment to the stepparent—to like the stepparent is to betray the natural parent.

Even when things go well for the child after a divorce, constant adjustments have to be made to institutions and organizations, which ignore children's living situations. Schools offer only one parent-teacher conference and one report card. Forms are designed for one home with two natural parents. Tickets for social events are offered to one family. When told to bring things "home," children have to choose which one. Separate gifts are made for mother and father. Working mothers have little time to bake for school functions, and custodial fathers often are expected to act like nonworking mothers. These attitudes and practices continually remind such children that they and their family are different from others.

Counseling Approaches

Magic Years Children

With all children the counseling task is to help them verbalize their distress and their conception of why their parents separated. With the very young remember that they often feel their behavior or thoughts caused the split. It is very difficult to convince them otherwise. Remember, however, that children can be helped to decenter by proper questioning, and efforts should be made to get them to look beyond their conclusions.

> ADULT: You've spilled your milk many times before—did Dad leave then? Did your brother ever spill his milk?

or

> ADULT: Have you ever heard your Mom and Dad argue? Do you think they argue when you're not home, or away at Grandma's? Ask your older brother sometime.

One real problem is that parents fight a lot over how to handle children. This contributes to the children's feeling that they're responsible.

> ADULT: Did your parents ever argue about your older sister? Who did they argue most about—you or her? Do you think she caused Daddy to leave?

Most important is counseling that reflects the child's universal feelings at this age level.

> ADULT: Sometimes you think Mommy will leave home, too, and

you'll be all alone with no one to feed and care for you. Lots of kids feel like that.

or

ADULT: Sometimes you think you'll never see Daddy again, that he'll get another son he likes better. Lots of kids feel like that.

or

ADULT: You often get mad at your mother's new boyfriend because now Daddy can't get Mommy back.

These comments are door openers. They are universal interpretations of the general concerns known to exist in children of divorce. They help get the children talking; they move one from the general to the specific so that one can learn their unique feelings and concerns.

Marshaling Positive Forces

Children need to be reassured that they will be taken care of, but that their mom and dad will temporarily be struggling with their own worries. Conferences with parents can help them clarify this to children, but often other adults need to support the children through this period.

ADULT: It's not that your mommy doesn't love you—she's just worried about how she'll manage without your dad and can't always listen to you. But she can still pay the bills and buy the food since Dad will be helping her out for a while. Maybe she'll take a job too. But she'll make sure you're taken care of. She won't leave you.

Children need to feel that they are not helpless about their situation. Task mastering helps them to overcome helpless feelings. But let the children choose the task.

ADULT: Mommy seems very busy now. Maybe you could spend more time with Mom if you helped her in some way. What does she complain about most?

CHILD: My clothes all over the floor.

ADULT: So she spends time picking up after you, or trying to get you to pick up, when she could be playing a game with you instead. Maybe you could be more careful about putting your clothes away?

Middle Years Children

Knowledge of the concerns of this age help to get a communication going. For example:

ADULT: I'll bet it's real hard getting mad at Daddy. You think he might not visit you if you get mad. Mom got mad at him a lot, and he left. Poor Mom, I'll bet she gets a lot of the anger you feel about his leaving, but blaming Mom hurts her and makes her unhappy. She's not likely to want to take you places if you're angry at her all the time.

or

ADULT: Taking sides with Mom against Dad helps you to be sure Mom will always love you. Do you think she might stop loving you someday?

Adolescents

Parents of adolescents can be encouraged to reassure their youngsters about their unexpressed worries such as financial ones, possible increases in responsibility, or changes in living conditions. Direct work with adolescents will focus on a number of issues: allegiance and loyalty, anxiety about their own future, precipitously changed perceptions of their parents, accelerated individuation of parents, or heightened awareness of parents as sexual objects.[7]

The adolescents' disillusionment with their parents and their rage at them prevents their realistic assessment of them. The counselor's gentle persistence in talking about parents can help the youths make more realistic assessments. The counselor can help adolescents to disengage from loyalty conflicts in which they find themselves. Since denial and withdrawal are additional defenses against experiencing the pain of family disruptions, confrontation is frequently employed.

When confronting adolescents, one needs to show that a particular behavior or attitude represents poor judgment in terms of *the adolescent's frame of reference.* Adolescents need to feel that they are in error by *their own standards,* not the counselor's.

ADULT: I don't understand why you're so angry at your mother when your father left her, and he visits you inconsistently. For a kid with your smarts, it would seem you have got it backward. I might be confused. Explain it to me so I'll understand how you see it differently.

or

ADULT: It looks like you'll never trust men because your Dad let you down. Have you known any men who have been trustworthy? Did your Dad ever let you down before?

Remember that adolescents who were attached to their parents prior to the divorce frequently become quite detached from them during the divorce. Nevertheless, these are the adolescents who look best during follow-up interviews.[8]

Crisis Preparation

Children's knowledge about the problems they encounter when their lives change after a divorce can help them prepare for future problems. One way to minimize short-term stress is to prepare the children ahead of time so that they will not be caught off guard by abrupt and unexpected events, and by *their reactions to them.*

ADULT: You know, Cassie, when your mom starts dating other men, you're going to compare each one with your dad and probably not like them. This will make mom unhappy.

or

ADULT: When your mom's new boyfriend gets mad at you the first time, you'll probably tell him "you're not my father" and feel like he has no right to get mad at you. This will cause some problems between you and mom.

More General Approaches

A major theme of this book is to provide ways to create a climate in which children undergoing a crisis feel understood and can communicate what they are going through. When children in crisis can direct their energies to deal with the crisis, they become less disoriented and are enabled to face daily tasks. Divorce makes many adults uneasy. Instead of acknowledging this and seeking further training, they simply say, "My job isn't to discuss problems with children. It's to teach math, reading, gymnastics." In adopting this stance they lose a valuable opportunity to help children. If you can help children to think productively about their personal problems, you can help them to free up energies to devote to other tasks. Let's examine some positive approaches, as well as some pitfalls, in working with children of divorce.

Be a Careful Observer

Most children have difficulty signaling their plight directly to you and may express their conflict about a divorce situation indirectly. Look for behavioral cues that reveal children's feelings by observing children over a period of time in several situations—work, play, and in individual tasks. Such observations permit construction of a complete picture of the total child and reduce the likelihood of basing judgments on a bad day.[9] Some things to look for include

- absentmindedness, or staring at the floor or out the window
- forgetfulness, such as not putting possessions away
- nervousness, or being fidgety—particularly in a child who has not shown this behavior before
- weariness, slowness, lethargy
- declining grades
- and excessive fantasy and play.[10]

Knowing something about children's families helps to relate these signs to a possible divorce. Many times children are referred to learning disability specialists for suspected "learning problems" which others falsely attribute to neurological disorders. What is really going on is that these children lack energy to focus on school tasks, have no motivation, and are conveying their distress indirectly.

Children's artwork or storytelling may refer to a divorce at home. One young child kept drawing monsters with different colored hair. Inquiry by the teacher revealed that Mom had a number of boyfriends, several of whom disliked the child. A seven-year-old wrote the following story, in which the flying dragon represents her stepmother.

The Flying Dragon and the Princess

This is a story about a good flying dragon and a princess. The princess is scared because she thinks the dragon is going to claw and scratch her. She will bleed all over. She will run away. She ran to the prince and he put bandages on her, but she still kept bleeding. She slapped his face—she ran to her mommy and had more bandages put on. She ran to a farm—it still kept bleeding— she ran away to her grandfather's and still bled—she went to her uncles—still bleeding. She ran back home—she went to the girl dragon—still bleeding—went home and told her mother that she didn't like her—then ran away and still kept bleeding.

She had an idea. She went up in heaven and told the lord and the lord helped her by telling her mother to do things for her and take off the bandages now. She went back to the dragon and said, "Next time will you be more friendly instead of scratching me!!" Her daddy just said—"Next time when you see the dragon, don't talk mean to her." The End.

Remember that stories like the above are fantasies. The stepmother may not be the dragon she is depicted to be; in fact, the child says it is a "story about a good flying dragon" who she then makes to be mean. Children's feelings are confused—treat them that way by remaining nonjudgmental. The "monsters with different colored hair" may have disliked the child because her loyalty to her father prevented her from behaving well in their presence.

Avoid Clichés

In chapter four we discussed the difference between making so-called sympathetic comments and providing true empathy. There are many handy clichés available to say to children about divorce. Avoid them. Let's look at approaches which obscure your understanding of children, as well as those which communicate your knowledge of what they are going through.

Be wary of making statements to children that place them in conflict about how they are supposed to feel or behave. For example, people have been known to make statements to children that can increase their conflict: "Now you can be the man of the house," or "You be sure and take good care of your daddy."

Children need to grieve the loss of their parent—they do not need their emotional energy consumed by unclear adult responsibilities. Children need to know that they are *not* taking their father's place, and that new relationships in the family will be established that will take into account the new situation.

Remarriage and the addition of a new parent create new stresses. Many times, however, adults will offer a "helpful" comment such as "Aren't you glad that you got a new stepdaddy? Isn't that nice!" This new development is definitely not nice. These children have now lost their mother to another partner. She may be enraptured in a new relationship, think and talk about her new partner continually, and be less available to the children than she was previously.

Adolescents often feel shame and embarrassment at their parents' divorce. Their family failed. To make them feel better, adults might say, "It's not your fault." Such comments do not rid the youngsters of their shame, nor do they encourage them to express the meaning of the event to them.

Keeping these pitfalls in mind, how do we communicate to children that we want to understand the impact this painful experience makes upon their life, and encourage them to tell us its unique meaning to them? How do we convey empathy rather than just say nice and polite clichés?

Encourage Verbalization of the Crisis

Recognize that children's minds may wander from the task at hand. Ask open questions that will encourage them to express what they feel. "It seems like you have a lot on your mind lately. You're not your usual self. Would you like to talk to me about it?"

Sometimes children will announce that their parents are divorcing. They are probably making this announcement because they want to talk about it, because they are concerned about it and want to get it off their chest. You might say to them: "It must be upsetting to you to have that happen. Maybe just before lunch or recess you can tell me about how this happened to your mother and your father."

In private you can explain that you like to know about children and their families. "Where is your daddy going to live? How much will you get to see him? What is mommy going to do? Is everyone being taken real good care of?" Such questions often will elicit both factual and emotional information from children, rather than force them into agreeing or disagreeing with clichés that are presented to them.

Realize that Children's Work Is Going to Suffer

Keep in mind that children's schoolwork is going to suffer, particularly new learning. Struggling to comprehend the meaning of events at home and the feelings they evoke, children have less energy available for work or for participating in structured activities. If you make demands of them without understanding their struggles, then both of you will be frustrated. Give them material that they like, typically activities that do not require sustained concentration, but which keep them occupied and minimize daydreaming.

Call a Meeting with the Parents

Children can blow out of proportion events surrounding a divorce. Meetings with parents can ascertain what is actually happening and enable those in the children's lives to communicate the truth to them.

The parents of Frank, a third grader, were divorcing. Frank's father moved to New Jersey from upstate New York. Frank believed his father's reason for the move was to obtain a higher-paying job. In school Frank constantly fantasized about trying to find a better job for his father in New York! Consequently, most of his schoolwork was left unfinished—he spent nearly all of his time devising ways to get his father back. After a conference with Frank's teacher, his mother explained to

Frank the real reasons for the separation and that getting his father a job in New York would not bring him back home.

Another valuable function of the parent conference is to convey your support to the entire family. Recognize that divorcing parents are unable to parent as well as you or they would like.[11] Suggest they read some books that will help them talk with their children, including those written for children which appear at the end of this chapter.

Discuss with the parents approaches you may employ to help the children through this difficult period, especially what you may do to help them express their feelings.

Bibliotherapy

Discussions with children about readings on divorce help give them a vocabulary for understanding and describing their own feelings. Point out to the children what seems obvious to you, but which may be unclear to them. It is truly surprising when we discover the facts about divorce that children don't know though we think they do. "A lot of kids are in the same situation. Their moms and dads had problems in getting along with each other, and so they got a divorce," or "Dave in the story had a hard time concentrating in school because he missed his dad so much." These readings help children to see the obvious things they don't see when embroiled in the actual situation, or which they never really thought about.

Identify Children for a Group

A number of children in a classroom or school may be preoccupied by divorce or separation. Teachers can take the initiative and suggest the formation of a group in which these children can discuss their concerns in more detail. The school psychologist, guidance counselor, social worker, or a professional consultant from outside the school could conduct such a group.

When a Referral Is Indicated

Allowing children to express their concerns to you does not mean that you are going to be their therapist. Well-meaning listeners can get in over their heads and handle a situation poorly. When the disruption in children's daily lives and functioning is severe, or when you feel uncomfortable discussing the kind of concerns that are brought up, refer children and their families to a competent professional rather than trying to assume the role of professional yourself.

Before you make a referral, find out firsthand about the effectiveness of the therapist. Former clients, colleagues, and a personal visit to the therapist are valuable sources of information. When appropriate, working with the therapist can be quite helpful: You may be able to furnish useful observations about the children and their interactions with others. In turn, the therapist can suggest strategies and approaches useful to you.

Paul was a sixth grader whose unhappiness was not helped by the attention of his teachers and neighbors. His parents had experienced a particularly painful divorce the previous year. During a meeting with Paul, his mother, and his three sisters, Paul's teacher noticed that he bore the brunt of numerous frustrations vented by the other family members. She suggested that family counseling might be helpful to get everyone through this trying time and provided the name of a family therapist in the community. One goal of the family therapy was to free Paul from the scapegoat role. When this effort was successful, Paul's work in school improved. Wisely, his teacher had left the intensive therapy to a professional.

Suggested Reading for Children

Brooks, J. *Uncle Mike's Boy.* Harper & Row, 1973. (Ages 11+; a boy's adjustment to a one parent home)

Gaff, B. *Where Is Daddy? The Storm of a Divorce.* Beacon Press, 1969. (Ages 4–8; portrays magical thinking, grief, confusion, and loneliness)

Klein, N. *Taking Sides.* Pantheon Books, 1974. (Ages 10+)

Lexau, J. M. *Emily and the Klunky Baby and the Next Door Dog.* Dial Press, 1972. (Ages 5–8)

Norris, G. B. *Lillian.* Atheneum Publishers, 1968. (Ages 9–12)

Smith, D. B. *Kick a Stone Home.* Thomas Y. Crowell, 1974. (Ages 11+)

·7·

Health Crisis

And does it not seem hard to you,
When all the sky is clear and blue,
And I should like so much to play,
To have to go to bed by day?

ROBERT LOUIS STEVENSON
"Bed in Summer"

At some time we all encounter children who are very ill. How do you explain heart disease to a five-year-old? What do you say to the teenage girl who is balding and overweight, side effects from her chemotherapy for cancer? Or how do you respond to the stricken faces in your group of ten-year-olds when one of them is having a seizure? Sometimes a child is dying—how do you deal with this very difficult situation?

While knowledge doesn't always lead to empathy, it dispels our fear of the unknown and relieves anxiety which interferes with being empathic. In this chapter we will review common experiences of children who are ill, such as how they perceive the treatment they are receiving, their experience of hospitalization, and the role they feel they play in their illness, and we will go into some specific diseases that our surveys indicate trouble direct care staff and parents. These disorders are epilepsy, sickle cell anemia, diabetes, asthma, heart disease, and cancer.

We present these diseases not so much to acquaint you with the disease per se, although such information is helpful in responding calmly and empathically, but to lead your thinking about the psychological effects of disease, particularly how developmental issues color children's interpretation of their disorder.

Epilepsy

Jimmy smelled that familiar unpleasant smell, felt the tingling in his legs, and heard the teacher's voice fade. Before he could speak, he lost consciousness. The child in the adjacent seat saw Jimmy's arm begin to quiver and then his whole body shake. The other children saw Jimmy fall from his seat and shake violently. He had difficulty breathing, and saliva collected in his mouth and ran from his lips.

Mrs. Brown quickly moved to help Jimmy, shoved aside nearby furniture, and turned him on his side so he did not choke on his saliva. When Jimmy's jerking stopped, he looked very sleepy and was taken to the nurse's office to rest.

Mrs. Brown simply told her class that Jimmy had a seizure, that he would need to take some medicine to prevent another attack; but if it happened again, his friends could help him to not hurt himself during the seizure. Two students near Jimmy's desk would be prepared to help the teacher place Jimmy on her coat, another was appointed to run for the school nurse, and one of his close friends was asked to sit and talk with him when he woke up. She added that Jimmy felt no pain and, in spite of the violent movements, slow breathing, and paleness, would not die, although he would need to rest when the seizure was over. She made it clear that, aside from the seizure, Jimmy was the same as the rest of the class and could continue to participate in all the regular activities.

Mrs. Brown was familiar with epilepsy. The year before, she had become concerned about one child who sometimes stared into space and rolled his eyeballs. Unlike a normal child's daydreaming, these episodes were brief, lasting no more than thirty seconds, and the child seemed confused following their termination. She discussed the child with the school psychologist who then referred the youngster to a pediatric neurologist. The neurologist identified the child's disorder as epilepsy. He had petit mal rather than grand mal seizures that Jimmy had experienced.

Let's look at the basic principles Mrs. Brown followed when she handled Jimmy's seizure. First, she gave an immediate, matter-of-fact explanation. "Right now Jimmy is having a short seizure. It won't hurt him and will be over in a few minutes. Then he may be tired, and we'll let him rest. Alice, when he is ready to work, would you please tell him what we have been doing? Okay, boys and girls, now let's get back to our reading assignment."

Second, she kept calm. If the adults can remain calm but concerned, the youngsters will model their calmness. If fearful and anxious, the youngsters will respond similarly.

Third, she was open and knowledgeable when the children asked questions after the seizure had subsided: "What causes seizures?" "Are they catching?" (No.) "Do flashing lights cause seizures?" (They can.) "Can you take medicine for them?" (Yes, it helps a lot but sometimes can't prevent every seizure.) "If Jim gets real mad at me, could he have a seizure?" (He could.) "Do lots of kids have them?" (Five out of 1,000.) Correctly answering these questions and reflecting the underlying concerns will help the children better understand seizures.

Fourth, Mrs. Brown knew that Jimmy could participate in most activities. During swimming, however, he would need to stay close to the edge of the pool while one adult was assigned to watch him. Consultation with his physician had revealed that swimming and climbing were the only activities that needed to be restricted and monitored.

Fifth, she was aware that epilepsy is no excuse for bad behavior. An adult may be reluctant to discipline a child with epilepsy for fear that the stress may aggravate the situation and trigger a seizure. But in general, expect the same from epileptic youngsters as you do others. Don't overprotect them.

In addition to grand mal and petit mal epilepsy, some children have psychomotor seizures. During these seizures, they behave in ways that do not relate to the task at hand. For example, they chew, smack their lips, or fiddle with their clothes buttons when they are doing a class assignment.

Clarify with a consultant which symptoms are those of the epilepsy itself and which are the child's reactions to it. For example, temporal lobe damage can cause not only grand mal seizures but also aggressive outbursts, bad smells, eating disturbances, ringing in the ears, poor judgments about size, distance, or speed, and *déjà-vu* experiences. These children may respond to their disorder with slowness and depression, anxiety and restlessness, and refusal to join clubs or groups, fearing the embarrassment of a seizure.

There will sometimes be children who use their epilepsy to control adults. Parents may give a special meaning to the seizures, which is then adopted by the child and generalized to other situations. For example, parents sometimes believe children have seizures to get out of doing something. When this occurs, children may give this same meaning to their seizures and try to bring about the conditions that produce seizures in order to gain certain ends. In this case the seizures become part of a larger picture that requires closer examination, and professional consultation can be helpful.

One goal of the counselor is to help children look objectively at their disorder. The story below (told by a therapist) conveys the irrational feelings that many children have about their seizures:

> The woman put a man on the table, cut his head open, inserted a hydrogen bomb, and sewed him up again, while the bomb ticked. The ensuing explosion killed all the men; all the women escaped unharmed.[1]

The child whose account this is will need considerable help to look more realistically at himself and his caretakers, and to see how he has intertwined his hostility at women with his seizures.

Sickle Cell Anemia

A serious, often fatal condition suffered by black youngsters is sickle cell anemia. Despite its widespread occurrence (3 out of 1,000), many do not understand the unfolding of the disease.

Arlene's birth was without incident, and she was judged to be in good health, the third child in a healthy family. Development proceeded normally until shortly after her first birthday. She seemed thinner and paler than other children and had more frequent colds. One cold hung on. She developed a deep chest cough, shaking chills, a sharp pain in her chest, and a high fever. She was admitted to the hospital with pneumonia and severe anemia. A blood study revealed a low red-blood-cell count and the presence of many sickled-shaped cells among the normal round cells. A screening test for sickle cell anemia was positive; Arlene had the disease.

She was placed in an oxygen tent where she was given intravenous fluids, penicillin to combat her pneumonia, and a blood transfusion. She improved rapidly.

Arlene's parents were shocked when their blood tests revealed that they were both carriers of the sickle cell trait. Both their other children were normal—why Arlene? The physician explained that the disease was inherited, carried by a recessive gene, and incurable. Somehow it didn't sink in, everything had happened so quickly. Arlene had just begun to be a personality in the family, no longer a dependent baby but a mobile, into-everything kid. Now she would have to be dependent again.

After they took Arlene home, her parents explained the nature of the disease to their other children so they wouldn't fear for their own health and also in the hope that they wouldn't resent the extra attention and special care Arlene would need. They explained that the red blood cells in Arlene's body had changed in shape from fat doughnuts to elongated sickles. These clumped together and cut off the blood circulation in Arlene's knees, ankles, shoulders, brain, and other areas. She could be in severe pain and lose consciousness at any time.[2]

Although Arlene's family took all the precautions recommended by the hospital physicians, several months later Arlene was readmitted to the hospital with a high fever, nausea, and vomiting. She was pale, and her eyes had a yellow tint. Treatment was similar to that during her first admission. Again she improved, but her right hand had lost its coordination, and her right foot dragged when she walked. A pediatric-neurological examination revealed partial paralysis caused by a blood clot in her brain. She needed physical therapy. Four months later, Arlene again was hospitalized, treated with intravenous fluids, and discharged.

By the time she was seven, Arlene had been hospitalized twelve times. Substantial damage occurred to her liver as a result of the repeated crises of sickle cell anemia. Each relapse was extremely painful. Obstructions of the vessels in her lungs brought episodes of severe chest pain, causing her body to twist and contort as she tried to breathe. As they witnessed these attacks, her parents experienced great anguish, and at times perhaps wished she would die to be spared such suffering.

Even though Arlene has a devoted family and received excellent treatment at the hospital, it is unlikely that she will live through adolescence. If she does, her crises may be less frequent and less severe since the disease seems to subside somewhat in adulthood.

The problems faced by Arlene and her parents are not uncommon among black Americans. Perhaps one in every ten American blacks carries the trait. Most of the carriers have very few sickle cells in their blood and experience no trouble with them during their lifetime. If two trait carriers marry, they can expect that one in four of their children will get this serious disease. The other two will be carriers and the fourth will be free from the trait.

But these are only the facts about the disorder. What about the psychological effects upon the child and family? Children need to feel their parents are protectors and providers, not painful punishers, and often idealize them as figures who have control over everything. When parents cannot prevent repeated pain, children become angry at them. Their own hostility frightens children because they fear their parents will respond in turn and abandon them. If they already have a strained relationship with their parents, they may believe the parents' inability to stop the pain is due to their anger at them for misbehaving. Interpreting the pain as punishment, they will struggle to no avail to discover why they made the parents so angry.

> ADULT: Arlene, sometimes I'll bet you think your parents could stop your pain if they really wanted to. Lots of kids think their parents are more powerful than disease.

or

> ADULT: Arlene, I wonder if you ever get mad at your mom because you have so much pain? You'd like her to kiss you and make it better, like she does to small cuts and bruises?

or

> ADULT: Sometimes when we get mad because of our pain, we think our anger scares away those we love and count on.

Children who experience continuous pain are constantly overwhelmed by anxiety, which lowers their coping skills. Children with predictable symptoms, such as asthma or seizures, have a better chance of assimilating the experience than children with an illness in which the symptoms vary.

External sources of danger, as real and serious as they may be, are not what makes an experience traumatic. Medical treatments and pain become manageable until they touch on emotional influences which transform them into experiences of punishment, assault, being robbed, mutilated, abandoned, or condemned. Pain is borne well when anxiety plays a minor role. Pain augmented by anxiety, even if the pain is slight, is remembered for a long time, accompanied by defenses against its return. In children anxiety is fueled by fantasies, a point made repeatedly in this book.

Arlene's family, and Arlene herself, will need continued help to keep her experiences of the disease anchored in reality, to keep the external dangers clear from, rather than confused by, her fantasies and interpretations. This is not an easy task when the disease is sickle cell anemia, a disease that strikes an already oppressed group.

Diabetes

Juvenile diabetes mellitus affects 1 in 1,000 school-age children. It is a disorder in which the body is unable to metabolize carbohydrates, particularly sugar, because of insufficient production of insulin, a secretion of the pancreas. A characteristic of juvenile diabetes, in contrast to late onset diabetes, is total lack of insulin. Lack of insulin causes blood sugar level to rise. Because this sugar cannot be converted into energy, a condition similar to starvation develops. Treatment includes the administration of insulin to make up for the body's inability to manufacture it. To regulate insulin dosage and carbohydrate intake, urine is analyzed to determine sugar levels.

Surprisingly, many diabetics know very little about the disease and its care. A survey of patients at home found that many—even long-term sufferers—made numerous errors in their disease management.[3] Studies done at camps for diabetic children revealed that patients and their families often lacked the basic facts about diabetes. What is needed are more thorough educational programs for diabetic children, their families, and those who work with them.

The treatment is ongoing. While urine samples typically are taken at home, some children need to test their urine at school. To avoid embarrassment, older children learn to take their urine samples between class periods. Adjustments in the dispensing of insulin have to be made when the children's diet changes due to particular circumstances: when the children forget their lunch and have to eat the school lunch (packed lunches are generally high in protein, whereas school lunches are usually high in carbohydrates); when they go on trips either with classmates or family; when they exercise excessively or irregularly (before eating); and when they are sick or upset about something.

Children go into insulin shock. Exercise results in a lowering of blood sugar and can cause shock unless the insulin dose is reduced accordingly, or carbohydrate intake is increased. Insulin shock is a serious condition which calls for the school nurse or other medical authority to be summoned immediately, but it can be prevented by informed teachers who know the symptoms of low and high blood sugar:[4]

> *low blood sugar* (usually develops suddenly)
> restlessness
> sudden change in behavior

sweating
pallor
tired or weak feeling
headaches
extreme hunger
convulsions
coma

high blood sugar (usually develops slowly)
dry skin
sweet or fruity odor to breath
excessive thirst
excessive urination
deep breathing
coma

Teachers should keep snacks which are quick energy sources available, such as candy bars or fruit slices, particularly on excursions in case they notice low blood sugar reactions caused by delay in mealtime or excessive activity. Snacks should always be given out when delays are anticipated. If there is doubt, always manage the situation as if it were a *low blood sugar reaction,* as dispensing sugar will cause no harm, while withholding it can have serious consequences.

The psychological impact of diabetes revolves around children's reaction to prolonged dietary restrictions. Children feel singled out, discriminated against, and deprived. Because they master anxiety by turning passive experiences into active ones, children may develop ascetic self-denial tendencies rather than accept the passive role imposed on them by dietary restrictions. Food is equated with love in our society. "Mom must not love me because she won't give me the foods other mothers give their children." Since mothers similarly equate food with love, their withholding of forbidden food is accompanied by anxiety and guilt. Food restriction can become a starting point for serious and prolonged eating difficulties and battles with parents. For remember that restrictions imposed by some illnesses have been commonly used as punishments for years—sending the children to bed, depriving them of their favorite food, confining them to the house. How can children think otherwise about their restrictions?

ADULT: Royce, you know, sometimes I think you feel your mom doesn't *want* you to have sweet things. You don't believe her when she tries to explain why you can't have them. You think she's just a mean mommy!

Asthma

Asthma remains one of the leading causes of absenteeism from school.[5] A child having an asthmatic attack can disrupt a structured event such as a camp-out or a little league game.

Asthma is defined as "breathing with difficulty." The difficulty results from a spasm of the bronchial muscle. After the initial spasms, thick mucus collects, causing further obstruction of the air passage. During the attack not all of the air that is breathed in can be exhaled, causing wheezing, hoarse sounds. An asthma attack can last for several hours or for several days.

Many believe that asthma is used by some children to avoid stressful situations or that it is caused by underlying emotional conflicts. These beliefs make it less clear how to react to an attack. Yet they are not supported by the facts. Close to two-thirds of children with asthma also have other allergies, and the majority have diminished symptoms when they reach adolescence, a time when emotional problems are intensified. Under stress children can have more frequent attacks, but the disorder itself is caused by physical, not emotional, factors.

When working with an asthmatic child, an attack can cause a crisis if you have not developed an alternate plan. Have a contingency plan. Make sure that there is another supervised place to which the child can be excused for the duration of the attack. Mention in a matter-of-fact way to the other children, "Jeff is having an asthma attack. He needs to cough for a while to clear his lungs, and after that he will be all right. He will join us again when he is ready. . . ."

Heart Disorders

Heart disease occurs in one of every thousand children and is a highly variable condition. Some children have a benign, self-limiting defect which doesn't interfere with their day-to-day functioning; others have a condition severe enough to be life-threatening.

Children are confused about the heart. When asked, "What is your heart?" children ages four through seven respond that "it . . . drums . . . hammers . . . ticks . . . helps us breathe." These youngsters are not certain whether animals and trees have hearts. Children ages seven through ten realize that "[the heart] makes you live . . . you die when it stops." Youngsters ten and eleven can explain about veins, valves, circulation, and pumping action, and know why death can result from heart problems.[6]

The child's physician is the best resource to explain the disorder and the effect (if any) it will have on the child's response to daily routine. Classmates should be helped to understand why the child may have a routine different from theirs when he or she looks and acts just like they do. This understanding can come after discussion about the heart and its functions. When we keep in mind that children really don't understand how the heart works, such discussions might prevent the teasing and ridicule often directed at children who are different.

A realistic understanding of the child's heart condition also prevents all who work with him or her from becoming overly apprehensive, overprotective, or from exempting the child from normal expectations and discipline. Many emotionally healthy, outgoing, social, and popular teenagers who have congenital heart diseases have definite plans for the future, including marriage. Their parents usually have given them as much responsibility and independence as their maturity and health have permitted, and from about ten years of age they have participated in discussing and planning their cardiac treatment.[7]

Cancer

> When my doctor told me I had cancer, I started crying. I thought, "Why did this have to happen to me? Why couldn't it be someone else . . . ?" I was sure I was going to die . . . when my doctor tried to tell me more about the cancer, I said, "Don't go any further, because I don't want to hear anymore."[8]

Cancer, more than the other diseases covered in this chapter, is a life-threatening illness. Often cancer goes into remission, making it difficult for younger children to understand their disorder. In addition, the term *cancer* itself is confusing because it refers to a number of different conditions: leukemia, tumors, Hodgkin's disease, or Ewing's sarcoma, among others. Each of these has a particular onset and course of progress that will vary from patient to patient. Despite the severity of cancer, there is hope for many who suffer from it:

> The poor prognosis of children with cancer in times past in no way compares with the hopeful outlook of the 1980s. Fully half

the children diagnosed this year will be cured of the disease and go on to live productive lives.

But for some reason, many health professionals do not seem to have integrated this hopeful attitude into their perception of patients with childhood cancer. Many assume that any child with cancer will have a painful and dismal existence and succumb to his disease—if not now, then sometime in the near future.[9]

In the winter of his fourteenth year, Steve was told that he had cancer—metastatic neuroblastoma. About two-thirds of these tumors are associated with the adrenal glands, and it is typically a disorder of early childhood.

During his first year of therapy, Steve received three cycles of combination chemotherapy at his hometown hospital. Each time the treatment helped to relieve pain and brought about some tumor remission, but only temporarily. Steve needed specialized care, and his physician referred him to a special hospital over 2,000 miles away from his home.

Specialists determined that Steve needed a very complex regimen of chemotherapy. The toxic side effects could be severe. At any time Steve's white blood cell count could drop very low and remain there for weeks. During this time any infection would require platelet transfusions to prevent hemorrhage. The drugs that Steve was taking could also be toxic, damaging the kidneys, bladder, liver, and heart. Thus, all possible side effects had to be taken seriously. Steve was assigned a primary-care nurse to provide continuity during his treatment.

Many chemotherapeutic drugs cause alopecia—hair loss—a particularly difficult loss for an adolescent. Steve wore hats, scarves, and sometimes a hairpiece. He eventually adjusted to his baldness. He joked that bald was "in," for after all, Kojak had become a national sex symbol.

During adolescence sexual development accelerates. Cancer treatments—surgery, radiation, and chemotherapy—affect all stages of development. (Steve looked much younger than his age because of his treatments.) Some of the adjustments Steve had to make were difficult, particularly the fact that he would probably never be able to father children. Many times he wanted to scream, "Unfair! Unfair!" And it was.

Steve's treatment was complex. Many daily routine tasks had to be efficiently scheduled, or they would not get done. Steve soon made it clear that he would not submit to this mechanical routine. Realizing that his desire for independence was normal, his nurse tried to work out a compromise with him. A personalized schedule seemed to be the solution. When Steve was permitted to have an equal say in decisions that concerned him, much of his frustration disappeared, and he continued in becoming more independent.[10]

The National Cancer Society has coproduced a picture booklet and audiotape called "Help Yourself: Tips for Teenagers with Cancer." The cassette tape has four sections: "The Day They Told You," "Your Family," "Your Treatment," and "Your Friends." Each deals with fears and issues found among teenagers with cancer. It is available free from the National Cancer Society, as are other booklets such as, "What You Need to Know About Childhood Leukemia" and "Chemotherapy and You—A Guide to Self-Help During Treatment." These booklets and the audiocassettes can be used in high school health classes to stimulate a discussion about this ominous disease. Such discussions not only help teenagers better understand their afflicted peers but also help prepare those who might later develop cancer.

Sexuality and reproductive abilities become concerns once adolescents realize they may live a productive life. Individual concerns can be handled through counseling:

ADULT: You know, Thad, you've never mentioned dating or girls in any of our meetings. Other teenagers I've worked with worry about whether they can have a normal sex life when they get older. . . .

Factors Common to Diseases

All the chronic diseases presented here have trauma associated with them that are not part of the disease itself. Medical treatments and hospitalizations are traumatic, parental reactions and the attitudes of others can affect children's adjustment, and children's own thoughts and feelings can influence the outcome.

Hospitals Are Scary

Many medical observers have emphasized the adverse effects of hospitalization on children. Anton Chekhov, the Russian writer and physician, knew this also. In *The Runaway* we read of a child's terror of a hospital and his flight from it:

> The latch creaked, there was a whiff of cold wind, and Paschka, stumbling, ran out into the yard. He had only one thought—to run, to run! He did not know the way, but felt convinced that if he ran he would be sure to find himself at home with his mother.[11]

Hospitalization fears can be decreased by familiarizing children with what will happen to them. A tour of the medical facility and participation in a puppet show depicting what they will experience during their hospitalization is helpful. A small stage on which some of the basic props of the operating room are displayed leads to discussion of their function and helps dispel the children's fear of the unknown. Children can be helped to write a picture story about "What will happen at the hospital." This can include a clear-cut explanation of the procedures to which they will be exposed. They'll learn what the X-ray machine does, the purpose of intravenous fluids, and the role of anesthesia.

Caretakers should know these procedures as well so they can talk intelligently with children as their fears come up. In some schools teachers have incorporated visits to hospitals into class lessons.

We must also remember that children often misinterpret events surrounding their illness. Many three-year-olds believe that women get pregnant from eating something, and they hold equally invalid views about sickness. Anesthetics can be viewed as oral attacks, motivating a child to refuse food. Others view treatments as bodily attacks and respond by spitting out the medication or by refusing to eat with a knife and fork. Accident proneness and self-injury also are common. Whether we believe in Freud or not, the fact is that male children about to undergo tonsillectomies are discovered to hold on to their penises more often than other ill boys. Operations and torture often are equated. Other fears are
- they are being punished
- they might die
- their parents will abandon them during the treatment
- they'll wake up and find something gone from their bodies
- loss of identity and unfamiliarity.

While surgery is particularly disturbing to children, most children under age four become extremely upset regardless of the reason for hospitalization. They display panic attacks, outbursts of anger when parents leave, depression, and eating and sleeping disorders. Many young children view their hospital experience as punishment for wrongdoing.

Hospitalized youngsters are concerned about the intactness of their body and become distressed at even minor injuries. If they insist upon Band Aids for the tiniest cut, imagine how anxious they must feel about an operation they don't understand and the separation from their mother.

In fact, separation from the mother is a greater crisis for children than being ill. The hospitalization occurs at a time in their young lives when anxieties are fed by fantasies of bodily harm and mutilation, of masked doctors and nurses wheeling them into an operating room for the great attack. They are unsure when they will return home and exaggerate how long it will be until they see their parents again. Only the mother's actual presence in the hospital can alleviate the anxiety of a child four years old or younger. Rooming in for mothers has been implemented in some hospitals, but not in others.

Hospitalized children deprived of the comfort and support of their mother react in a predictable way. First they protest and strongly display their distress. When parents visit children in this initial stage, the children release a flood of tears and protest. In the past this observation had led nursing staffs to ban parents from the ward: "They upset the routine." "Their visits stir things up." "The children are calmer without them."

When their protest fails to bring the return of the mother or ensure her presence, children show increasing helplessness. They become withdrawn and apathetic and cease to demand their mother's attention. The uninformed believe that their distress has finally lessened.

The third stage is denial. The children show interest in their surroundings and appear sociable. When the mother comes to visit, the children act as if they don't know her and no longer cry when she leaves. They feel so numb that they are even reluctant to leave the hospital.[12]

Older children typically experience hospitals as unfamiliar, frightening places. They panic—and to control their panic, they either think about things at home or they display fantasies of being omnipotent and all-powerful. They brag or boast of their accomplishments, or make some up. While they don't need their parents' continual presence, time between visits seems endless.

If a child on the unit says, "I miss my mom," and the nurse replies, "Don't worry—she'll be here at three o'clock," the nurse has lost an opportunity to be empathic with the child. Before responding, allow children to fully express their fear, then focus on their feelings before providing adultlike reassurances:

NURSE: It's hard to feel good when your mom's not here.

CHILD: I'm afraid something will happen to her. (Since the child is sick, she worries Mom can get sick too.)

NURSE: Then you'd be all alone in the hospital where no one loves you.

CHILD: (silence)

NURSE: If Mommy did get sick, who else would come and visit you? Why don't you ask Mom about that when she comes in at three; ask her "Who will visit me and take care of me at home if you get sick too?"

Single mothers with no support from extended families will need help from hospital staff in answering this question. Typically, they reassure the child that they will not get sick or have an accident, explaining that they cannot catch the child's disease. While such statements are helpful, magic years children often disbelieve them. If the parent can find someone whom she and the child both know can "take her place temporarily," then the child will worry less about her also getting sick. Perhaps the child's classroom teacher could be asked to fulfill this rarely needed role:

PARENT: Miss Jones, Greta is really worried that I might get sick and she'll be all alone in the hospital. Could I tell her that if this happened, you'd visit her and bring letters from me to read to her? It would really help ease her anxiety.

Some parents actually are ill when their child gets sick. They will have to work out some meaningful alternative to their visiting.

Often sick children express their worries indirectly. They act nervous, wonder what time it is, want to watch a favorite television show, or become nervous when it's not on. Those around them need to read these cues and respond accordingly. Responses should include efforts to help the children feel more control over their life.

ADULT: Lots of kids worry that everybody's forgotten they're in the hospital. Do you ever worry about that?

CHILD: (Expresses worries.)

ADULT: What do you think you could do between visits to make you feel better . . . write a story for your school newspaper about your illness? That's a good idea, and it would help other kids who might have to come here, too! Make a drawing of your house, to remind you of home—that's a good idea too.

Contact with a single doctor and the assignment of nurses to specific children rather than to units help develop a stronger bond between patients and staff and encourage the expression of feelings, resulting in less anxious children. Association with another child who has coped with a similar ordeal can have therapeutic effects.[13] Such exposure helps to replace massive denials or exaggerated fears with realistic fears and expectations.

Children should become involved in their own care. The youngsters should retain a sense of their bodies as their personal property. Create a climate in which children become active partners with the treatment team rather than passive victims.

The Child's Awareness of Fatal Illness

The death of a child is particularly difficult to accept because it means unfulfilled promises and dashed hopes. To defend ourselves against such pain, we may avoid dealing with children who have fatal illnesses or rationalize that they are unaware of what is happening to them, leaving them to face their fears and anxieties alone.

The conspiracy of silence surrounding dying children has harmful effects. Despite valiant efforts to shield children from their prognosis, the false cheerfulness or evasiveness of adults betrays anxiety. Children almost always sense this and may feel that an open expression of their fears will meet with disapproval. Consequently, they don't let others know that they suspect something's wrong. They play the game by the others' rules. Research has shown that children with fatal illnesses not only are more anxious than other hospitalized children but also dwell more on their condition. When they made up fantasy stories, they presented themes of loneliness, separation, and death— even though none had expressed these fears directly to the hospital personnel. Witness these stories created by children who were dying and had not been told about it:

This is about a woman. She's somebody's mother. She's crying because her son was in the hospital, and he died. He had leukemia. He finally had a heart attack. It just happened . . . he died.

Then they took him away to a cemetery to bury him, and his soul went up to heaven.

The woman is crying. But she forgets about it when she goes to bed. Because she relaxes, her brain relaxes. She's very sad. But she sees her little boy again when she goes up to heaven. She's looking forward to that. She won't find anyone else in heaven—just her little boy that she knows.[14]

Another child related:

The little boy had to stay in the hospital because the doctor wanted it. He got a shot in the back; a big needle. He was scared of shots, and he didn't want it. And the doctor did it hard. His lungs are gone—he can't breathe. His lungs got worse, and he didn't get well. He died and was buried with a big shovel.[15]

Most distressing was the dying children's belief that nobody cared, a belief resulting from misinterpretation of the parents' and the staff's uneasy silence and feigned cheerfulness. These children equated lack of discussion with lack of love and felt utterly abandoned.

Many dying children need to know what will happen to them and need opportunities to discuss their fears and anxieties with those close to them. Children from religious families can talk about death within the religious framework. Any religious discussion can also emphasize the acceptability and appropriateness of feelings of anger and despair.

Some opening statements in talking with children who are dying appear below:

ADULT: Lots of sick children worry about dying. Mothers and fathers find it hard to talk to children who have such worries. They love their children very much and think such talk will make them sad. So children with such worries often feel awfully alone with their thoughts and concerns. I'd be glad to talk with you about such things. I've talked with other children who worried about death. In fact, maybe I could get one to come over here and talk with you. Would you like that?

or

ADULT: Eileen, you probably know that some children with your disease die. But no one's ever talked straight to you about death. Since I've worked with other sick children, I know they worry about such things, and I also know their parents are so pained by such talk that they avoid it. They hope that if they don't talk about it, it won't happen. Sometimes kids feel the same way. But I know that deep down they need to talk to somebody about this fear we all have when we're really sick.

Sometimes a simple, "Alan, do you ever worry about dying?" is all that is needed to open floodgates of expression.

Discussion of impending death with children is a complex issue. For some the imminence of death need not be the focus. With many serious diseases, nobody—not even the world's best medical specialists—knows what the ultimate outcome will be. Some cases of leukemia, cancer, and serious heart conditions fall into this category. Regarding these instances, one medical expert on leukemia has written:

> It appears that there may be at present excessive emphasis on the preparation of the family for the early death of a child, and insufficient attention given to the emotional aspects of "living" with this chronic disease.[16]

Discussing death with a five-year-old who has leukemia and who may live until adolescence may generate despair and rob the child and his or her family of hope. Helping the parents and child interpret their fears of death should not replace encouraging the family to plan for years of excellent health. As in all crises, marshal positive forces.

Adolescence

Most adolescents fear not living up to the image our society values: attractiveness. They wonder if their looks, their personality, their clothes, or their athletic ability measures up. Many adolescents build self-esteem through "the body beautiful." Sickness and hospitalization are a threat to that shaky self-image. Place adolescents in a hospital for treatment of an illness or accident, subject them to medical procedures which may change their physical self, and you may introduce a deep, traumatic blow to their self-esteem.

Compounding this threat is adolescents' tendency to reinterpret the world from a sexual framework. They embellish their problems with sexual connotations. As children, they could say to themselves, "I don't get along with Bob and Ralph," and let it go at that. As adolescents, they are overly sensitive to their functioning as a sexual being: "I don't get along with Betty. I must have sexual problems."

Because they place adolescents' sexual identities in jeopardy, health crises take on a new, deeper meaning: "I will not be intact" after the illness, operation, or hospitalization. Such thoughts rekindle a deeper fear of abandonment or being unlovable.

Adolescents' newly developed ability to think abstractly is twisted by a threatening illness. The way a given disease appears to the observer often bears little resemblance to its appearance to adolescents. For example, youthful diabetics have grossly inaccurate concepts about the nature of their disease, even after they complete a thorough instructional program. They give bizarre explanations when they try to explain what is happening inside of them. Those who spend considerable time with seriously ill adolescents should be familiar with the physiological details of a disease so misconceptions can be corrected as they surface.

Any worries over impending surgery or medical procedures should be taken seriously, even when young persons' concerns seem needlessly exaggerated. Do explain sensitively and in depth,

- what is wrong
- what is known
- what is not known
- what may be expected from medical treatments
- what is uncertain. (Instead of being hidden, doubts should be shared honestly.)

Give the youngsters ample opportunity to express fears, ask questions, and review anything that remains unclear to them.

Hospitalization interrupts adolescents' moves toward becoming their own persons. As patients, they must face events over which they have little or no control, be separated from family and friends, and submit to dependence and invasion of privacy. They may perceive hospitalization as a reminder of the poor hand life has dealt them, and those around them must bear the brunt of their outrage, resentment, and bitterness.

What are some of the ways in which adolescents handle illness and hospitalization?[17]

Adolescents intellectualize. This defense is well known to health professionals, who themselves use intellectualization as a major defense against anxiety, speaking in a clinical language designed to distance them from pain and suffering. Intellectualization is conveying what you *think* about something, rather than how you *feel* about it. Adolescents who intellectualize may find themselves favored by health professionals.

Nurses, physicians, teachers, and parents can recognize that beneath the intellectualization lie burning concerns: "Will I still be attractive and acceptable to others?" "Will my life change drastically?" or even "I know this is a simple operation, but is there a chance I won't make it?" For example, when adolescents preparing for heart surgery express a keen interest in cardiovascular functioning, physiology, and the details of the surgical procedures, they are intellectualizing. They are really seeking reassurance about their survival.

Intellectualization can be positive when it provides the youths with a greater sense of control, enabling them to relate more confidently to their condition. It is not helpful when used excessively or when it cuts off expression of feelings. Reflective statements communicate that you understand the deeper message: "Nancy, you are concerned about how your heart works. I wonder if deep down, you're worried about how things are going to turn out and if we'll be around afterward to help?" First, let the youths express their concerns, then offer factual information and reassurance.

Adolescents worry about seemingly less important matters—they *displace.* It is not easy for adolescents to cope with mounting fears of the unknown while waiting for test results, for doctors to determine the problem and the course of action, for surgery, or for the path the disease itself will take. Adolescents are *now* oriented; to have patience is unbearable. Under the circumstances, they displace their intense concerns about themselves onto other matters. Adolescents about to undergo major surgery may seem calm and coolly indifferent to the impending operation, yet be highly preoccupied about missed schooling, hospital food, roommate problems, who is caring for their pets or possessions, an expected visitor, or some other unrelated matter. Displacement generally is a useful coping mechanism—it forms the background of recreational therapy programs.

Adolescents who are ill get angry, and their anger becomes everyone's concern. Failure to control the youngsters by normal approaches results in increasing frustration. Doctors, nurses, and other adults may experience the youths' hostility and provocations as an unwarranted rejection of their efforts to help. How understandably human it is to respond to angry and insolent adolescents by becoming punitive in return!

Confronting or punishing youths for their anger may intensify objectionable behaviors and result in power struggles. The approaches outlined in chapter eleven, "Defiant Children," may be helpful, particularly: physical gestures, providing alternatives, I-messages, and getting to the root of the problem. Flexible limit setting and a sense of humor are basic approaches in working with adolescents.

The Dying Teenager

During teenage years, uncompromised idealism is at its peak and the search for values is expressed both within traditional and nontraditional religious systems. Many invest death with some sort of physical continuity and meaning, along with the recognition that physical death is irreversible.

Health care providers, in relating to patients in an intellectual way, may miss the opportunity to meet the spiritual needs of adolescents. Even when they are full-time employees, members of the clergy usually function independently of other hospital personnel, making their rounds or being called only at the request of the patients themselves. Usually they are excluded from deliberations about patients, even those with strong religious ties. Such exclusion denies religious adolescents an avenue to express their concerns, since they typically avoid seeing mental health professionals. Pastoral counseling may be as essential for the well-being of dying adolescents as any medical or psychological intervention.[18]

Empathy: Looking Beyond the Illness

Children's physical helplessness in the hands of doctors and nurses makes them particularly vulnerable when they are ill. We must listen to children's concerns, understand their interpretation of these events, provide them with realistic information at a level they can comprehend, and encourage them through these stressful times.

When we work with children who are very ill, we need to look at more than just the disease. We need to discover the unique ways in which children view their symptoms, their fantasies, and their thoughts about what the disease is doing to their body. This depends not only on the developmental level of children—magic years, middle years, or adolescence—but on their relationships with family and friends. Keeping these things in mind enables you to counsel children suffering from any childhood sickness.

Suggested Reading for Children

Chase, F. *A Visit to the Hospital.* Grosset and Dunlap, 1957. (Ages 4–8)
Collier, J. L. *Danny Goes to the Hospital.* Grosset and Dunlap, 1970. (Ages 5–8)
Deegan, P., and Larson, B. *A Hospital: Life in a Medical Center.* (Ages 10–12)
Sharmat, M. W. *I Want Mama.* Harper & Row, 1974. (Ages 4–8)

·8·

Handicaps

In nature there's no blemish but the mind;
None can be called deformed but the unkind.
SHAKESPEARE, *Twelfth Night*
Act III, Scene 4

Handicaps not only restrict opportunities, but also separate people from others. Philip, the boy with a clubfoot in W. Somerset Maugham's *Of Human Bondage,* deeply felt this distance:

> ... But meanwhile he had grown horribly sensitive. He never ran if he could help it, because he knew it made his limp more conspicuous, and he adopted a peculiar walk. He stood still as much as he could, with his clubfoot behind the other, so that it should not attract notice, and he was constantly on the lookout for any reference to it. Sometimes they seemed to think that it was his fault if he could not play football, and he was unable to make them understand. He was left a good deal to himself. He had been inclined to talkativeness, but gradually he became silent. He began to think of the difference between himself and others.
> ... Philip passed from the innocence of childhood to bitter consciousness of himself by the ridicule which his clubfoot had excited.[1]

The handicapped youngster lives a life of continual crisis, of upset. Beginning at birth, his intentions are thwarted, his expectations that he will be like others and accepted by them go unfulfilled, and many of his feelings remain unexpressed. Although many suggest that handicapped persons learn to accept their condition, in reality this does not happen. One experienced social worker said: "I've never found the concept of 'acceptance' helpful—I've never met a handicapped person who has 'come to grips' with his condition."[2]

Meeting a handicapped youngster who displays mastery and competence in selected areas, who makes friends and enjoys life, can be inspiring. Behind such youngsters are families that provide warm, accepting, unpitying relationships at home, where reasonable expectations are blended with an acceptance of limitations.

Unfortunately, many lack support. Parental differences of opinion are more pronounced, child abuse occurs more often, divorce rates are higher, and hospitalizations and separations are more frequent than in families with nonhandicapped children. Being different and unable to master what others accomplish easily is difficult for anybody, but without adequate support a child is doubly handicapped. These youngsters need careful watching, empathy but not pity, understanding without overindulgence, acceptance but not resignation.[3]

In the past decade the status of handicapped children in our nation has changed considerably. Previously, handicapped children were separated from others—hidden in the privacy of their own homes or in special schools or state-supported institutions located in secluded rural areas. Parents challenged this inequity in the Supreme Court and won the right for a free public education for handicapped children. In 1975 Public Law 94–142 was enacted, a law which guarantees every handicapped youngster an appropriate education at public expense. Since then programs have been established in which handicapped youngsters are placed within regular classes (mainstreaming) or attend special classes in schools that allow for association with nonhandicapped children.

But social acceptance cannot be legislated, and many handicapped children remain alienated from their peers. Even adults who work well with nonhandicapped children are less effective, uneasy, and often afraid when they discover they are to work with a handicapped child. One experienced teacher confessed, "I admit it. I was frustrated, afraid, and angry when told I'd have a handicapped student in my class."[4] Or what do parents say when their child invites a classmate who has cerebral palsy home for lunch? Having to relate to a handicapped youngster becomes a crisis for adults. Learning more about handicapped children, the feelings they evoke in ourselves and others, and approaches to employ, can turn potential crises into constructive experiences.

How does it feel to be handicapped? Perhaps only those with handicaps can truly understand.

• Most handicapped children feel helpless. They can't master simple, "normal" tasks or participate fully in everyday activities. Helplessness breeds depression.

• Retarded children experience a vague awareness that they do not live up to everyone's expectations. While they struggle to count to ten, others are reading books. As their peers take dance lessons or play fast-pitch little league, they grapple with basic body coordination.

• Children with physical handicaps, especially those in institutions, need privacy. Having undergone so many treatments in their short lives, they feel a tremendous sense of personal violation.

• Physically handicapped children in group homes or residential schools have their every weakness, strength, and need charted into plans and objectives. For every plan, there is someone to monitor it, check off when objectives are met, and devise new ones. Imagine how it must feel to have your every move followed so closely.

• Emotionally disturbed children need care, affection, and love, in addition to limits and structure. Yet their disruptive behavior repels others and makes them disliked and avoided by others.

• Physically handicapped youngsters feel embarrassed. People stare at them in public, whisper about them, and point them out in a crowd.

• Handicapped children living at home lack socialization opportunities. They feel left out, alone, isolated, and different.

Magic Years Children

We sometimes forget that a handicapped child eight or nine years old, and even older, can still display characteristics of a much younger child. This is especially true for youngsters who are retarded.

The chief developmental tasks of earlier childhood rarely are mastered. Children with mobility disturbances have considerable difficulty separating from parents. In normal childhood the sense of individuality and autonomy is developed by moving away from the mother and then returning periodically for emotional refueling. Physically handicapped children cannot do this. In fact, when they are young they become anxious about their mother's comings and goings because they cannot creep or scoot around to keep in visual contact with her. For blind children learning to be a separate person is hampered by always having to be within earshot of their mother; deaf children become anxious when their mother disappears from view. Consequently, such children will remain overly dependent upon their parents even when the latter make a concerted effort not to overprotect them. In addition, handicapped children's need for assistance with personal hygiene, dressing, and eating keeps them dependent well beyond the period for nonhandicapped children—sometimes for life.

Nonhandicapped children entering the magic years already have experienced a sense of individuality and self-control which lead to feelings of achievement and pride, with occasional feelings of shame and self-doubt when they temporarily lose control. Their physical independence has allowed them to shift from being passive to being active, to take charge of many activities, which contribute significantly to their mastery of anxiety and development of feelings of self-worth. They have moved through the "terrible twos" when they cried, pouted, and in other ways defied their parents, and have developed verbal communication skills and mastered body control. They can stand on their own two feet, express their desires, and actively clamor for adult attention. Their energies are free to develop an inner language, to fantasize, to wish, to hope, to dream.

In contrast, handicapped children have mastered few if any of the basic tasks, leaving them little energy to grow in other areas. If they are language-impaired or deaf, they may continue to express their anger and frustrations physically rather than by talking them out. This severely strains their relationships with other people. Because they cannot express aggression appropriately, it surfaces indirectly through soiling, wetting, or refusing to be toilet trained, making it difficult to know if they can't be or won't be trained. While many nonhandicapped three-year-olds begin to feel inklings of pride and achievement, for handicapped youngsters there is only shame and self-doubt.

Most handicapped children receive intensive instruction in basic academic readiness skills, self-help skills, and mobility training through interdisciplinary efforts such as in infant stimulation programs, preschool classrooms, and special class placements. Despite the richness of these programs, many professionals are at a loss when asked how to help the young child emotionally. Because they can't play or can't talk, approaches used with nonhandicapped children often are inappropriate. More efforts need to be aimed at parents and other caretakers (such as teachers and child care workers), educating them about normal development and how the children's handicap results in their particular developmental problems. Parents need information about how bonding and attachment take place in normal infants, and how their children's handicap interferes with such processes. For example, blind infants cannot gaze at their parents, deaf infants cannot hear their mothers' "coos," cerebral palsied infants cannot cuddle, and cleft-palate infants cannot suckle.

Recommendations given to parents include the following. Nonmobile infants should be within their mothers' eyesight at all times and when they are ready to separate, their mothers should leave them for short periods, but remain in visual contact, and then return at regular intervals, or when they see the child is agitated. Parents of blind children are encouraged to make more voice contact, since blind infants will smile at the sound of a parent's voice as the sighted child will to seeing their face. Other nonvisual methods of communication are recommended.[5]

Direct work with the child involves reflecting feelings they do not express, clarifying procedures, tests, hospital visits, and other disability-related activities for them so their fears are kept realistic.

ADULT: Billy, the people at the hospital need to take a picture of your tummy. They have cameras that can take pictures through skin. Isn't that amazing! But they need your tummy empty to get a good picture. That's why we won't feed you dinner or breakfast.

Remember from the last chapter that young children often misconstrue treatments as punishments. Stretching and exercising muscles can be quite painful to cerebral-palsied children. Their resistance to physical therapy is understandable, but it may be increased by their interpretation of the event.

ADULT: Chris, I know it hurts when I stretch your muscles. But I'm not mad at you, and you've been a good girl. We need to do this or your muscles will get hard and tight like dried up bubble gum or clay, and then they won't work well. When you continue to chew gum or handle clay, it stays warm and soft and can be worked with—the same with your muscles.

Universal fears of being to blame for their disability, for accidents resulting from the disability (spills, falls, family troubles) should be expressed for them and their misconceptions corrected.

Parents need opportunities to express their attitudes about and their reactions to a child's disability. They often are unable to do so with friends and relatives, who are jubilant and boastful of their own non-handicapped children and unwittingly insensitive to the special pain that comes with being the parent of a handicapped child. Indeed, this "chronic sorrow" is best alleviated by meeting with parents of youngsters with a similar disability. Parent groups help parent and child, since the child's reactions are largely related to the parent's response. Anxiety, denial, embarrassment, and defensiveness are attitudes easily communicated to these children.

Middle Years Children

Middle years children need to keep physically active while engaged in counseling sessions. They fiddle, pace, climb, push toy cars, squirm on chairs, draw, paint, sing to themselves, and generally keep busy and appear distracted throughout a conversation. This helps them manage the anxiety generated by hearing or discussing their worries. Children master their anxiety in many ways, all of them motor: they may inhibit action, cling to a protective adult, escape from the situation, show exaggerated courage, or turn a passive experience into an active one. But the physically handicapped children's motor inability means that they cannot handle their fears the way most children do, and as a result, they lose still more self-esteem. When mobile children become too anxious, they often leave the counselor's room, which is a strong, indirect message to go easy. Nonmobile children can't do this.

You must observe subtle signs of increased anxiety when counseling nonmobile children. Slight increases in spasticity (muscles that work against one another), lip chewing, tongue rolling, head movement, etc., suggest that the children's anxiety is mounting. Reflect that they're getting upset by this talk, but that it's important to continue. Let them know that if they get too upset, however, to raise their hand or give some other sign, you'll see if there's something you can both do together to help them be less upset, but you'll continue to talk anyway.

ADULT: Nina, I can't always tell when what I say makes you upset, and sometimes you're not always aware either. With kids who can walk I notice they move around more, fight, or open and close drawers when I talk about something upsetting. When I remark that maybe what I'm saying is too upsetting, they usually agree. You and I are going to have to discover what you can do when you are upset or nervous so I can be on the lookout for it and back off a bit.

Other themes emerge when counseling handicapped youngsters. Arguments are more frequent in their families and often pertain to disability management issues. The children blame themselves for the disharmony.

Perhaps more important, however, are the core issues for the middle years handicapped child: (1) an unconscious feeling of incompleteness which often expresses itself in attempts to compensate for the handicap; (2) hopes for a normal body, often revealed in fantasies that exclude the handicap; and (3) repeated grieving for a partly ruined body.

As children talk about their fantasies, they lose their symbolic meaning, resulting in painful disillusionment because it means abandoning the dream which keeps alive the hope of normality. You need to help children manage the feelings aroused by looking at the three core issues as well as to hold out hope and help them see their positive features.

ADULT: I hear from your mom that you talk a lot about being a great swimmer some day.

CHILD: Yeah—I'm going to be in the Olympics.

ADULT: I admire your courage, Tom, but I know your motor problems bother you a lot. Lots of handicapped kids I know wish they were more normal, like other children. They feel less whole, somehow imperfect, so they pretend to be good at something.

CHILD: I'm not pretending! I swim every day, and I'll be a great swimmer—you'll see!

ADULT: What we want to do and what we can do are not always the same. You are learning to swim, and you can have fun swimming, but a world champion you'll never be.

CHILD: Yes I will. You wait, you'll see!

By the age of seven most handicapped children, previously educated in specialized centers, will have been transferred to public schools where they are placed in classes for the handicapped and mainstreamed for part of the day, or are mainstreamed into regular classes for the entire day. For the first time in their lives, they are in the minority and subjected to the harsh reality of being different. Yet their own attitudes about their disability will greatly influence others' attitudes toward them. Their attitudes, however, are colored by the thinking skills that characterize middle years children. Recall that they tend to jump to conclusions from false premises. Perhaps the most self-damaging conclusion they make is that others relate to them in terms of their handicap alone. For example, when a crippled boy and his father were turned away from church, the boy thought crippled children were not allowed. What the sign said was "No Children Allowed at 11:00 Mass."[6] Such conclusions even characterize the thoughts of many disabled adults. One blind man expressed his discouragement when a woman refused to answer his letter because he was blind. Nevertheless, this was his own conclusion; she may have had other reasons.[7]

Help children decenter—to look at other possible reasons why people may react to them as they do. Your task is to help children deal with real reactions to their disability, and to the way they present themselves to others. Suggest and role-play simple explanations these children can give to other children about their handicap and health needs. They can be as simple as these:

CHILD: Will you help me find the door? I can't see, you know!

or

CHILD: The reason why I talk funny is because I was born with a hole in the top of my mouth. Doctors sewed up the hole, but not perfectly. I take speech therapy to try and learn to talk better.

or

CHILD: I talk funny 'cause the muscles that control my tongue don't work. Hold down your tongue with your finger and try to talk. See how hard it is! While my tongue is not held down, it's something like that for me.

Preparation for a Crisis

Readying children for incidents they will probably encounter softens the shock that paralyzes problem solving. They can be told stories in which the main character's experiences are those they will face. Children can role-play or rehearse through playing with dolls or making art possible responses on their part that will increase their mastery of a situation. Focus on

- teasing
- insincere sympathy and pity ("Oh, you poor child!")
- being misunderstood
- tactless questions
- curiosity
- other's fear of disabilities
- staring
- talking behind their back.

Children should also be prepared for their own reactions to activities of others, such as their feelings about
  • genuine offers of help
  • desires to be treated like anyone else
  • inferiority feelings
  • idolization of normal students. ("I want to do that.")
ADULT: Your physical difficulties will make kids uneasy because kids are often afraid of what's different. If you can put up with their teasing for a while, their uneasiness will go away as they get to know you, and they eventually will come around.
Reviewing with children how they will present themselves to others also lets you learn their views of their disorder, views which you can then correct.
ADULT: Craig, if you had to explain your epilepsy to another child who just had his first seizure, what would you say to him?

Did I Cause It?
Magic years children often believe they are to blame for their disorder ("I've been punished for being bad") and attribute magical powers to their parents ("My parents must have wanted me this way"), and efforts to convince them otherwise are difficult. Similar efforts prove more fruitful in the middle years when such ideas are held but are capable of being modified.
CHILD: (Her play or indirect expressions suggest she is asking, "Am I to blame for my disorder?")
ADULT: We don't understand how you got that way or why this happened to you, and we wish we did but we don't. But we do know it didn't result from wrong things you did, or what other children like you did or thought!

Will I Die?
Not only are children with handicaps subjected to frequent doctor visits or hospitalizations, they are more prone to illness and suffer more when they are sick. They often worry they will die, but rarely do they directly express such fears.
ADULT: Scott, it seems as though you're worried about dying. That's a sad thought. It isn't easy for any of us to talk about dying. You have been doing so well lately. I wonder what made you think of dying right now. . . ?

CHILD: (Lets adult know why—saw a television show about a dying child, a friend died, had a dream about death, overheard his parents talking about ill grandmother, etc.)

ADULT: You must be feeling real scared to worry about death. No one on earth knows how long they will live, but we hope and expect that you will be with us for a long, long time.

Many handicapped children fail to understand their treatments and read sinister meaning into even a simple doctor's visit. They have difficulty grasping what they cannot directly observe or experience, but they can be helped to understand by careful explanations. Remember always to discern the basis for children's questions as they may mask other more basic questions which need to be brought out.

ADULT: I'll try to answer your question, but first tell me what made you think of it . . . tell me what *you know* about it.

Sometimes questions are not questions but merely signs of frustration. Answering them factually results in a missed opportunity for providing empathy.

CHILD: Why can't I move my arms better? (Child demands after repeated bumpings.)

ADULT: It's pretty frustrating not being able to get your hands to do what you mind tells it!

Bibliotherapy

Middle years children are ready for exposure to public figures with similar disorders and can read, or have read to them, selections from books by handicapped people. For example, Raymond Goldman's description of his reaction to leg braces at age eight can help children realize that their feelings are shared by others.[8] Some notable figures with handicaps who continue to inspire us include Robert Lewis Stevenson (who had tuberculosis), Charles Darwin (who was so sickly he could only work two hours each day), Lord Byron (had a clubfoot), Edgar Allan Poe (had a lung condition), Kant (had gout), Aristotle and Demosthenes (had speech defects), Nietzsche (had a frail body), Goethe (who had confirmed chronic pain), Beethoven (who was pockmarked, snubnosed, and deaf at age twenty-eight), Franklin Delano Roosevelt (had polio), Lou Gehrig (suffered from Lou Gehrig's disease), Winston Churchill (who suffered from stuttering), and Flannery O'Connor (who was crippled by lupus).

Consulting with Others

The counselor can assist parents to respond empathically to children. Often parents and other caretakers witness children's rejection by others or their failures at mastery. They may quickly offer "cheer up" comments rather than empathic ones. Instead of saying "Don't worry, you'll make other friends," adults can learn to make appropriate empathic responses:

ADULT: You must feel awful. I know it's hard for you, but some day things will get better. I admire your courage. It's a brave child who tries as hard as you do!

All adults need to understand the basic rules for talking with handicapped children:

1. Don't immediately ask questions about the handicap.

2. Don't continue talking about the handicap unless the children express an interest in doing so.

3. Don't try to change the subject if they bring up their handicap.

4. Talk with the children in privacy, not in the presence of others.

5. Do consider the children's mood.[9]

The principle underlying these recommendations is that disabled children should determine when and how a discussion of their handicap should *start* and the *course* it should take.[10] Remember that rarely will children directly relate their desire to discuss their handicap. They will give covert clues that they are ready. When adults are very close to children, their mentioning the unmentionable can relieve the children of their communication fears and their silence about the unknown.

Counseling Isn't Magic

A ten-year-old child was referred for couseling because she refused to wear leg braces, preferring a wheelchair. She said the braces hurt her legs, but others felt she had become hopeless about herself and had given up. If she continued to use her wheelchair for much longer, she would not be able to walk. Taking away the wheelchair did not work, as she still refused to put her leg braces on and only crawled around when possible. Rather than being worked with in couseling, the girl was referred to a residential center where she was forced by trained professionals to wear leg braces, something the family had been unable to make her do. The counselor knew that he could not guarantee that the girl's motivation would change, even though the braces needed to be worn immediately to keep her muscle tendons stretched so they would not atrophy.

Adolescence: How Can a Blind Boy Be a Member of a Gang?

In our chapter on adolescence, we stated that the capacity to construct ideals, or contrary-to-fact situations, develops at this stage of life. Adolescents can conceive the possible, meaning that the future becomes as real as the present. Another feature of adolescent thought is the capacity to evaluate one's self from the viewpoint of others. They can think about what others will think of their looks, their personality, or their talents. Because of these skills adolescents are capable of looking at discrepancies between what they are and what they wish to be, differences between the ideal and real self. Since they now have the capacity to see other possibilities in the future, they embark on self-improvement programs. The fat thirteen-year-old works at becoming a thin fourteen-year-old. Hair styles take on excruciating importance. Diet and exercise programs are initiated, and makeup and clothes are taken seriously.

The nonhandicapped adolescents' concern about their appearance and people's judgments of them heighten their social sensitivity. Imagine the handicapped adolescents' concern! They have deep fears of rejection from their contemporaries: "How do I behave and look to others? Do I seem gross and disgusting? How do I look when I'm having a seizure? Do I make strange noises?" Such fears are rarely expressed. Instead, handicapped adolescents work hard to project a cheerful front by bottling up their feelings. Help them express their worry, resentment, and shame either directly to you or to a trusted friend or family member.

Physically handicapped adolescents usually cannot release bodily tension through sports, active exercise, or dancing. They are prone to explosive release through babyish tears and tantrums and need help in dealing with the embarrassment and shame caused by such outbursts.

ADULT: You know, Mark, sometimes you feel bad about your hot temper. But remember, other kids can go outside, scream, stomp around, and you can't.

Handicapped children who have been relatively happy and optimistic will experience their first real depression at adolescence. Handicapped adolescents often see no way to improve their situation: they see a future that offers little opportunity to decrease the discrepancy between the real and the ideal self. The future looks bleak, and hopelessness is added to longstanding feelings of helplessness.[11]

Sexuality becomes extremely important to adolescents. While parents are concerned about their nonhandicapped adolescents' emerging sexuality and place various restrictions upon their social activity, most find outlets for sexual expression. This is not true for many physically handicapped or retarded adolescents—they are forced by circumstance or parental supervision to live by a different set of rules. Some of the restrictions they face are

1. No sexual expression with another.
2. No need for sexual information because you'll never make use of it.
3. What you do learn about sexuality won't pertain to you.
4. You may not go anywhere without a chaperone.
5. Because you're less attractive, you won't get much physical affection from others.
6. Parents will intrude more into your privacy.
7. You won't have much opportunity to be with members of the opposite sex.
8. Sexual literature will be difficult, if not impossible, for you to get.

If physically handicapped or retarded adolescents live in a group home or institution, they are likely to have still more rules added to those above.

9. No privacy.
10. No locks on doors.
11. Do not look at pictures of naked men or women—they will be taken from you.
12. Do not express interest in pregnancy—you may wind up being sterilized.
13. Remember that someone is always watching you. Masturbatory sexual expression can get you into trouble.
14. You may be placed on birth control.
15. Forget about marriage and long-term relationships.

Many cerebral palsied adolescents, while capable of sexual responsiveness, are incapable of masturbation because of their spasticity. Some enlightened agencies are looking into ways to help such individuals develop their sexuality, even constructing apparatuses for masturbation, but communities surrounding these agencies may not be so tolerant. Neighbors have been known to call and complain to group home parents when they see wheelchair couples making out on the lawn.

Counseling handicapped adolescents about sexuality is a difficult task. The restrictions placed upon their lives limit their possible solutions to problems. How does an unattractive but warm and bright cerebral palsied adolescent deal with the cold fact that intimate relationships will probably always be denied her? In fact, the more independent the severely palsied adolescent becomes, the less attractive she will be. In group homes, there are usually staff who will groom her, such as combing her hair and doing her nails. If she lives in a supervised apartment and is more responsible for her looks, she typically cuts her hair very short because this requires less care, yet this can make her more unappealing.

Handicapped adolescents may become so anxious in finding someone to love that they become overly aggressive in attempting to court anyone of the opposite sex who shows an interest. This eagerness frightens or repels potential partners, driving them away.

Often physically handicapped adolescents set very high goals for themselves, such as desiring to date only nonhandicapped individuals. Since physical conformity is the essence of social appropriateness at this age, handicapped adolescents are rarely seen apart from their deformity. Consequently, they rarely attract their ideal date. Handicapped partners are viewed as second best, and heterosexual relationships they engage in are considerably strained. "Since I need somebody, I'll settle for Joe." How would you like to have a "settle for" relationship?

Counseling handicapped adolescents is a struggle. Often they can't communicate clearly, and one hesitates to keep telling them to repeat themselves. Their depression is understandable, sometimes contagious. You wonder how you can help. You feel hopeless. Don't! Be a good listener as you would with any adolescent. Consult with other professionals who work with these youngsters and who can suggest things you can accomplish. Set goals as you would for any nonhandicapped youngster. Be direct.

ADULT: Juanita, many times I can't understand what you say and I know that frustrates you, and you give up trying to tell me. But I won't let you. I'll keep after you until I understand. Sometimes you'll have to show me what you mean, or use your communication board. We have plenty of time here to talk about you and your problems. It's important that you be understood, but it will be hard for both of us sometimes.

Encourage other adults to be honest with handicapped youngsters they encounter.

ADULT: You know, Brian, often I can't understand your speech, and I hesitate to ask you to try again because I get uncomfortable doing so. Don't let me get away with that, because I'd like to get over my anxiety and talk to you more.

A big issue for handicapped adolescents is their dependence on adults. Because they often feel so alone, they seldom dare to openly assert themselves to adults for fear of abandonment. It is extremely difficult for them to disagree with people upon whom they depend, to develop increasing responsibility for themselves, and to be on their own. They assert themselves in inappropriate ways, such as subtle defiance—being slow, taking longer, etc.—maneuvers characteristic of younger children. Deal with these issues openly to help them express undelivered communication, and even suggest ways to be appropriately assertive.

ADULT: You know, Bob, sometimes I think you clown around and tell jokes about people's mistakes because it helps you to feel one up on adults. I don't think I've ever heard you get openly angry at adults. Maybe you feel you'd lose our friendship. If you let us know how angry it makes you sometimes to need us to wait on you, I think we could stand it. We might get angry back, but so what!

The language we use with handicapped youngsters often makes them feel even more subservient. Parents and caretakers can be alert to communication of this nature and stay away from it. Statements like "Put on your sweater; it's cold," or "Finish your juice, it's time for school," are examples of overbearing communication. Instead, say, "It looks cold outside. Do you think you'll need a sweater?" Or, "Shall I put your juice in the refrigerator for later, or do you want to finish it now?" Encourage minor decision making even when you're asked for help. "Shall I wear this sweater?" can best be answered with "Wear whatever you feel you look best in."

Practical Advice

Remember that couseling isn't just talking about feelings. Sometimes direct advice is helpful. One handicapped youngster resented being bathed but was afraid to say so because he was warned about breaking the glass shampoo bottle. Suggesting a plastic-bottled shampoo solved the problem.[12]

Suggest materials that will assist the adolescents' efforts at autonomy. They can subscribe to *The Independent,* a magazine published by the Center for Independent Living, a collective of multiple handicapped individuals in Berkeley, California. Arlene E. Gilbert's book, *You Can Do It from a Wheelchair* (Westport, Conn.: Arlington House, 1974), gives detailed instructions on how to get up after falling, how to vacuum from a wheelchair, and so on. Help handicapped youths construct networks of people to assist them with the small but necessary tasks that must be done when living independently. In most communities there are agencies whose purpose is to help develop such support systems. Encourage adolescents to seek out such assistance, or to continue if they have already done so. Bibliotherapy is also useful. Some first-person accounts by handicapped individuals appear at the end of this chapter.

Marshal Positive Forces

Perhaps the most important goal of couseling is to help adolescents change their definition of self from a self-defeating to a self-benefiting one. This switch involves a change in orientation from "doing" to "being." This is a difficult adjustment for adolescents because their normal peers strongly hold to a doing orientation, and rehabilitation programs often focus on behavioral goals. Handicapped adolescents have to learn to value things in themselves. As long as they measure themselves against the achievements of the nonhandicapped instead of against intrinsic standards, their self-concept will suffer. Yet many of the handicapped have done this, including Helen Keller, famous for her line, "Let me be judged by the same standards as others."

Stimulate a change in orientation from doing to being by encouraging adolescents to keep a diary, remember dreams, learn a new word each day, take photographs, write poems, greet a person they dislike, write a letter to their congressperson about something they really care about, find a pen pal, send audiotapes to friends, choose a foreign country to visit and learn as much as they can about it (later they can worry about how to get there), see a foreign film, ask other people what they enjoy, become an expert on something, find out what others dislike about themselves, list areas in which they like to make decisions.[13]

The Covert Crisis:
Being the Sibling of a Handicapped Child

You may learn that one of your students or clients has a brother who is retarded or a sister with cerebral palsy. At this discovery, you may become uncomfortable: "What will I say? Perhaps it's best to say nothing . . . I don't want to open up that can of worms!"

How many adults would say to a youngster, "I was visiting the rehabilitation center over at the hospital. I met your brother's physical therapist there. Have you ever been there with your brother? Have you seen the exercises your brother does when he visits the center?" Probably not many would.

Yet how different it is if a youngster has a brother who is a football player! Our shyness disappears. We think nothing of saying, "I saw your brother working out at the YMCA yesterday. He sure is a terrific football player! You must be very proud of him."

Siblings of handicapped children make sacrifices and adaptations. They receive less attention and must show considerable responsibility, which can engender enormous resentment and anger toward their handicapped sister or brother. They need to acknowledge the negative side that coexists with the caring and love they feel for their handicapped sibling.

A discussion group at the Bronx Center of the United Cerebral Palsy Association of New York included the brothers and sisters of the handicapped children attending the center's program for preschool and school-aged children. Members talked about how they coped with the daily demands at home. One girl described how she kept herself busy with outdoor activities until her handicapped sisters were nearing bedtime and her parents could devote more time to her. A boy explained how he provided his sister with a substitute activity that usually worked to keep her out of his books and homework assignments. In addition, the members read books and articles written by or about siblings of handicapped brothers and sisters and went on special field trips.

Mainstreaming

Mainstreaming is an attempt to overcome the separation of handicapped youngsters from their peers. However, mainstreaming—placing children with special needs in a group of any normal children—has triggered a lot of debate. Perhaps no other educational concept has been so emotionally charged. There is a crisis about mainstreaming because many individuals—children and adults alike—are unsure of how to handle it.

Michael takes a special bus to school. Actually, it's a van, smaller than the large bus the seventh-graders take to school. Michael is a "slow learner" and needs a self-contained class. If you could read his file, you would see him described as "educable mentally retarded." Today Michael is dressed in his best school clothes, and as his van pulls up to the parking lot several children announce: "Here comes the retard bus. Nah, nah, nah, nah. . . . Re-tard! Re-tard!" This singsong chorus stabs Michael like daggers. He starts to cry, but holds it back. "Come on, crybaby. Can't you take it? Nah, nah, nah . . ." The teacher on playground duty has a crisis on her hands, one concerning both herself and Michael.

Despite snags and failures, mainstreaming is a noble, democratic idea: all children are entitled to an appropriate education that includes activities with nonhandicapped peers. Mainstreaming gives handicapped children a chance to feel at one with others. Retarded adults, when asked about their school days, respond that they disliked being segregated from other children and wished they had remained in a regular class.

The teachers' utilization of procedures to prepare nonhandicapped children for mainstreamed children should be geared to *children with a disability* rather than to *disabled children*—"to the coping aspects in the situation rather than to the succumbing aspects."[14] Consider the manner in which a mother of a handicapped child spoke to a kindergarten class the day before her daughter was to start school:

> MOTHER: I have a little girl just your size, named Karen. She's nice and laughs a lot and has freckles and pigtails. Now God didn't make Karen's legs as strong as yours, so we have to help them get strong so she can walk. Some children wear braces to help their teeth, and Karen wears braces to help her legs. There are some things she can't do and some games she can't play. Sister will let you help her once in a while, but don't spoil her.[15]

These words prepared the class to meet a child much like them, yet different in certain ways, who is managing her difficulties so she can be part of a group.

Enlist the help of youngsters who might show positive interest in the mainstreamed child: "Let me push the wheelchair!" Take them aside privately and suggest, "Look, we're going to have a new student join our class. Some of the kids will tease him. But maybe you could help by . . ." By capitalizing on the positive interests of other students, the mainstreamed child can be helped by them.

Mainstreamed children—whether a slightly handicapped child in a regular classroom, or a physically imparied child in a dormitory—frequently are the targets of scapegoating. Unfortunately, handicapped youngsters often are the butt of the anger and frustration other children feel toward authority figures. Sensitivity, combined with firmness and good timing, is essential. You want to prevent scapegoating, but you don't want to overprotect children. Other children will pick on them at recess or after school if you protect them too much in class.

Make it clear to your group that insults are not tolerated. Everyone deserves respect, and firm consequences await those who show disrespect. Comments or judgments about another's appearance, school work, or athletic performance are unacceptable. Stress that everyone proceed at their own pace, because every human being is unique and special.

Many handicapped youth attend clinics or programs to receive various therapies. You have a "hidden team" available to help you. Seek out and take direction from the professionals who presently, or previously, worked with these youngsters. Talk to the physical therapist, the speech therapist, the social worker, the occupational therapist. The more you consult, the more you learn about the child and what works successfully.

Any handicapped child can be mainstreamed: children with cerebral palsy, the deaf, the blind, the partially sighted or hearing impaired, those needing crutches or a wheelchair, children with epilepsy. In each case, discuss the youngster's impairment with the group in a matter-of-fact way.

Suggested Reading for Children

Carlson, E. R. *Born That Way.* New York: John Day, 1941. (severe spasticity)
Goldman, R. *Even the Night.* New York: Macmillan, 1947. (learning to walk with leg braces)
Guy, A. W. *Steinmetz: Wizard of Light.* Alfred A Knopf, 1965. (Ages 9–12; dwarfism)

Killilea, M. *Karen.* Englewood Cliffs, N.J.: Prentice Hall, 1952. (The classic story of a girl with cerebral palsy)

Savitz, H. M. *Fly, Wheels, Fly.* John Day Company, 1970. (Ages 10+; paraplegics)

Smith, G. *The Hayburners.* Delacorte Press, 1974. (Ages 9–12; mental retardation)

Stein, S. B. *About Handicaps: An Open Family Book for Parents and Children Together.* Walker and Company, 1974. (Ages 4–8)

Vinson, K. *Run with the Ring.* Harcourt Brace Jovanovich, 1965. (Ages 12+; sudden blindness)

Viscardi, H. *A Man's Stature.* (Story of courage)

Werfield, F. *Cotton in My Ears.* New York: Viking, 1945. Hearing disability.

Wolfe, B. *Don't Feel Sorry for Paul.* J. B. Lippincott, 1974. (Ages 8+; prosthesis)

·9·

Child Abuse

The plant cut down to the root
Does not hate.
It uses all its strength
To grow once more.

ELIZABETH COATSWORTH
The Fair American

The weekend is over. It is Monday morning, and Carl is at school before the doors have opened or the teachers have arrived. Throughout the morning he is anxious and preoccupied. Only later in the afternoon does he begin to settle down. One winter day it snowed so heavily that school was closed, but Carl came to school anyway. He was the only child present.

Every day Carl carries his gym shoes with his books so he can remain on the grounds after classes. Throughout the week, he lingers after school every afternoon until he is asked to leave. Friday afternoons are particularly difficult because he does not want to go home. He worries about getting hurt. Carl is an abused child.

By now most people are aware that child abuse is a significant part of our culture. Estimates of incidents are between 200,000 and 500,000 cases a year. This figure could approach one-and-a-half million if severe neglect and sexual abuse are included in the total.

Suspected abuse and neglect evoke a crisis in the helper: Do I intervene or not? Can I document what I think is going on? If my intervention backfires, will it be taken out on the child? Besides these practical problems, issues of a more philosophical nature arise. For example, intervention attempts to alleviate harm, but it can violate the rights of privacy when harm is not substantial.[1]

Strains that Can Lead to Child Abuse

Single parents are overrepresented among abusive and neglectful parents. Many of them are adolescents, and more and more adolescents are becoming parents. For example, 30 percent of the births in New Orleans in 1982 were to teenage mothers. We know from our discussion of adolescents that most of their thoughts center on themselves and that they can be irrational and impulsive. Typically, they want the children to grow up so they can get on with their young lives. Consequently, they have grossly unrealistic expectations for their infants. Surveys of adolescents reveal that most expect children to be toilet trained before they are able (as early as six months of age), to walk earlier than possible, and to talk before they are ready. When children don't reach these milestones as expected, adolescent parents take it personally: "This child is deliberately defying me!" One teenage mother thought her infant was deliberately disobeying her because she repeatedly dropped objects from her high chair onto the floor. When adolescent parents' futile attempts to accelerate the development of their children are met with resistance, an interaction occurs which results in abuse. "I just couldn't stand his crying, and when he finally stopped I felt relief," a young mother admitted. The child stopped crying because he was beaten unconscious.

Adolescents have particular difficulty with an infant's demands. Teenage mothers have their own needs which are unmet and have little energy to meet the needs of a growing child. Usually a first unwanted child is followed by another, and the likelihood of abuse increases as the responsibilities rise. When the twenty-five-year-old mother of three beats her youngest child, we often forget that it all began when her needs went unmet as a teenager and, in search of love, she became a young mother.

Different factors interact to produce abuse. Prematurity, mental retardation, physical handicaps, congenital malformities and other disabilities cause increased stress in parents and therefore are ever-present in abused populations. Vulnerability in the infant, such as low birth weight or colicky behavior, can be heightened by a separation from the mother after birth. The mother herself may come from a poor environment and may be experiencing significant stress in her marriage.

Nevertheless, just because these factors are present does not mean that abuse will occur. "There is a complexity and subtlety of the many processes that interact to create the abuse."[2]

How Abused Children Feel

One of the things we sometimes fail to appreciate is that almost all children—no matter how abusive the parents—want to love their parents and remain at home. We may "objectively" judge the home life as unfit. Yet to the children their home offers as much love as they have ever known in the world, and they are afraid to leave this security. As the Wizard of Oz said to Dorothy when she wanted to go home, yet loved the Land of Oz: "I get it—you prefer the security of misery to the misery of insecurity!"

Abused children feel they are the cause of their abuse. They are yelled at and punished so frequently and told so many times that they are bad when they disobey or irritate that they come to believe it.

Typically, frequent screaming, tension, and upheaval characterize abusive families. Abused children are often demeaned by hostile name calling: "devil," "bastard," or "whore." The affectionate nicknaming so common in healthy families is not present. The children are threatened with removal, eviction, or abandonment by their parents. When this happens, the children become painfully aware of their predicament. As one British eight-year-old said: "Nobody bloody wants me."

Abused children suffer from inconsistent and inappropriate punishment out of proportion to their behavior. Often normal behavior is regarded as a nuisance to the parents: "This child is out to get me!" claims a tired parent when her noisy child is simply playing like a normal six-year-old. A child may be hit for a relatively minor action. Abused children learn to suffer silently. They often do not cry when punished, because if they did, parents would then beat them for crying.

Abused children are angry and full of rage. (One child said, "What makes me angry is when my father puts my head in the toilet."[3]) However, they have learned to suppress these powerful feelings at home. They must deny the bitterness, resentment, fear, anger, and hatred that they feel toward their parents because expressing these emotions could cause more abuse. And they feel guilty because they fail to feel the full love they know they should have toward their parents.

Perhaps the greatest problem of abused children is the parents' expectation that they will nurture them. This role reversal is doomed to fail: what four-year-old or eight-year-old or even ten-year-old can ever hope to meet the insatiable needs of the deprived adult?

No matter how well the abused children behave, they can never please their parents or meet their unrealistic expectations. They can dot every *i* and cross every *t* and still fall short. Their best is never good enough. They are always doing something wrong.

In families in which child abuse occurs, the children are blamed for all the woes. Frequently, they are viewed as the source of marital problems, economic problems, even medical problems: "I wouldn't have this cold if I didn't have to work so hard to be able to feed you." Abused children take the blame when their parents erupt. "Don't cry or I'll lose control and spank you, and it will be your fault."

Is it any wonder that some abused children withdraw? Any playtime activity may be perceived by the parent as a disruption, a direct attack. Consequently, abused children are afraid to try new things, afraid to explore, and afraid to volunteer unless asked. Since they are failures at home, every activity is a new threat to them.

Abused children need their parents and want to love them. But as they draw close to the parents, their violence pushes them away. They love and hate their parents at the same time and are forced to bear this painful ambivalence in solitude. Often these children provoke others in order to relieve the tension inside. Abused children often become defiant children, easily stimulated to tantrums and attack upon anybody who comes near.

How We Feel

News of child abuse shocks us. We feel indignant, outraged, and impatient. Talking with children who bear bruises from the previous evening can tear your heart out. Child abuse is cruel. It is unfair. But it is a crisis that many who work with children will encounter.

Sometimes we fail to be sympathetic with abused children because they are typically the children who attempt to abuse us. Violence begets violence. Children learn aggressive behavior from aggressive parents. Because interest in and empathy for others is learned from empathic and caring parents, abused children are predominantly concerned with their own welfare and frequently seek it at the expense of others. Their frustration tolerance is low, their feelings are high, and their actions run rampant. As a result the teacher, child care worker, or other professional is too busy trying to manage these children to feel much sympathy for them. We address this topic more specifically in chapter eleven, "Defiant Children."

Enormous amounts of time and effort are needed to make an impact on abusing families. Our common reaction is to want, indeed demand, that change come immediately. To witness suffering, especially in innocent and vulnerable children, is draining—but even more draining is harboring false expectations that our interventions will instantly rectify the situation.

Most child protective agencies remain overburdened and understaffed and are unable to attract highly trained personnel. They can place abused and neglected children only temporarily and lack the capacity to provide the intensive, long-term clinical support necessary to treat these children and their families.

Short-term treatment approaches are not satisfactory. Even intensive long-term treatment may not allay the powerful cultural and personal factors that contribute to abuse. A teacher usually has a child for an entire year; it generally takes that long for the abusive parent to develop a working relationship with a treatment agency.

One organization that makes an impact on abusing parents is Parents Anonymous, a self-help group similar in organization and philosophy to Alcoholics Anonymous. Yet even this very effective organization reaches only a few. Parents must decide to join and to commit themselves to the group. Change requires a period of support and encouragement and may end up being only minimal. As one abusing parent said, "Since I joined Parents Anonymous, I don't beat my kid anymore, but I still don't like playing with her. Every time I say we have to stop, she carries on and cries and I wish I hadn't started playing with her in the first place."

Once we enter the world of abused children, it is easy to become angry at the parents. A normal response is to want the children taken away. Unfortunately, acting on these angry impulses does little to help either the abused children or their family. A mature response needs to also take into consideration the world of the abusing parents.

How Parents Feel

No matter how poor, how deprived, or how overwhelmed, most parents would rather not abuse their children. They become frustrated, they can't control their frustration, and they take it out on the youngster. They feel ashamed and guilty of their actions, but they can't seem to help themselves, and may lack empathic skills.

Most abusing parents lead lives in which their own needs for safety and love are not met and never have been. "Wanting" characterizes their lives. Most have lost significant others early in life. An early death of a parent or a difficult divorce chokes emotional fulfillment during childhood and takes an even greater toll years later. Abusing parents grow up with unmet needs and look to their own children to satisfy their emotional deprivations. Instead of wanting to give, they expect to receive: "I have never really felt loved all my life. When the baby was born, I thought he would love me; but when he cried all the time, it meant he didn't love me, so I hit him."[4]

Frequently, abusing parents are poor; poverty breeds frustration. They suffer the violence, humiliation, and despair which accompany poverty in our society. They feel unable to meet life's daily demands.

Parents who abuse misunderstand the basic nature of children. When they were growing up, they lacked a positive role model of parenting. To be good at parenting parents must express love, show tolerance, and serve as examples. Most parents who abuse were raised without seeing these in practice, and many were abused themselves.

One father whose severe disciplining included forcing his son to kneel on carpet tacks explained,

> It may seem cruel to you, but as children this is the type of punishment we received, my wife and I. We were just using the same type of punishment. If we did not care about him, we would not do this.[5]

Parents who are abusers suffer.

> Child abusers are going through hell. We have a vision of how powerful our anger can be, the concept of where our anger will take us if we are pushed too far, and the constant dread . . . we will be pushed too far. [Abuse is not a singular incident but usually part of a consistent pattern.] We don't like being child abusers any more than society likes the problem of child abuse.[6]

Some child abusers would like to give their children up for foster care or even adoption. Unfortunately, their relatives pressure them to keep the children without supporting them. Giving up the children means loss of whatever little love they do get from their extended family. As one grandmother said to her daughter, "You give away my grandson and you're not welcome in my house anymore." Other statements are less direct but convey the same message: "Anyone who would put their child in a foster home is an unfit parent." Consequently, they keep the child in an effort to please their parents, but they find themselves continually criticized for mishandling the child.

When You Suspect Child Abuse:
Interviewing Children

Many adults feel uncomfortable when talking with children about suspected abuse. Some of these approaches might help.

First, mention that you see an injury on their body that may need attention. "Herb, I see you have a bruise on your arm. Should I have the nurse look at it?" Children who are reluctant to talk about their injury or to see the nurse are more likely to be those who have been abused.

Now the interview becomes more difficult. Most children are reluctant to take the blame for something that they didn't do. The adult can make statements that imply the child caused the accident, such as, "I guess you fell off your bicycle," or "I guess you lost a fight with some other boy," and note the response. Sometimes it works to simply say, "I guess your mom or dad must have gotten real mad at you for you to have a bruise like that—what did you do to make them that mad?" If the child responds with, "I didn't do nothin', and she hit me with the broom!" be empathic and reflect how angry she must feel at being hurt. Remember also that sometimes it is relatives or baby-sitters who abuse children, particularly in sexual abuse.

Children often reveal abuse through notes to teachers that are hastily written and unclear. When you go to talk with them about the note, they have second thoughts, sometimes saying they made it all up. They worry about the consequences of what they have done in a moment of desperation and clam up. They worry their parents will get into trouble, that they will be sent away, or that the abuse will get worse. No amount of reassurance can get them to change their mind.

In the vast majority of cases, children who mention, no matter how briefly, that they have been abused are telling the truth. Take them seriously. While your interview may get you no further, a thorough investigation needs to be made.

Never reassure children who report abuse to you that they won't get into trouble. Often they will. What you need to reflect is how difficult it must be for them to tell you this information, to risk getting hurt more, and how you hope you can assist them, but you can't make any promises. Remember, make no promises. Most likely the children will continue to be abused, and you want their trust throughout their ordeal so you can help them to deal with their painful environment. They won't turn to you if they think you lie.

ADULT: Maria, I'm glad you told me your dad hit you. You are angry at him and know I'm your friend. I'll have to talk to your dad about what you told me, and I can't promise he'll listen to me and not hit you again. He'll probably get angry at you for telling me. I hope I can convince him you're scared and need help. If he hits you again, someone else might have to come to your home and ask him if you need protection from him—sometimes we need protection even from the ones we love.

Many children from abusing families have been instructed *never* to mention abuse to outsiders. The parents hit the children, realize the mistake, and order the children to tell *no one.* "I'll hit you harder next time," or "You will be sent away for good." In addition to fearing harm, the children now worry about being sent away from home. They will be reluctant to provide you with a straightforward explanation about their bruises. Respect their position and terminate your interview.

There are other occasions when children will tell you about the abuse once but never again. One fourth-grade boy told his social worker that during a party at home his father's friend had burned him with a cigarette. The next day the boy had changed the story. "I backed into the cigarette accidentally." Later it was discovered that the father had threatened, "Say that it was an accident or I'll whip your butt good."

Once a protective service agency becomes involved, the children usually are blamed for the predicament: "If it weren't for you, I wouldn't be in this trouble," the parent wails. "And we wouldn't have people checking out our house for child abuse. So shut up. You misbehaved, you got your lickin', *now shut up!*"

Sometimes child abuse is a no-win situation for everyone involved. If the abuse goes undiscovered, it continues. But if discovered, sometimes parents can retaliate in greater force against the children. Keeping this in mind will help you understand children's reluctance to talk with you about their bruise marks.

Reporting Abuse

Most state laws require that suspected child abuse or neglect be reported, and the procedures vary from state to state. Some agencies funnel all reports through a specific individual: the principal, program director, school nurse, guidance counselor, designated social worker, etc. Reporting suspected child abuse is a serious obligation, and persons mandated by law to report it leave themselves open to legal penalties if they fail to do so. This creates a dilemma for many workers when abuse is only suspected: "Will I do more harm than good by reporting this abuse?" Even if the abuse is substantiated, workers may question the effect of reporting on their relationship with the children and their families. If you face such a dilemma, seek out the support of your colleagues. Consultation with a mental health professional experienced in the area of child abuse can assist you in making the best possible decision, and support you throughout a difficult situation.

Reporting parents for child abuse when you have struggled so hard to establish a relationship with them is a frustrating requirement. Arrange for the principal, or another authority, to report the incident so that you might maintain your relationship during this period. Initially, the parents' anger will be directed at the entire school. Wait patiently, send positive notes home, inquire about the parents' welfare, tell them you miss them, and eventually your relationship with them may be renewed.

Interviewing Parents

Call a conference with the parents when you suspect neglect or abuse. While it is easier to simply call and officially report the abuse and hope the parents will think someone else is responsible, your own feelings about the parents will remain colored by impression rather than by fact. Suppose the parents actually aren't responsible. Talk with one of the parents first, even if you are required to report the suspected abuse. Explore the possibility that someone other than the parents is responsible. Sometimes it's siblings, baby-sitters, neighborhood children, or relatives.

ADULT: We've noticed lots of bruises on Glenn lately. Is he playing places he didn't used to, perhaps with older boys? He won't tell me how he got them.

PARENT: I don't know—I certainly don't abuse him. I smack him when he's bad, but I don't abuse him.

ADULT: Well, I hope you can find a way to prevent it. If it gets worse, we're obligated by law to report it to Child Protective Services who will then come to your home and investigate the report. We certainly don't want to do that if you can handle it.

Such an interview alerts the parents, without accusation, to provide better supervision of the child, or if they are to blame, to curb their own impulses.

Sometimes children will tell you their parent hit them. If the bruise is serious, you must report the incident. Always call the parents first and ask for a conference. If they refuse, explain that by law you have to report the incident to Child Protective Services. If you can be of help, you will visit their home with the Child Protective Services worker. They will often hang up on you. Be prepared for their anger and respond empathically.

If the bruise is not serious, keep after them for a parent conference to explain some recent problems you've had with their child. Stress that it's really important that you see them, but don't mention exactly why. At the conference, express that you're troubled by their child's recent communications.

ADULT: Tim's been telling me that you hit him. This must have been hard for him to say 'cause I know he loves you. He's bragged about you before. What do you suppose is going on with him now? Is anything different going on in his life?

Sometimes children's play reveals concerns that require exploration with parents.

ADULT: We're somewhat concerned about Elliot. His play with dolls suggests he has some worries. He took a large man doll, pulled down its pants, and placed it on top of a baby doll he laid face down. When I said the baby must have been scared, he quickly stopped playing. Do you think he's been playing with larger boys who have sexually molested him?

Sometimes the parents realize who the abuser is, don't say anything, but correct the situation on their own. They supervise the child more closely, severely admonish an older brother, kick the uncle out, or restrict visits to the grandfather—all done without your awareness.

Make sure all your interviews with parents start out in a nonaccusatory fashion. While this is rare, children sometimes try to elicit sympathy in ways that can get their parents in trouble. One child would change into filthy, ragged underwear, find some reason to see the school nurse, and then when she asked him to disrobe, he would "allow her" to discover his filthy underwear. He would then tell her his mother was too drunk to do the wash or too poor to buy him new underwear. Three children in a local children's home would hide their sweaters and socks during the winter so teachers would say, "What kind of a place is that children's home anyway, that they let children come to school dressed like this?" These children figured that if the home was forced to close, they could go home.

Parent-Teacher Conferences About Other Issues

Most parents come to conferences anxious. They want to hear that their children have done well. If the teachers think the parents will challenge them, they are apprehensive. In a conference with a suspected abusing parent, anxiety will run high with both sides fearing each other. The parents expect to be scolded by the teachers for neglecting the child, and the teachers expect the parents to criticize their approach with the children. Both will be defensive and both could respond to this defensiveness by taking the offensive: "I'm going to be attacked anyway, so I'll attack first." The teachers want to convince the parents that their disinterest and neglect contribute to their problems with the children, and the parents want to avoid being reprimanded, so they blame the school for improper care or instructions: "What does he do here? Seems to me he hasn't learned anything." With this tack, an unproductive conference will result.

To avoid unproductive conferences, teachers can resist the temptation to defend themselves when attacked, and simply reflect the feeling the parent is conveying. "You're worried that Karin's not progressing fast enough, and her education is important to you. I can understand that!" or "Do you have any suggestions for me, things you feel are important for her to learn?" Let the parents be right to avoid an argument. Your goal is to establish a relationship with them, not to defend your teaching skill. Insisting on being right yourself will cost you the relationship and might make things harder for you in the classroom. When the parents learn that they are not going to be attacked, they will lighten up considerably and stop resisting you. Then when you show them the children's good work and don't emphasize the bad, they'll ease up more and eventually you'll both begin discussing the children's real problems as partners rather than as opponents ready to square off. Of course, if you can start out talking about the children's strengths, so much the better.

Remember, don't let your anger get in the way! If you continually harbor anger toward abusive parents because the situation is not changing as fast as you would like, your effectiveness as a resource person will be diminished. The parents will feel your anger and avoid you. You will lose an opportunity to understand the family and be viewed by them as a source of support.

Another consideration is whether to call parents whom you suspect are abusive when the children have displayed inappropriate behaviors. With most parents, it is helpful to alert them to behavioral difficulties so that a consistent approach can be planned. When you know that children's parents have abused them, you should also remember that abuse occurs when the parents feel let down. Assess the situation thoroughly before you call parents in to discuss their children. Never discuss over the phone. As a general rule, avoid telling parents about the children's failures since the children's failures are parents' failures, and this feeling contributes to abuse. Send them regular notes about what they do well, no matter how insignificant. Many times you will want to write angry letters home, both about the children and the parents' seeming disinterest. You must restrain yourself—ventilation of anger on the parents can cause them to direct their anger toward the children.

Below is a letter written to a parent. At first, the writer wanted to chastise the parent for his uncooperative behavior, but instead tried to be more constructive:

Dear Mr. Jones:

I understand that one motive for your recent call to us was a visit from Child Protective Services regarding your difficulty with Tony. It would seem that you are under a great deal of pressure now from CPS, your ex-wife, family court, in addition to the problems with Tony, which can be overwhelming, such as his refusal to listen, his extreme restlessness, and so on.

I would think you might need some rest from Tony just to keep your new family functioning. Astor Home in Rhinebeck runs a specialized foster home program for emotionally disturbed children which is supervised by a clinical staff. Foster parents are carefully selected and specially trained to handle disturbed kids, their problems following visits to parents, relating to schools, etc. Perhaps you might want to discuss such a service with us when our worker visits you. We know you want to be a good father and probably feel that Tony is best served at home with you. Sometimes, however, relationships get so strained that people need a break from them to work them out.

If you're not ready for such a step, then we will work with you to help Tony at home.

Becoming Too Involved

In working with parents of abused children, nonprofessional counselors often face this dilemma: "Where do I draw the line between working with these parents and providing therapy for them?"

Often these parents are more open and frank in talking with the empathic nonprofessional counselor than with the mental health worker. They realize that the former is less likely to confront them or try to make interventions in the home. Parents often view social workers as watchdogs. They are usually afraid that their children will be taken away if they discuss their true feelings about them or incidents that happen at home. They dread the thought of being labeled "bad parents."

A short-term ventilation of parents' feelings with you might be helpful, but if this continues over a period of time it may undercut the relationship they are building with their therapist.

An empathic attitude that shifts the parent back to the mental health professional is often the most therapeutic stance:

TEACHER: Mrs. Harrison, you and your family have been under a great deal of stress lately. It sounds as though you feel overwhelmed, but you keep on trying. I appreciate your coming in to talk with me. But I want to encourage you to share your concerns with Mr. Samuels, your social worker. Since you will see him every week, I'm sure he can be a big help to you and your family.

It may be helpful to set up a meeting with yourself, the parent, and the social worker. In this way, you can gently define your role as one related to school matters, and the social worker's role as one concerning family problems and deep-seated personal issues.

Helping Abused Children

Professional Treatment

Abused children convey a general feeling of depression, unhappiness, and sadness. They have problems forming attachments, as well as detaching from others. They can be aggressive, have poor self-concept, and have trouble relating to peers. But worst of all, their capacity to trust others is impaired.[8]

Individual treatment of the abused child often takes two approaches: individual play therapy emphasizing a safe environment in which to express feelings, and therapy that educates the child to better cope with the reality of the abuse.

Many abused children have been deprived of the love and attention that all of us need. As a result they require a warm, nurturing relationship over a long period of time to help heal their wounds. In the safety of therapy, children will open up and reveal their feelings about being abused. In play the abuse situations can be recreated and discussed with the therapist.

Most abused youngsters believe at some level that they are the cause of the abuse. Abused children typically misbehave. This becomes a vicious circle: the children are abused, which leads to increased misbehavior. The parents, already with low stress tolerance, become even more abusive; children act out more, until their misbehavior becomes the "cause" of the abuse.

Many clinicians emphasize to children that perhaps their mom or dad is sometimes unreasonable and that the abuse would happen to them anyway. The goal of this tactic is to keep the children from internalizing the feeling that they are bad or worthless. They are not to blame. Unfortunately, the children typically feel at fault, and efforts to convince them otherwise fall on deaf ears. Another approach is to get the children to verbalize the things they feel cause their abuse. While the question, "What did you do that made mom so mad?" may seem harsh, it needs to be asked so the children can begin to understand their role in the abuse.

One goal is to alert children to the cues that precede abuse by their parents and to the role their behavior plays in the parents' anger. If children are abused after parents fight, then they can remove themselves from the room rather than stay around to see how the fight develops. If their mother storms around the kitchen or living room when she is angry, then they can leave that area and to go their room. If their father comes home drunk and hates to see the television on, they can quietly read a book instead. These timely actions give children more control over the situation.

Abusive parents make unrealistic demands on their children. Even with professional intervention the demands may continue, and when the children fail to meet them they are abused. Some therapists teach children to meet these demands in order to dodge the abuse. If Ed's father beats him and keeps on beating him until he cries, then Ed can learn to cry right away. If Janice's mother gets mad at her for not cleaning the kitchen table, then she should clean the table. If Bobby's mom doesn't like him to tease the cat, then Bobby should not tease the cat. Educating children in this way gives them more power over a situation in which they were previously helpless. Since helplessness is a cornerstone of depression, this approach helps lift the children's unhappiness.

The Nonprofessional Counselor

Professional treatment requires a significant investment of time and energy. The approaches we have described must be repeated over and over again, with slight variations like in the theme of a symphony, for children to make them part of their thoughts, feelings, and behavior. What can the nonprofessional counselor do to help these children?

Empathic statements communicate to abused children that they are understood and not alone. On Monday morning a teacher might pull fidgety Alice aside and say, "I know it must be hard for you to concentrate today." Or the recreation aide after school might say, "You'd probably like to stay here longer, but the basketball game is over. I know that you don't want to go home right now, but it's late, and it's time to leave."

Build in daily periods of intense physical activity in which these children can release their tension and aggression appropriately. You can also help these children by giving them I-messages. Let them know how their behavior affects you. For instance, help them see some of the things they do in your presence that infuriate you. If they do these same things at home, they are significantly contributing to their abuse. Teach children to see the relationship between their behavior and the feelings they evoke in adults:

ADULT: Leroy, I get very angry when I'm called names. I don't like being called a buffalo face. I get angry when you are disrespectful toward me.

or

ADULT: I wonder if your mommy gets mad when you call her names? Then she gets so angry that she hits you. You know your mommy has to learn not to hit you when she's angry. But you have to learn to change your behavior too and not call her names.

Developmental Considerations

Keep in mind children's developmental levels when you talk with them. Children in the magic years will attribute the parents' abuse to what they do. You can gently emphasize, over and over, that mom or dad has problems and that they are not to blame. Nevertheless, this message may not become incorporated into their thinking. Perhaps the best thing to do is to work with the protective service agency to guard them against abuse at home.

While children in the middle years believe they cause some of their parents' problems, it soon dawns on them that they do not cause most of them. They know they are not responsible for everything that's not working out. Discuss with the children the difference between problems they contribute to and problems beyond their control. Seek professional consultation. Since the children will probably tell the parents what you have discussed, be careful not to blame or disparage the parents.

Special issues arise in talking with abused adolescents. Their attitude is exactly the opposite of that held by magic years children: they know they are not the cause, blame their parents totally, and may refuse to acknowledge or discuss their role in the matter. "It's all their fault. I'm just gonna get the hell out of there."

Abused adolescents may confide in you that they plan to run away. In general, don't try to persuade them otherwise—there is no better way to inspire them to leave. Perhaps these youngsters should run away and thereby call attention to themselves and to their family. It is their way of saying, "Things are seriously wrong here, and we need to find solutions."

Be empathic with adolescents in this situation. Explore options with them. But try not to encourage or discourage them in either direction because you can never fully understand the condition in which they live. Your role is to help them make an intelligent decision. Appropriate self-disclosure may be helpful, not in the vein of "I can tell you what to do" but rather "I can appreciate the difficulty of your situation. I've had a slightly similar experience myself. . . ."

If there is a theme for this chapter, or indeed this book, it is that "things take time." Many who work with children are so busy planning activities and implementing them that they have little time for a heart-to-heart talk with a child. If you can listen to abused children and let them talk their feelings out, you help support them and lead them to a greater understanding of their lives. Likewise, if you have referred abused children to a mental health professional, beware of the illusion that therapy will work miracles with these children and their families over a brief period of time. It won't—but it is the most constructive approach to date in helping to break the vicious circle of children abuse.

Suggested Reading for Children

Bradbury, B. *Those Traver Kids.* Boston, Mass.: Houghton Mifflin, 1972. (Ages 12+)
Coolidge, O. E. *Come By Here.* Boston, Mass.: Houghton Mifflin, 1970. (Ages 11+)
D'ambrosio, Richard. *No Language But a Cry.* New York: Doubleday, 1970. (Ages 13+)
Greene, B. *The Summer of My German Soldier.* New York: Dial Press, 1973. (Ages 12+)
Rabe, B. L. *Rass.* New York: Thomas Nelson, 1973. (Ages 12+)
Smith, D. B. *Tough Chauncey.* New York: Dial Press, 1973. (Ages 12+)

·10·

Foster Care

They are behind you
They are holes
Holes in the snow
Holes in the sand
Holes in the mud
Your feet made the holes, lots of holes
So your mother can find you.

A FIVE-YEAR-OLD

Most children who enter foster care have attempted to cope with early life traumas (such as death of a parent, divorce, separation, surgery, health problems), all of which impaired their capacity to deal with subsequent life tasks. Some children, however, are placed following an unsuccessful adoption or a remarriage which created a stepparent situation. Because of the numerous crises these children have experienced, counseling them includes all we have discussed before plus children's reaction to placement itself.

Many children will need only temporary foster care until the crisis which brought about the breakdown of their own family has been resolved. But others can never return home and need to be cared for until they are placed for adoption. A large and increasing number, because of their age, intellectual level, or family status, face long-term care. This group includes those referred to child care institutions or group homes.

Natural parents usually have strong feelings about their children's placement. They feel relieved—yet ashamed, hurt, and angry at the same time. Their guilt often is unbearable. Mothers whose children are placed because of neglect feel empty and numb; everything seems beyond their control. They have to prove themselves all over again. Others feel isolated, lonely, and inadequate, and expect punishment for having allowed their children to be taken from them. Some express fear that when their children are grown, they will retaliate for this wrong.

The inequities and irrationalities of the foster care system are enormously frustrating for children, parents, foster parents, and everyone else involved in the situation. Often the goal of foster care for children is unclear. Children are transferred from one foster home to another out of fear that attachments will develop. This attitude implies that attachments to nonbiological adults are suspect, but we forget that children are capable of numerous attachments. English children are attached to their nannies and their parents. Kibbutz children are attached to the group as well as to their parents.

Any children in foster care for over two years obviously have a troubled relationship with their parents. If their parents' commitment is minimal, they need attachments to others. "But won't the foster parents have difficulty returning the children if they're attached to them?" Yes, but they can remain involved as "aunts" and "uncles" throughout the children's youth. Most foster parents grieve when children leave, but most are able to let go and say good-bye, acknowledging their contributions to the children's lives.

In this chapter, we draw from the work of Robert L. Geiser, who has written compassionately and insightfully about foster care in his book, *The Illusion of Caring: Children in Foster Care.*

How Foster Children Feel

How children feel upon entering foster care depends upon many factors. One is the children's prior placement. Children who go directly from their own home into foster care are usually from a background of chaos and disorganization, from a family that has threatened them with foster care as a solution to their problems—"Shape up, or we'll kick you out!" Once in foster care, these youngsters try to eliminate the behaviors that led to their placement. When successful, disappointment awaits them when they discover that often they still can't go home. Hence, the terrible conclusion: "I'm away from home to stay; I thought it was only temporary."

Children who go from an institution to a foster home can experience a crisis of unfulfilled expectations. While in the institution, their all-absorbing wish is to return home. They expect their placement to improve their family situation—they would then return home and receive the love and attention they miss. When they are discharged from the institution to a foster home, they discover their family remains unchanged and that problems still abound. Their dreams are shattered. In discussing reactions to hospitalization in chapter seven, "Health Crises," we described children's movement through three stages: protest, despair, and apathy. Children who are removed from their parents respond similarly.

When children who have some attachment enter foster care, they cry, often alone and unobserved. While their sorrow expresses their pain and loss, it is also a cry for the lost parent, a last-ditch plea for reunion. When their cries go unanswered, they actively protest their placement with rage and indignation. Such children are prone to defiance and acts of physical aggression. Help them verbalize their frustration:

ADULT: You're real angry at having to leave home. And you're not even sure who you're angry at—your parents for sending you away, yourself for not pleasing them, or us who have taken you in. Probably everybody.

or

ADULT: It's hard to express your anger at your parents for sending you away because you might worry that they'll never take you back. It's easier to get angry at us because you didn't want to be here in the first place.

or

ADULT: We know you're real upset and angry at having to come here. It's all right to be angry, but you need to talk about your angry feelings. It's not all right to smash things and hit people. We can't let you do that.

If these interventions are effective, the children's protest will become more verbally controlled and communicative and less physical. When the anger cannot be worked through, the emptiness that accompanies despair causes greater distress than the anger, because the latter at least implies hope of reunion.[1]

To ward off emptiness, loss, and despair, most foster children resist discussing their home or parents because it evokes too much pain. Discussing their family life when they're not a part of it adds insult to injury. But some discussion is necessary.

ADULT: Remember when you first came here? How angry you used to be? We talked about your anger at your parents, at us, at yourself.

CHILD: I don't care.

ADULT: That's just it. We think you care very much, but your anger didn't get your parents back. Have you given up hope? Do you think you'll never get home?

CHILD: I don't care.

ADULT: Maybe your parents won't be able to take care of you every day. Maybe visits will be your only contact for some time. I don't know. But others care about you, too—teachers, us, your friends.

CHILD: You do not! You do this for money.

ADULT: Yes, we get paid for taking care of you. (Say no more.)

CHILD: Yeah, but not much, I'll bet.

Children in foster care often harbor feelings of revenge. Many are reluctant to write their families, particularly when they aren't written to. Encourage them to write. It keeps alive issues which have contributed to their placement and allows feelings to surface that can be discussed with you. Or their refusal to write can be addressed.

ADULT: You won't write your parents 'cause they haven't written you. You think they should write you first—you're the one away. I can understand that feeling, but it's important for you to tell your parents that. Maybe they think you're happier here! Sometimes parents get discouraged, too, and feel they're no good, that their child is better off without them.

After despair comes apathy, a listless going through the motions of routine tasks, withdrawal from people and activities. Some children even try to make believe that their parents are dead. In this condition, the children are more manageable, and you may be tempted to view their "calmness" positively. Be wary.

> With his feelings hidden, a frozen smile on his face, he goes about his daily routine. Some say that he has settled in, finally accepting the separation from his parents. They are mistaken.[2]

Your interventions may keep children from reaching this stage, but that means you need to be prepared to tolerate despair and protest.

Some children secretly are relieved to come into foster care. Living with an unpredictable family situation is extremely stressful, and the safety and support at another home can be a blessing. Some children's best days will be their days away from home, and they know it. Friendships with foster parents, child care workers, teachers, and therapists, along with weekend visits to parents who are on their best behavior, can be a better life for many children. Most parents intend to do the right thing, but intentions aren't always enough. Children who are away from a disorganized, overwhelmed, and rejecting home are free from the daily ridicule, criticism, and unpredictability we discussed in the last chapter.

Other children resist foster or institutional care because they are more controlled in such settings. They desire to return home not because they suffer from severed ties with loved ones, but because they get their way there more often. They come home when it suits them, go to bed when they want, and have no responsibilities. In short, they are unsupervised and omnipotent. Often these children are referred to institutions. While we know that the structure and routine is good for them, they don't. We suggest approaches for working with these children in the following chapter, under the section "Understanding and Enabling Extremely Defiant and Physically Aggressive Children."

"I Am Bad"

Children's age at placement plays an important role in determining their attitude about separation:

• Children who have a sibling born shortly before they themselves are placed may conclude that their anger toward their mother and the new baby was the reason they were sent away.

• Children placed at one month of age may later decide that they cried too much and that's why their mother placed them.

• Children placed at the end of first grade reason that their failure to be promoted had so shamed their parents that they no longer wanted them.

These young children all conclude they are no good. Older children can also feel responsible for being placed:

CHILD: The only reason I can think of for my mother not to want me is if there is something terribly wrong with me or terribly wrong with her. Either way, I've had it.[3]

or

CHILD: I figure that I must have done something pretty bad for my mother not to want me. I was only ten days old when my mother got rid of me. The only thing I can think of that a ten-day-old baby could do wrong was to cry a lot. I've thought back as far as I can, and I don't remember crying that much.[4]

Children in foster care expect rejection. Sometimes the wait for the rejection is so intolerable that they bring it on themselves: "There, now I can relax. The worst is over."

Children often blame themselves for their placement because active blaming is preferred over helplessness: "I caused it." Is it not better to be a strong and bad somebody than a weak and good nobody? It's difficult to work with children who are convinced that they are monsters.[5]

Magic and middle years children experience loyalty conflicts about placement and attempt to draw adults into these conflicts. Young children express great ambivalence toward foster parents. Some fantasize about returning home while hoping that their foster parents will replace their real parents.

In working with foster children, avoid telling them "You've never had it so good. Your real mother is irresponsible, not as nice as your foster mother," or "You should be more appreciative—you're lucky to be in such a nice foster home." Such comments are not helpful. They may be true, but they do not contribute to the children's belief in themselves as worthwhile persons. To feel worthwhile, children need to feel loved by their parents or someone in their past. Trying to convince them of the unworthiness of their parents takes away their belief that they are lovable. By criticizing their parents, you criticize the children. If their parents are no good, then they are no good: "If my mother does not love me, then I am unlovable."

> But we are so much a part of our parents that to attack them is to villify ourselves. To admit that they were neglectful is to affirm that we are worthy of neglect. To want to be other than like them is to aspire to be nobody at all.[6]

Foster children often "split off" an image of their own mother as a good mother. They develop an idealistic view of her and try to make their foster mother into the bad mother. Let's look at this phenomenon in more detail.

Splitting

For foster children, love and hate become intensified. The hate for the parents is fueled by the additional resentment of being placed. The desire to love and be loved by parents grows because it is unsatisfied. As these two opposing forces become stronger, their resolution becomes increasingly difficult, making the children more anxious, uncomfortable, and guilty. These children can't reconcile the two opposing sets of feelings they have for the same parent, so they devise a way to sidestep the whole conflict. They *split the feelings* into separate parts and attach each feeling to a different adult. They now feel only one way about each of the two mothers (or fathers) in their life.[7]

What happens most often is that love is felt for the lost parents, to the point of overidealizing them, and hate is expressed toward their present caretakers. This process can be accelerated if caretakers make negative comments about the natural parents or overly positive comments about the foster parents. In working with foster children, adults should reflect how disappointed they must feel to live in someone else's home, or in an institution, and how they must miss their real mother.

CHILD: When I go home, my mom lets me stay up to eleven o'clock. And she's not always telling me to pick up my clothes.

ADULT: (Tempted to say that the mother provides no structure, replies.) Your mom has different rules. It must be tough to follow two sets of rules. You probably feel we treat you unfairly, but remember that my own children follow the same rules as you do. When they grow up, and when you grow up, you can make your own rules too.

CHILD: I like it a lot better at home. I wish I were home instead of here—I hate it here.

ADULT: It's hard living away from home. We wish you could have what you want too.

CHILD: My mom says she's taking me home next week.

ADULT: Wouldn't that be something if she could! I'll bet she sure wants to. She feels bad at not being able to care for you.

CHILD: She really is!

ADULT: When I hear from your social worker, we can both pack your bag. I'll miss you when you go.

By reflecting foster children's feelings, you help free them to accept the foster mother or child care worker as a not-so-bad person. If you tell them how good the foster mother is, they automatically defend their own mother. This can produce further splitting and jeopardize their placement.

Things Seem Overly Important to Children in Placement

Foster children often seem greedy. Having things becomes important. Remember the little girl in chapter one who got angry because her ill foster mother would not give her candy from the bedside table? Material possessions become equated with love. Sometimes when foster children are unable to get something, the pain of being unable to feel close to their parents comes up. Getting things, collecting things, squirreling things away become an obsession. Sometimes foster children take, or ask for, relatively useless objects. One little girl in our program asked for nearly everything in the offices and classrooms. The staff wanted to say, "You can't have anything in here." Instead, we allowed the girl to collect discarded objects such as dried up pens, paper clips on the floor, fallen thumbtacks, old memos and flyers from the bulletin boards, or worthless items like bottle caps and twigs from the playground. We alerted the foster mother, who then proudly examined the girl's daily scavengings when she returned from school each afternoon.

Marshal Positive Forces

Children in foster care need to find positive qualities in their natural parents or other relatives so that they can experience these qualities in themselves. If the parents are seen as losers, they view themselves as losers.

Assist children to find these positive qualities. Almost paradoxically better relationships with foster parents will occur. Children say to themselves, "If my parents have some lovable qualities, then I am lovable, and if I'm lovable, I can be loved by the foster parents and other adults." Thus, they open themselves up to the foster parents.

Often we shudder when children in foster care express love and admiration for their parents. Does this mean they will grow up to be just like them? When a six-year-old expresses admiration for his father's strength (a father who used his strength to rob people and is in prison), does this mean the boy will grow up to be a mugger? Or when a teenage girl whose mother is a prostitute goes boy crazy, does this mean she will end up like her mother? We fear that these children will become like the "bad parts" of their parents. We are reluctant to tell the children good things about their parents because we fear we will encourage their identification with the bad qualities as well. These fears are unfounded and prevent our enabling foster children to discover who they are. Two examples of positive statements to these children are—

ADULT: You're getting to be strong, just like your dad. He was a good athlete, both at football and baseball. Maybe if you practice a lot, you can get to be a good player, just like him.

ADULT: You have pretty eyes, just like your mom.

The importance of such statements to children cannot be understated.

> Most foster children cannot identify with adequate adult models that they see around them because they have not let go of their parents. Until these children can relinquish the past, they cannot take from the present or the future. This does not in any way mean that children must be helped to "forget" their parents. On the contrary, they must be helped to remember, know, and ultimately accept their parents as they were. They must be helped to a new and different love toward their parents, not one which rises out of unfulfilled need and deprivation, but one which expresses compassion and acceptance. This partly means they must come to see their parents as being unable to care for them, not as unloving.[8]

Children's identification with parents includes identification with their attitudes. If parents feel helpless, hopeless, and desperate, children must be helped to see things differently. The problems and confusing behaviors of their parents must be made understandable:

ADULT: It's really hard to want to be close to your mom and not have her close to you. How awful you must have felt, and still feel, being unloved by your mom. But she had many problems and couldn't express her feelings for you.

or

ADULT: How frightening it must be to live with parents who can't always show their love. You must want to run away, but that would be scary 'cause you'd feel terrible alone. Other people do not easily replace the ones we love, and sometimes we won't let them.

Help foster children find positive qualities in themselves. It's difficult for them to feel self-confident when they feel demoralized. They make many disparaging comments about others and eventually about themselves. Begin by reflection.

ADULT: You feel pretty discouraged about yourself today.
or
ADULT: You've seemed pretty hopeless about yourself lately.

Remember our fledgling artist, Freddie, in chapter four? It does not help him when others claim "But you're so good," when he feels so bad. If you reflect his discouraged feelings, he can look at himself more objectively and realize that he's not so bad after all. Then you can reply with, "Perhaps you'd like some help with that," or "Try again, maybe with a few suggestions from me, you can make it better."

When children feel discouraged, it further alienates them to hear, "You did okay yesterday." In their hopelessness, they want to feel understood, to be in communication with someone, to feel connected. When you sense their message and are able to reflect it back, they will feel less hopeless, will judge themselves less harshly, and will try a task again.

Avoid false praise. Often children make scribbles on a piece of paper, and well-meaning adults will praise them for their wonderful production. While such praise might be appropriate for three-year-olds, it certainly isn't appropriate for older children whose scribbles resulted from minimal effort. Observing adults were shocked when such a drawing was shown to another, who replied, "That's junk, and you know it. Come on in the kitchen and I'll show you how to make some good drawings." The child initially resisted but then complied, and for months after, continued to ask her foster mother, "When is Mr. Lenox going to visit me again? I want to draw with him." Children know when they have really tried and when they haven't. They will accept praise even when it's hollow—but they won't grow from it.

Praise children's efforts rather than their results. Sometimes when you praise results, children fear they won't produce the same result again, and their motivation wanes.

ADULT: Mark, you put a lot of work into that English assignment. We appreciate such effort. Keep it up, even though we know it's hard. You can send it to your mom.

Adolescents in Foster Care

Foster parents, despite their name, rarely parent adolescent foster children. They function more as adult siblings.

Adolescents cast the final vote that determines whether or not they will stay in a foster home. They see the placement as being their choice and will run away from it if they don't like it. Many do run away and ultimately live in group homes or institutions. The adolescents who choose to stay in a foster home have usually decided that staying with a particular family will make a difference in their life. They have given up on the notion that parents or parent figures can be helpful to them, so those who relate to them as a parent usually are unsuccessful.

Teachers and other adults working with adolescents in foster care should know that their placement will not greatly influence their relationship with them. They have already decided that they have to finish high school (or whatever else it is they've decided to do), and they will stick it out in the home, provided they perceive the foster parents as fair and reasonable. Encourage them to talk to other adolescents about their parents' rules.

Visitations: Anxious Reunions

Most children in foster care display problem behavior before or after a home visit with their natural family. Teachers may experience frenzied, chaotic behavior from foster children on the Friday afternoon before the visit or on the Monday morning after the visit. Unfortunately, in most cases teachers are not informed. Caseworkers from the social service agencies that place children usually are too busy to call and say, "Johnny will be visiting his natural parents this weekend. . . . He's been in the foster home for three weeks now, and we're going to start his visits this weekend." You need to take the initiative to find out when visits occur.

Know which type of visit is planned. Generally, there are three types of visiting arrangements: parental visits to the foster home, supervised visits in the office of the social worker, and visitation in the home of the natural family. (The last type can be one-day visits, overnight visits, or weekend visits.) Equipped with this knowledge, you can adjust your expectations of the children before and after the visit. If children are visiting their parents on Friday and become highly anxious, you can change the demands you place on them. Or when you've learned that on the Monday following a visit they will be edgy, you can modify their activities accordingly. This information will help the social service workers to determine the children's reaction to their visits.

Why is visiting so traumatic? Primarily because it releases the children's fantasies about reunion. Reunion holds forth the expectation that the loss will be undone. ("Mom will love me better than she did in the past." "I will behave better than I did before." "My visits will put things right.") With time away from home, parents become idealized, imbued with magical curative powers. Visits shatter this illusion.

Reunions reveal reality. The children discover that their parents still have problems. Mom will have changed too much or too little. Dad will criticize them more. Mom will be reminded of how "bad" they were—that they didn't live up to her expectations. Or the children fear they will do all the wrong things and never be able to go home for good.

Visitations make parents and children aware of how they are growing apart. They are no longer sure how to relate to each other. Intimate communication between parents and children are nourished by togetherness and are diminished during separation. The mother now undervalues her importance. What exists is an "altered state of togetherness." Both parents and children have the same apprehensions and expectations about reunion. Child care workers, foster mothers, and even therapists have witnessed this altered state on numerous occasions and have wrongly attributed it to bad parenting. "The mother doesn't really care; she only comes up here for a trip to the country. Look how she ignores Tammy and talks to others." She is not ignoring, and she really does care. But she is uncomfortable, and she doesn't know how to reach her child.

Reunions serve as painful reminders of past rejections and contribute to feelings of self-doubt. Both parents and children can be reluctant to reach out to one another for fear of rejection. The children's attachments to surrogate parents warp the quality of their reunion.

Concrete changes threaten foster children—a new sibling, a mother's new boyfriend, or a remarriage. Issues from the past are compounded by issues in the present.

Help the children stay grounded in the facts, as their intensely experienced ideas may become confused with reality. When children are caught up in the past, they have a distorted view of the present. Help them understand and accept the past—to relinquish what was, or what might have been, and affirm what is.

How We Feel Toward Foster Parents

People become foster parents for different reasons. Some become foster parents for altruistic reasons, out of a genuine desire to help children. Others want another child to add to their own fulfillment. Still others need the extra income that comes with taking in a foster child.

Unfortunately, foster parents with financial motives are judged harshly by other people in the children's lives: "They're just doing it for the buck!" Interestingly, many altruistic foster parents become quickly disillusioned when they discover that love does not significantly change the child. They fail to see the fruits of their labor and give up quickly. Many foster parents whose initial motive is financial approach the tasks as would a professional and are able to manage the child effectively in spite of "not getting much back," as often happens before children become adjusted to the home. Examine your own judgments about people who take in children. Have empathy for the foster mother, who herself is going through some rough testing from the child.

Foster children need firm controls. Most children are placed because of difficulties with parents. Many are unmanageable and need a home with supervision, support, and controls. Typically, children learn to control themselves by wanting to please a loved adult. Children, not wanting to lose their mother's or father's love, learn to control their impulses. When children enter foster care, they are unsure whether anybody really loves them. They find themselves in a new home with strangers, people whom they have no desire to please. Many of these youngsters behave worse soon after placement.

When foster parents are firm and the children's behavior is more compliant, the children become more receptive to love and affection. These controls can seem unusually strict to outside observers who unfairly criticize foster parents. Children in placement may try hard to discredit their foster parents so they can return to their natural parents. They will take advantage of judgments they sense you have about the foster parents. During this testing period they try and align other adults against the foster parents. They may tell you their foster mother does not feed them, or they may put on old, dirty clothes to make it appear as if they are not being cared for.

When this happens, unsuspecting adults can make hasty judgments about the foster family without checking things out. Some youngsters are adept at orchestrating teachers and even staff members of social service agencies against foster parents. One eleven-year-old boy in foster care announced to his teachers and classmates, "You know, I have to eat in the basement." Everyone became concerned, and a call was made to the caseworker to further investigate his claim. It turned out that the family had remodeled the basement as a living area for everyone in the family; the rooms upstairs were used as a showcase when there is company.

Talk with foster parents as you do any parents, treating them with respect and listening carefully to their point of view. If they are involved in the work for financial remuneration (as you may be also), treat them as professionals who in most cases will do a good job with the children.

Foster parents sometimes take abuse from natural parents who feel guilty that they can't take care of the children, or fear their loss of the child's love. Consequently, they try to demean the foster parents in the child's eyes: "You don't have to listen to her, she's not your mother." They will criticize the foster parents in front of the child with comments such as

• "You've been beating my child. I'm going to sue you!" (From an abusive mother)

• "I don't like her dressed in blue. I never liked blue on her."

• "What the hell right have you to cut my child's hair? I want him to have long hair, not short hair."[9]

Foster parents need support so as not to return such anger, and to feel appreciated for their work.

Professional Therapy with Children in Foster Care

The behavior of many foster children suggests they could benefit from professional counseling. The problem, however, is that professional counseling can dilute the relationship with the foster mother. Now a third adult is added to the children's lives! Theoretically, a professional therapist is a neutral figure who helps children sort out their feelings about the two parent figures in their lives. What sometimes happens is that the therapist becomes a third parent figure—one who can take children out of their dilemma—and the children's confusion multiplies. Teachers, child care workers, or nurses have more clearly defined roles. Although children may be attached to them, they know these adults work with many other children and are not going to take them home. But the therapist sees them alone—the seed for fantasy. If the therapist has not worked with many foster children before, he or she may never know that such fantasy exists and the "therapy" will not be therapy at all, but simply fuel for confusion. Consequently, don't immediately seek psychotherapy, but realize that you can be of significant help yourself.

·11·

Defiant Children

. . . Perhaps we have not fully understood that anger is a
secondary emotional cover for hurt.

CHARLOTTE PAINTER

"So does your mother!" one angry little boy taunted another.
Hurtful words which resulted in the swinging of fists, kicking,
biting, and possible injury for all participants.

The playground aide who witnessed this episode tried to keep the
boys from fighting, but they wouldn't stop. She frantically called to
another student, "Jimmy, go get the principal. Hurry!" This seemed to
be her first, last, and only course of action.

Similar scenes take place everywhere—at camps, day care centers,
community parks, child care facilities—anywhere that children are
present in groups.

Defiant children tax the patience of even those near sainthood.
Angry children have a way of irritating the calmest, most tolerant
adults. They know the adults' sensitivities, and they know how to manipulate these to their own advantage. If unchecked, defiant children's
anger can escalate to the point at which they damage property or hurt
others.

The goal with defiant children is prevention: If you can make the
right moves early in the game, defiant youngsters can control their
anger. Some approaches emphasize physical defense training but fail
to focus on effective verbal techniques that can also be therapeutic.
Most defiant children can be prevented from acting out physically.
Common sense as well as the professional literature suggest effective
ways to defuse situations involving defiant youngsters.

Defusing Violent Situations

Separate children from their audience! Fanfare adds fuel to the fire and can keep a fight going. In the musical, *West Side Story,* two reluctant young gang members were literally pushed into a fight by one of their peers. Neither youth really wanted to fight, but someone in the crowd poked one of them, and a battle ensued. It is a common ploy of gangs to encircle potential contenders so they cannot escape—a fight has to take place.

An audience can heighten youngsters' anxiety. In any group activity or situation, one effective technique to prevent defiance from escalating to physical aggression is to handle the situation in as much privacy as possible. This helps dilute the intensity of feelings. Youngsters may need to save face for their audience, and this need can become their motivation to fight. A display of bravado might not be needed if they talk with an adult in privacy. Privacy also accentuates the relationship between adults and children, providing children with an external source of reassurance, guidance, and control.

One resourceful teacher used an ingenious method to keep a youngster from becoming aggressive. Terry, a fifth grader in her special education class, was being extremely belligerent and did not want to talk with anyone about it. She declined the teacher's offer to leave the room and pull herself together. "You go pull yourself together yourself!" Terry snapped. In response the teacher invited the rest of her class to follow her to a different room. All of the other students left with her, and Terry soon found herself in an empty classroom. She calmed down.

In educational or treatment settings, the staff may wish to devise a plan for dispelling the audience effects if a fight begins to develop. One staff person can be designated to counsel the anxious and defiant youngster, while other individuals can disperse the onlookers.

Another preventive technique concerns having only one adult communicate with the defiant, upset youngster. Teachers, child care workers, and nurses often ask, "Shouldn't we all work together to try to calm Peter down . . . ?" The answer is no. If more than one adult talks at the same time the child typically shuts everybody out and becomes even more belligerent and violent.

If you can establish one-to-one contact with angry children, usually you can calm them down. Through this personal contact, these children come to view you as an ally who will help them control themselves—even though they may verbally attack you. They can follow your cues—your demeanor, your physical gestures, your tone of voice—in regaining their composure. When three or four adults are talking at once, the children fail to establish contact with any of them, and their defiance escalates.

The Use of Interpersonal Space and Physical Gestures

Training in the helping professions emphasizes that helpers should "get close" to persons being helped. The physical display of affection comes naturally in working with children. In the language of feelings, a sincere hug or pat on the shoulder can communicate more to the child than hundreds of words.

When children are angry, however, touching them can increase the likelihood that they will lash out physically. Angry children need their own space, an area to occupy by themselves, or at least a physical distance of several arms' length from others so that they do not feel encroached upon. The research by ethologists suggests that all animals— even as sophisticated a species as we believe ourselves to be—will lash out with explosive power and energy when they feel trapped or cornered. Angry youngsters often misperceive a friendly pat on the back or touch to the arm as aggressive acts and respond accordingly. Feeling the pat was a shove, their reasoning goes, "They hit me first, now I'll hit them back." Be very careful about gestures you make toward defiant children. Children in crisis generally feel a loss of security and control. If you approach them calmly and act self-assured but not overpowering, angry children are reassured.

Your physical posture lets these children know that you are there to talk with them and to understand them. One way to defuse defiant children's anger is to stand at least one arm's length away from them. In doing so you respect their personal space. In response they do not feel intimidated. They know you will not use physical violence.

Some counselors and teachers directly face those with whom they are talking. With defiant children this approach is likely to communicate to them that you are ready to square off. Don't face these children directly. Stand near them at an angle, or sit down near them, in as relaxed a manner as possible. You are now at their level and not towering over them. This communicates that you are with them to spend time together in constructive problem solving. Making a nonthreatening or conciliatory gesture invites the youngsters to respond to you in a similar way.

For example, when we place children who have lost control in isolation, we usually enter the room ourselves shortly after placing them there. We quietly sit on the floor some distance from the child while he or she usually remains standing. Similarly, when a youngster threatens with a bat, we quickly and quietly get other children away and take a passive stance well away from the potential bat swinger, either going down on one knee or placing our hands in our pockets. This gives the youngster space to back down while saving face. It communicates that we don't intend to attack or take away the bat. The youngster is scared as well as angry; both feelings need to subside before the bat will be relinquished. Sometimes simply turning and walking toward the building with a "Come on now, let's go inside" comment will induce the child to follow with the bat hung at his or her side.

One caution about assuming a passive position. Once one of us entered the time-out room and sat down on the floor to talk to a small and extremely bright seven-year-old. The boy had an explosive temper and had lost it. At first he remained distant, then he approached and realized that he towered over the reclining psychologist. His feeling of omnipotence overtook him, and he struck a brutal blow. The error was not knowing that this small boy took advantage of the weaknesses of others—he had been referred for hitting his teachers and throwing chairs at adults, including his mother. Sitting on the floor actually invited attack from this little child. Know your children!

When the child has calmed down, interview him or her about the behavior. Although there will be resistance because the interview attempts will be interpreted as scolding, be empathic and you'll make headway.

When defiant children are not in a crisis state, their bodily preoccupations can offer an entry point for establishing a relationship. Violent youth tend to regard their bodies as "instruments of destruction, as magnificent representations of self."[1] Sympathetic and genuine comments of concern about body scars, disfigurements, bandages (however small), recent scrapes and bruises will often elicit a friendly acknowledgment from the youngsters. How many times have we said to a child, "Don't make such a fuss. It's only a small cut." Pay close attention to small cuts, put bandages on them, and show concern so as to initiate and motivate a relationship through caring. This positive interest approach includes comments about attractive physical features as well. Bestowing compliments, however, is sometimes counterproductive with adolescents. They may perceive such flattery as an attempt to con them.

"I-Messages"

Angry children become angrier when they are ordered to do something. Orders or commands take the form of statements such as, "You stop that!" "You know better than to...," or "You are acting like a baby!" as well as hundreds of modifications of these admonitions.

I-messages are less apt to provoke resistance and rebellion. To let children know how their behavior affects you is far less threatening than to suggest that there is something bad about them. For example, you could tell the child with the bat:

ADULT: I'm not happy about getting hit on the head, but I'm willing to talk to you from here and see what made you so angry. You can keep your bat for now, but let's talk.

Personal I-messages often serve as an introduction to dialogue and discussion.

One unruly youngster began to recklessly sort through all of the glassware assembled for a seventh-grade chemistry lab exam. A teacher's warning, "Don't you do that!" might cause the student to be more careful, but more likely it will prompt him to further flaunt his behavior and lead him to break the glass. If instead the teacher says, "Robert, please. I'm getting nervous. I'm afraid somehow a glass will get broken," there is a good chance that the student will put the glassware down.

Almost paradoxically, I-messages often deescalate a crisis. Both people are on an equal level of respect, and this in itself takes the edge off a potential confrontation.

> It takes a certain amount of courage to send "I-messages," but the rewards are generally well worth the risks. It takes courage and inner security for a person to expose his inner feelings in a relationship. The sender of an honest "I-message" risks becoming known to the other *as he really is.*[2]

Extremely defiant children should know that their violence elicits fear reactions in others. The adult can use I-messages as well as appropriate self-disclosure. Many ask, "Why should adults tell defiant children that they make us afraid? If the children know this, they will act tougher and more aggressive." On the contrary, youth often act tough to cover up their own fear of us. If we feel fear but express something else, they'll get tougher. Expressing our fear in a noncombative stance takes away their need to be more aggressive.

Clarifying Intention and Motivation

Youngsters five and six years old are particularly prone to eruptions of hostility that seem irrational or even incomprehensible. They are often incapable of judging why someone bumped or pushed against them. Often they perceive an accident as a personal affront or hostile attack. Children at this age are unable to form correct judgments of other people's motives unless they are assisted to do so.

Jackie, a five-year-old girl enrolled in a Head Start program, erupted into a temper tantrum when three-year-old Lillian collided with her while they rode their tricycles on the playground. She screamed at Lillian, scared her off the trike, and chased her up the monkeybars. Upon catching up with Jackie, her teacher explained that Lillian was a little girl who did not yet know how to ride her trike as well as Jackie did. The collision was an accident. Lillian did not mean to bump into her. She was sorry. After hearing this explanation several times, Jackie settled down and returned to her group.

Aggressive children beyond the magic years also misperceive the intentions of others more frequently than nonaggressive children. They respond to ambiguous situations with aggression not because they simply don't understand another's motives, but because they attribute hostile reactions to others: "Because I'm always angry, others are always angry at me." Whereas nonaggressive youths first judge events to be accidental.[3]

When aggressive children are accidentally hit or pushed by another child, they infer that the other had *meant* to do that. Counseling middle years aggressive children should also include a thorough discussion of the difference between an accidental and a deliberate act, with reference to the child's own pervasive anger:

ADULT: David, just because you're angry at other kids doesn't mean they're always angry at you. Sam wasn't even thinking about you when he ran into you in the pool. He was thinking about swimming and didn't even see you.

Offending children should also be included in the discussion to communicate to angry youngsters that the former's intent was not hostile.

While violent adolescents know the difference between accidental and intentional behaviors, they are quick to see themselves as being challenged. They interpret others' remarks as belittling even if the others were only boasting or insisting on their own viewpoint in a discussion. They view these comments as challenges to their self-esteem. Their pride is at stake, and they feel called upon to repeatedly prove themselves. The incidents that spark violent attacks often are trivial. When they are angry, violent adolescents aim to hurt others with little regard for the consequences, but later they realize that fighting can get them into serious trouble.[4]

In such situations adults have to back off quickly, or swiftly remove other children who are the target of the aggression.

ADULT: I realize you feel Patrick insulted you and you'd like to hurt him for it. But consider the source—it's only Patrick. To hit him might make him look like he's right, and you know he's not. He probably didn't mean anything by it anyway. It was just a thoughtless remark.

Directive Techniques of Prevention

The setting of limits, if done in a responsible and consistent manner, is an effective way to curtail crisis situations with violent children. When children are losing control of themselves, they look for someone to provide them with limits. Limits make them feel safe. They define what they can and cannot do. One caution in limit setting: Be prepared to enforce the limits you set. Failure to do so will cancel out your effectiveness. Make sure the limits you set are enforceable and reasonable.

Many teachers make defiant children "sit minutes," either inside or outside the classroom: "If you don't finish your work, you'll have to sit for two minutes." This type of limit setting has three advantages. First, it specifies to the children what they can and cannot do. Second, it gives them private time to pull themselves together. Third, it's no fun, and the children soon wish to return to the group activities, this time with improved behavior.

Another effective technique is to provide alternatives. If defiant children are given the option to choose from alternatives, they will feel less confronted and ordered about. They will feel they have some say-so in the decision. Often they choose one of the options, and the crisis is avoided.

For example, an anxious, uneasy child arrives in class and announces that he is not going to do any work that day. If the teacher responds, "Oh, yes you are! Sit down at that desk and do your math, right now!" the student may walk out the door. But if the teacher says, "You can do your math. Or maybe you'd rather do your language lesson first. Which of these would you like to choose?" Given these choices, the student may pick one of them, and a crisis will be defused. Keep things simple for the child; don't provide more than two or three options. Most important, let the child know what the consequences will be if he declines to accept the choices offered.

Get to the Root of the Problem

Remember that children who come in angry come in with a problem. Problems typically render children helpless. They respond to helpless feelings with efforts to feel in charge, and often their take-charge methods result in conflicts with authority. While adults can make compromises with defiant children, the children's need to feel all-powerful may override these efforts. Adults must help these children to verbalize what is bothering them so that the cycle of defiance can be broken.

When under pressure, we often forget basic principles. Remember that our goal is to understand children, to burrow beneath the surface talk and deal with their real problem. Children are adept at throwing up smokescreens when they are troubled about something. Side-step the diversions and get to the root of the problem. Empathy is essential.

For example, if a child has just cursed a classmate over a seemingly trivial incident, you might want to say, "Cursing isn't nice," or "Cursing is against the rules." You would have missed the boat. The real issue is not the cursing, it's the child's anger. You need to find out what is bothering him.

> ADULT: Gee, Mike, I'm concerned about your anger. I may be wrong, but it's over something that doesn't seem important to me. I wonder what you're really mad at. Could it be . . .

An empathic approach can often cut through the angry words and threats and help children become aware of the real reason for their fury.

Most angry and defiant children are bewildered and confused. Their emotions surge up within them in a frightening way. Amidst this jumble of conflicting emotions, they experience difficulty controlling themselves. When children can sort out their confusion and label the different feelings that contribute to their bewilderment, they can control themselves better.

When you are faced with screaming and cursing children, realize that many times the anger is not the result of the momentary frustration they experience, but the end result of deeper and entirely different issues. The anger is a displacement. When these children discover what the real issue is, they usually calm down. Often their discovery follows your remarks to them, but they will rarely acknowledge you guessed correctly. They go away silent, and you wonder what the "exact thing" was you said that turned the tide. Their only response is, "I want to go back to class, now."

One child care worker described how she penetrated a young girl's smokescreen of defiance:

Shannon, a newcomer to the residence, was having difficulty feeling accepted by the other children. Just before Shannon entered the residence, her grandmother died, and Shannon had apparently never verbalized anything about this death.

The pressure of withholding (not ventilating) these two issues surfaced during an incredible physical outburst when she threw things all over her room. This occurred after she was informed that she could not go on a field trip due to an incident that had occurred during school. She wanted me, I thought, to restrain her guilt at possible responsibility for her grandmother's death. We had discussed this before at great length in a team meeting, so I was aware of it.

My partner took all the other children aside and I directed Shannon to her room. She kept yelling, "Let go of me!" even though I wasn't even touching her. You could tell that she was trying to set me up for a physical confrontation.

Finally, Shannon broke down and started to cry. She embraced me and began weeping about how she loved her grandmother. This was totally unrelated to how the incident began—being refused permission to go on a field trip. This was her way of letting things out. Then she cried about how nobody liked her in the dorm, as well as how her grandmother didn't really like her and that's why she left.

During this incident, I felt like I had provided a safe outlet for Shannon.[5]

Listed below are some common themes which emerge in our crisis counseling sessions with children. As the children's messages unfold, the meaning of their tantrums becomes clearer.

• A privilege is taken away from a child. The child perceives that there was some unfairness, and his anger erupts in another setting.

• Similarly, a child does not get his way in one situation and his anger at this carries over into another situation.

• A child wants to avoid an unpleasant situation that is coming up in the near future. Perhaps she doesn't want to go to gym or swimming; or perhaps it's Friday afternoon and she doesn't want to go home.

• Traumatic past events can interfere with a child's daily functioning.

• A child misses a significant adult in his life, either to death, divorce, or other separation. He harbors anger over this loss.

• A child acts aggressively when her academic work is not matched to her ability—whether it's too easy or too difficult, or not matched to her perception of her ability (which is usually markedly different from reality).

• Missing a meal makes a child anxious and angry.

• A minority youngster or socially deprived child experiences anger and suffering over the intolerable living conditions in his home or neighborhood.

• A child who is being abused at home comes to school angry and takes her anger out indirectly on others. She lashes out at the teacher and other students.

• In residential treatment centers or foster homes, many outbursts are triggered by problems at home or contacts with home.

• A child tests a new situation.

• A child is apprehensive about leaving a situation that has meant security to him.

Children who are prone to angry outbursts usually are those with low frustration tolerance. Such lack of tolerance can be situational (death or divorce in the family) or could be the result of long-standing problems. With chronic thwarted intentions and unfulfilled expectations, children develop a set of attitudes that influences their thinking when they are frustrated:

• The task is too hard.

• It is easier to do tomorrow.

• I deserve good things to happen to me.

• Other people should make life easier for me.

- I can't do that because I'm stupid.
- I must have certainty to perform well.
- I must have what I want *now*.
- I can't do what I don't want to do.
- There is an easier way to do this.
- I have a right to dump my angry feelings on people.
- I can't stand to be anxious.

When children are about to erupt, you can't attack these attitudes, but you can work from them to defuse the situation.

ADULT: Look, Kim, if you're really that angry you can do that work later. Choose something else for now.

or

ADULT: Okay, don't do them all. Do the first three.

or

ADULT: Wally will pitch it better next time, or I'll pitch a couple for you that will be right over the plate.

While such tactics can make you feel you're backing down, not doing so will result in an escalation of anger. By backing off and taking another tack, you gradually get the children to work at adult-initiated tasks. You are capable of flexibility—they are not.

Know Your Children

Understanding defiant children will help you deal with them. But understanding takes time, and time is a scarce commodity. Teachers in large school systems may see as many as one hundred different students a day. Nursing staff in a hospital may find children entrusted to their care before the needed background material has reached the unit. Even small, intensively staffed programs, because of the volume of service demands, can find it difficult to acquire a sound knowledge of each child.

Taking the initiative and identifying the children who may be "at risk" in regard to defiant outbursts are preventive measures. Some things you should know about the children in your care include

- issues they are facing in their lives
- positive qualities they respond to
- their families
- when ignoring is helpful
- what activities and materials are reinforcing for them
- their abilities and how they can be led to succeed
- the time of day when they seem most prone to aggression

- who their friends are, and those with whom they don't get along
- their condition of health or their medical history.

Thoughtful reflections on these questions can prepare you to avert a crisis situation in the beginning stages of a child's defiant behavior.

Many times children in special education settings are receiving medication to help them respond to the program. Know when children are on medication and what to look for when it works. Seek consultation. For example, if children are taking Ritalin, missing their dosage in the morning may make them inattentive by the time they arrive at school. This in turn may make them more defiant and prone to become involved in disruptive incidents. Knowing this helps you to plan your intervention strategy.

Because we really don't understand how most psychotropic drugs work, careful monitoring is essential. If a dosage is off by the smallest amount—even a few milligrams—acting out behavior on the child's part may increase. If a child has been placed on one of the major tranquilizers such as Mellaril, Haldol, Stelazine, or Thorazine, it is extremely important to fine-tune and calibrate the proper dosage. Some medical authorities say that in no other branch of medicine, except perhaps treatment for allergies, is the range of side effects and behavioral responses to dosages as variable as in the field of psychiatry. A doctor must continue to carefully adjust each prescription in response to regular feedback from those who have the most contact with a child. Sometimes busy physicians do not have the time to initiate contact with those in the child's life who may be a resource in evaluating the medical plan. You may need to take initiative in this area.[6]

Another related area is the significant amount of substance abuse by today's high school and junior high school students. Students sometimes come to class under the influence of marijuana or some other narcotic substance. Particularly with defiant children, being "stoned" may make their adaptation to the classroom more unpredictable. Knowing that students are involved in substance abuse contributes to a better understanding of them and can help you make more effective interventions should they become defiant or unruly.

Knowing Yourself

Equally important as knowing your children is knowing yourself. Recognize the situations or the particular children to which you're especially vulnerable.

Psychodynamic therapists emphasize countertransference, which occurs when children make the adult feel emotions not warranted by the situation. For example, you might feel generally irritated by particular children and not know why. Perhaps you view their barrage of defiance as a deliberate attempt to show you up, when it is actually the children's way of boosting their own feelings of inadequacy.

Violent youths stir up many feelings in helpers. Because they often respond to sympathy and reason as contemptuous efforts to control and dominate, even professionals reject them as "untreatable" and refer them to security settings. Those required to work with violent youths often experience a strong desire to punish them. They heap restrictions, suspensions, time-outs, and isolations upon them: "Dick needs to learn not to hit people. He should be restricted from all fun activities until he shows a willingness to deal with his problems without fighting." Heavy punishment of defiant children often only makes them more defiant and delays the application of an effective course of treatment.[7]

Sometimes we want to send defiant children elsewhere, but it may not be in their best interest to transfer them to another program. Sometimes we must make the best of troublesome children in our care whom we secretly wish might be reassigned elsewhere. In such cases seek help from your colleagues.

It is comforting to recognize that perhaps all who work with defiant youngsters have found themselves in situations in which adult composure had nearly been lost. In crises query yourself about the variety and intensity of emotions triggered in you by the children with whom you work.

• Are there children toward whom I feel an immediate, intuitive aversion?

• Are there children that make me exceptionally angry?

• Do I feel especially drained after working with a particular child?

• Are there children that I'm afraid of? Is this fear well grounded?

• Am I experiencing a bad day and thus am not responding to the child as I normally would?

• Do I find myself being sarcastic toward a child or about a child, particularly in a noncrisis situation?

Thinking about such questions helps you determine if you are losing your objectivity, and taking out your feelings indirectly and inappropriately on the child.

Another way to better understand both children and yourself is to examine the role of antecedents and consequences in crisis situations. Very few defiant children explode simultaneously, in a vacuum, without connection to other people or events. When the crisis is over, sit down with other people who are involved in the situation. Ask questions of yourself and your coworkers:

• What was the chain of events that led to the children's defiance?

• What effect, positive or negative, did my intervention have on this process?

• Could I have done something differently?

• What were the core issues being expressed by the children in their torrent of angry words and actions?

• What approaches can be used in the future?

Getting Assistance

Knowing yourself means knowing when you need a backup person. Rather than being a sign of defeat or failure, it is a sign of strength to know when you need help. No one can handle repeated crises without being affected. Many people in teaching or the helping professions feel both a need to help others and a need to set exacting, demanding standards for their own performance. Yet even with the best intentions and crisis intervention skills, encounters with defiant children may not work out the way we want or expect them to. Sometimes the situation is out of control—by definition, that's a crisis! Asking someone to step in for you at a time of weariness or frustration can be beneficial for both you and the situation. Doing this prevents bitterness and burnout.

Physical Interventions

Most children in regular schools rarely require physical intervention to keep them under control. Verbal techniques usually are enough to prevent a tantrum from escalating into a full-scale physical confrontation. In addition, legal statutes must be carefully considered before making a decision to use physical intervention.

Children referred from public schools to special settings—hospitals, special education classes, residential schools, or day treatment facilities—often are seriously imparied in their ability to control themselves. They possess the capacity to harm. As a result, there are situations in which a nonphysical crisis intervention approach is clearly inappropriate. When children hit or throw objects at others, verbal interven-

tion will often be ineffective and can make the situation worse. Therefore keep the following points in mind: (1) Always remember that any
physical intervention has as its goal the *care and treatment* of the children. That way the intervention is more likely to be therapeutic. (2)
Know safe restraining and carrying techniques which will convey to
the children that you are in control of them. This requires special
training, practice, and certification. (We recommend the training program offered by the Crisis Prevention Institute.)[8] (3) Be decisive and
don't show ambivalence when you restrain a child. Children are extremely sensitive to cues and will often intensify their defiant behavior
if they sense uncertainty. (4) Once you begin a physical intervention,
be capable of carrying it through. (5) Have a partner, a person available on call, or be part of a team in carrying out the intervention. (6)
Provide intensive follow-up counseling. Talk with these children about
what has happened. Explain to them why the adults needed to use
physical restraint. Help them look at ways of handling their frustration
in a nonviolent manner in the future. Make the crisis a tool in teaching
children to be more effective in dealing with important life issues.

Understanding and Enabling Extremely Defiant and Physically Aggressive Children

Children deal with anxiety by attempting to actively handle the
events that they experience. The crises described in this book generate
great anxiety in children. Children who have been abused, or sent from
foster home to foster home, or who have experienced the death or divorce of their parents without adequate support, may deal with their
sense of helplessness by becoming aggressive themselves. They need to
feel powerful to cope with their sense of vulnerability and aloneness.
Interestingly, 75 percent of extremely defiant children—those placed in
special settings—are boys.

These children often internalize a view of adults as policeman/ag-
gressor rather than as protector/provider. They weave a protective co-
coon: They anticipate blame, accusation, and punishment and forestall
them by being threatening to adults. To be controlled by others is to be
humiliated.

Because of the absence of nurturance, protection, and prideful experiences of pleasing and being pleased, defiant children feel rage characteristic of earlier phases of their development. They scream and flail
like two-year-olds, and they can be dangerous. Their rage blocks the

development of conscience. Fear of punishment does not deter their misbehavior, and they are not easily socialized. Aggression is readily displaced onto others. When they hurt another, they show no sign of remorse, concern, or empathy with the victim, since they do not expect like responses from others when they are hurt. Their fantasy is limited to the violent kind—Batman, Superman, and the Hulk are their models.

These children often require a structured and controlled environment. They need

• to be protected and rescued from situations in which they feel frightened
• to avoid experiences involving loss of face
• to have restraints and prohibitions that are predictable
• to have punishment limited
• to talk about frustrations
• to have a broadened horizon of "do's"
• to expand concrete skills
• to have dependable relationships with others
• to receive nurturance and acceptance along with clear, consistent, and well-defined limits.

Adults may balk at the thought of protecting extremely defiant children, but sometimes that is precisely what these children need. They usually start fights because they fear attacks from others.

Our initial rescue attempts can be as simple as breaking up fights without placing blame and administering to cuts and bruises no matter how small. Refrain from comments like "Big boys don't cry," or "Don't be silly. A tough guy like you doesn't need a Band Aid for that tiny scratch!" They've been rebuffed in that manner too many times before. Let them cry and give them a Band Aid! When you impose limits on their aggressive behavior, stress that you want to help them to stop hitting and learn to talk about their anger, rather than continually punish them.

When children begin to develop internal controls, you will find them checking with adults before they do things. ("Is this right?" or "Can I . . . ?") Their ability to delay their action marks the first step in the development of control. It reflects their desire to please rather than their fear of punishment. When they lose their temper, it will be less violent. They will be more focused on others and will sound possessive: "My friend . . . ," "My teacher . . . ," "My counselor. . . ."

Sometimes adults are frustrated at this stage because these children act like babies one moment and tough guys the next. It's difficult to baby a tough guy. Don't respond to babyish behavior with sarcasm. Allow it, even encourage it. Your commitment will be tested; the children will demand that you stay with them, guide them, and tolerate their moodiness. Stick with them. With your support, they will eventually begin to concentrate longer, take pleasure in activities, and control themselves to please you. Remember—they've never pleased anyone before.

As your trusting relationship matures, the defiant children's conscience will develop and their control of impulses will increase. With control comes satisfying involvement in activities and investment in learning. They begin to feel they want to do what the caring adult wishes. They develop trust in their good impulses and in their ability to control or mitigate their aggressive urges.

Throughout this process remember that every setback is difficult for defiant children. Since they expect failure, they see every new activity as a threat. Reflect these feelings and encourage growth: "It's real hard for you to try new things because you will feel bad if you fail. But you need to try. I'll stick with you no matter what."

Working with extremely defiant youngsters is time-consuming and emotionally draining, but even the smallest successes make it worthwhile.

Don't Give Up

In this chapter we have presented approaches that nonprofessional counselors, as well as parents and professionals, will find helpful. Unfortunately, there will be children for whom none of the approaches seem to have a significant effect. Some children live in areas of such intolerable poverty and social deprivation that even the most skilled helper will feel powerless when faced with the defiance and aggression that are engendered. Sometimes you can do everything right, and it's still not enough. We are reminded of the story, *Ciske, the Rat.* Here, a teacher visits a jail in which a pupil to whom he has devoted much attention is imprisoned. The boy had murdered his mother:

> I saw Ciske sitting on a wooden bench. He was swinging his legs, exactly like a boy who is momentarily bored during vacation. Here he was, my pupil. I had given my whole heart to the boy and had been unable to prevent fate from striking him down.[9]

We cannot protect children from life, and we can't always shield ourselves from failure and disappointment. But never underestimate the value of one positive relationship in the life of a child. Most defiant children can be taught cooperation, and the energy and activities of even extremely defiant and disturbed youths often can be rechanneled in positive, constructive directions. Keep trying.

· 12 ·

Alcohol Issues

> When you play dominoes, if one piece falls it
> can knock over all the other pieces. Alcohol
> is like that, too.

At first we were going to title this chapter "Working with
Children of Alcoholics." Especially during the past decade,
there has been a movement among mental health professionals to
address the specific needs of "children of alcoholics," both child
and adult. In thinking about the topic, however, we realized that
alcohol affects not only those individuals where it is a family
concern, but each person must decide whether or not to use alcohol
as part of growing up. Alcohol affects many people also through the
numerous tragedies that are associated with it. For example, over
20,000 persons die each year in alcohol-related accidents. Alcohol
is also implicated in many situations of violence involving weapons.
All of these things make it clear that anyone who works with
children and adolescents will at some point be talking with them
about alcohol. Whether as teachers in class, therapists in a counseling session, or parents, this is one topic that cannot be avoided.

Because alcohol lowers inhibitions, it is also associated with
child abuse—both physical abuse and incest. Consequently, readers are referred to the chapters on "Child Abuse" and "Sexual

Abuse" for further interventions when these are occurring in conjunction with alcohol. Interestingly, mental health professionals themselves may gloss over the role of alcohol in an abusive situation. For example, in one large agency twenty child abuse reports were examined to see if the clinician discovered an alcohol problem. Only in *one* of these was alcohol viewed as a problem. The research would suggest that a large number of these twenty cases would have alcohol problems, and it seems that the clinicians were not asking directly about this.

Recent surveys indicate that over twenty-eight million Americans have an alcoholic parent. This means that in a typical group of children, one in eight will come from a family where alcohol is a major concern, and studies also indicate that these youngsters are much more at risk in developing alcohol problems themselves.

Mark Twain wrote eloquently about the impact of alcohol on children in *Adventures of Huckleberry Finn*. Huck's father was an alcoholic—a "mean drunk" who used to hit Huck. Huck Finn was the "child of an alcoholic" almost a hundred years before this phrase came into use in clinical work.

In this chapter, we examine how alcohol usage affects children in families, and study supportive stances that can be taken with these children. We also consider other ways that alcohol affects the lives of children and adolescents, and how to talk with them about this. For concerned adults as well as counselors and therapists, it is important to understand the role of Alcoholics Anonymous and Al-Anon, so our chapter concludes by reviewing the principles of these very helpful organizations.

How Children Feel

Children in all age groups regress to the magic-years level thinking of "I caused it" when they try to figure out why it is that mom or dad drinks. Many alcoholic parents reinforce this false belief by their accusations aimed at the children. Many children try to think of ways that they can help stop their parents from drinking. One little boy poured his father's hard liquor down the drain when his father was away; thinking that this would help, he became even more disillusioned when he received a beating from his father. The mischief of childhood, rollickings between siblings, or understandable crankiness all become, for the child, reasons why the parent drinks too much. In all instances, children believe that they are at fault for their parents' drinking, a belief laden in stress and anxiety.

The Magic Years

Many parents think children who are this young do not notice parental drinking. They do!—and often attribute their own misdeeds as the cause of this.

Further, they are not exposed to appropriate models of parenting. A young boy will think that yelling is part of normal masculinity if his father is always yelling. One four-year-old boy came with his family to see the therapist; he had been referred because of his belligerent behavior in school. During the family meeting he turned to his mother and swore. The therapist was at first taken aback, but regained sufficient composure to ask, "Who else speaks like that?" to be answered with a resounding, "Daddy!"

Because alcoholic fathers often fail to perform many of the normal parenting tasks, the child's separation from the mother is hampered by the father's unavailability and disorganized behavior.

When it is the mother who is alcoholic, the child often never learns what it means to have a loving and giving mother. The parental drinking causes both emotional and physical distance, and this can cripple emotional development.

Sometimes both parents drink. (In fact, some relationships have been based on drinking. Some couples have met in a bar and much of their relationship involves shared inebriation.) For children with parents in these circumstances, life is indeed difficult.

Even more serious is the posttraumatic stress disorder that can occur in families with severe alcoholism. Timmen Cermak has written about how alcoholism in a family can have a more traumatic effect on a child than participation in warfare does for the adult. In "A Time to Heal" he writes:

> Being subjected to combat in Vietnam and being held hostage in an alcoholic home as a child are both stressful enough to create symptoms of post-traumatic stress disorder. Luke, the Vietnam veteran, continues to have vivid images of the smells and sounds he experienced as he knelt next to his buddy and saw his shredded windpipe filling with blood. You may have vivid images of the smells and the sounds you experienced as you knelt next to a

drunk parent in the middle of the living room floor, listening carefully to his breathing, wondering if he were still alive. You may have carefully covered your parent with a blanket and sat there shivering with fear while you waited for someone else to come home. The degrees of stress that children of alcoholics experience must be understood through the eyes of a child, not just through the eyes of an adult.[1]

Adults always need to remember how traumata are magnified many times in the eyes of a child. For example, one man received a medical discharge from Vietnam because the fighting reminded him of his early childhood as an abused child, and evoked flashbacks of being hit by his mother with a stick. Because he was a helpless child when his mother hit him, this was even more frightening to him than the actual experience of combat.

The Middle Years

A common characteristic of nearly all middle years children is the tendency to try to cover up the parental drinking when talking to outsiders. In one group for Children of Alcoholics, all the youngsters in the group acknowledged that they would "lie" to cover up for their parent's alcoholism. One little boy used to say that his father was "sleeping" and kept his playmates away with that excuse, adding that his Daddy worked very hard on his nighttime job.

Children in the middle years have been learning about alcohol through the media, through programs in school, and from discussions with adults in their lives. A recent study of over 800 children ages ten to thirteen indicated that:

• Most know that alcoholism runs in families.

• Most children in the fifth, sixth, and seventh grade think that alcoholism is a bad habit; even 37 percent of eighth graders say that it is a bad habit rather than an illness.

• Most children think people become alcoholics because they do not care about themselves. Only 40 percent recognize a connection between alcoholism and different body responses to alcohol.

• Most agree that alcoholics need help to stop drinking.

• Most think that those who live with alcoholism are lonely, angry, and sad.

• One-third of children think that families without alcoholism are problem-free.

• Most children say they can help their friends by talking with them about ways children can help théir alcoholic parent stop drinking.

• Most children do not know that there are nearly thirty million children of alcoholics in the United States.[2]

There are important implications for counselors from these findings. On the positive side, children acknowledge the risk of alcoholism that runs in families. However, most middle years children display a remarkable naïveté about the nature of alcoholism. They tend to equate it with a bad habit, or view alcoholism as something that "bad" people develop or that those who have "bad" children acquire. Here again we see the regression to thought patterns of the magic years. Some youngsters even confuse alcoholism with other diseases, such as AIDS, and wonder if they can catch it.

"Children also need to know that children cannot make their parents stop drinking," writes Migs Woodside in her article, "What Children Believe." "This myth puts an unbearable burden on children of alcoholics. . . . There is no magic cure to end parental alcoholism, but with education and prevention, children's pain and suffering can be relieved and the risks of future alcoholism can be reduced."

Children in the middle years may have specific questions about alcohol, and supportive adults can answer their questions with as much information as possible.

It is disconcerting to learn that many children learn to drink during their preadolescent years. It is now known that:

• Nearly 100,000 ten– and eleven-year-olds reported getting drunk at least once a week in 1985.

• About one-third of fourth graders (nine-year-olds) said children their age pressured others to drink beer, wine, or liquor, and this figure increased to 80 percent by high school.

• At present, first drinking usually occurs around age twelve, in contrast to age thirteen to fourteen in the 1940s and 1950s.

• A child will see alcohol consumed an average of 75,000 times on TV before he or she is of legal drinking age.[3]

In all of the above ways, alcohol affects not only children in families where there is alcoholism, but exposes children in all families to the effects of alcohol, and will cause them to have questions about these effects on the caring adults in their lives.

The fear of being found out is a common fear of middle years youngsters in alcoholic families. At a day treatment center, one eleven-year-old boy never brought the friends he made at school home because of his father's explosions and tirades while drinking.

In fact, *shame* is one of the most important issues to deal with in children of all ages who have an alcoholic problem in their family. Their shame makes them feel different and alienated from others. It makes them feel unworthy of the friendships or relationships that are so crucial to growing up. Their shame leads them to feel that they are unlovable and the cause of all their family problems. A sensitivity to and understanding of the shame that runs in families where alcoholism exists will be immensely helpful to those who work with these children.

Withdrawal is another common response in middle years children. Since children are too small and powerless to change the situation in an alcoholic family, and do not yet have the skills to leave the family (as an adolescent might), they are apt to remove themselves emotionally from other people and events. This state of apathy can become chronic and can generalize the school and other social relationships.

Adolescence

Adolescents experience an incredible pressure to indulge in drinking behavior. The media constantly are bombarding them with images that drinking is sexy, prestigious, and the "in thing" to do. Every year it seems that younger and younger children experiment with alcohol. Some observers of the social scene have noted that as drug usage has declined from the late 1960s and early 1970s, abuse of alcohol has increased. For many teens, learning how to drink is viewed as one of the rights of passage into adulthood.

Teenagers who have grown up in alcoholic family systems may react to continued parental drinking as "the straw that breaks the camel's back." Many times this will add to or precipitate the desire to run away. The normal "disillusionment" of adolescence is magnified many times when a teenager finally concludes that one of his parents has had a lengthy problem with alcohol. In the story of Huck Finn, it appears that Huck spent his entire life from adolescence on running away from the effect of his father's drinking.

Unfortunately for Huck and the other teens like him, when you "run from" something you consolidate your identity around "avoid-ing" and not on constructive "doing." Growing up in an alcoholic family can engender an outlook of avoidance rather than participa-tion or commitment.

It is helpful for adults who work with adolescents to understand also some of the facts of alcohol as related to usage by adolescents. The National Council on Alcoholism reports that:

• About 10,000 young people aged sixteen to twenty-four are killed each year in alcohol-related accidents of all kinds, including drownings, suicides, violent homicides, and injuries from fire.

• Lower expectations for the future, as well as alienation and boredom, are associated with those who drink.

• Alcohol-related highway deaths are the number one killer of fifteen to twenty-five-year-olds.

• It takes less alcohol to produce impairment in youth than in adults.

• Of 27,000 New York public school students, grades seven through twelve, 11 percent describe themselves as being "hooked" on alcohol, with 13 percent admitting to attending classes while "high" or "drunk."[4]

Especially in view of this last statistic, it is important to look for alcohol issues in those students who are at-risk for dropping out. There are many dropout prevention programs that are being de-veloped in high schools, and many of these have strong links with Al-Anon and with alcoholism counselors in the community.

Involvement in Alateen

Making teenagers aware of Alateen, and of specific Alateen groups in the community, can provide these youngsters with a sometimes-invaluable resource in coping with a drinking problem in the family. The following narrative, printed with permission from Al-Anon Family Group Headquarters,* while directed at teenagers themselves, also provides adults who work with them a view of how these teenagers feel about drinking in their family.[5]

*You may contact Alateen or Al-Anon by looking in your local tele-phone directory, or writing: Al-Anon Family Group, P.O. Box 862, Mid-town Station, New York, NY 10018-0812.

Do You Need Alateen?

Do you have a parent, close friend, or relative with a drinking problem?

Do you feel you got a rotten break in life?

Do you hate one or both of your parents?

Have you lost respect for your nonalcoholic parent?

Do you try to get even with your parents when you think they have been unfair?

Are you ashamed of your home?

Do you wish that your home could be more like the homes of your friends?

Do you lose your temper a lot?

Do you sometimes say and do things you don't want to but can't help yourself?

Do you have trouble concentrating on school work?

Do you resent having to do jobs around the house that you think your parents should be doing?

Are you afraid to let people know what you're really like?

Do you sometimes wish you were dead?

Are you starting to think it would be nice to forget your problems by taking drugs or getting drunk?

Is it hard for you to talk to your parents? Do you talk to them at all?

Do you go to extremes to get people to like you?

Do you believe no one could possibly understand how you feel?

Do you feel you make your alcoholic parent drink?

Do you get upset when your parents fight?

Do you stay out of the house as much as possible because you hate it there?

Do you avoid telling your parents the truth?

Do you worry about your parents?

Are you nervous or scared a lot of the time?

Do you resent the alcoholic's drinking?

Do you feel nobody really loves you or cares what happens to you?

Do you feel like a burden to your parents?

Do you sometimes do strange or shocking things to get attention?

Do you cover up your real feelings by pretending you don't care?

Do you take advantage of your parents when you know you can get away with it?

IF YOU ANSWERED "YES" TO SOME OF THE ABOVE QUESTIONS AND ARE CLOSE TO SOMEONE WITH A DRINKING PROBLEM, ALATEEN MAY HELP YOU.

Alateen, Al-Anon, and Alcoholics Anonymous

Sometimes the best thing that a concerned adult can do is to refer a child, teenager, or adult to one of these programs. Alcoholics Anonymous is a group program for adults with alcohol problems. Alateen focuses on teenagers who have a drinking problem. Al-Anon is for family members and friends who may be affected by the heavy drinking of someone they love. These meetings are free and are sponsored by a wide range of organizations across the country. Many times there will be a weekly listing in the neighborhood paper concerning all the meetings in a given area.

These three organizations center around "twelve steps" such as these in AA: The first, "We admitted we were powerless over alcohol," through the last, "Having had a spiritual awakening as a result of these steps, we tried to carry this message to alcoholics, and to practice these principles in all our affairs." Probably the best way to experience the twelve steps is to attend an actual meeting of AA, Alateen, or Al-Anon, or to accompany someone you are concerned about to one of these meetings.

Suggested Reading

Ackerman, R. *Children of Alcoholics: A Guide for Parents, Educators, and Therapists.* Second Edition. New York: Simon and Schuster, 1987.

Alcohol Fact Sheet. New York: National Council on Alcoholism, 1976.

Black, C. *It Will Never Happen to Me!* Denver: M.A.C., 1981.

Brooks, C. *The Secret Everyone Knows.* Calif.: Operation Cork, 1981.

Coates, M., and Paech, G. *Alcohol and Your Patient: A Nurse's Handbook.* Toronto: Addiction Research Foundation, 1979.

Forrest, G. G. *Diagnosis and Treatment of Alcoholism.* Springfield, Ill.: Charles C. Thomas, 1975.

Gravitz, H. L., and Bowden, J. D. *Guide to Recovery: A Book for Adult Children of Alcoholics.* Holmes Beach, Fla: Learning Publications, 1985.

Hornik, E. L. *You and Your Alcoholic Parent.* New York: Association Press, 1974.

Ryerson, E. *When Your Parent Drinks Too Much: A Book of Help for Children and Teenagers.* New York: Warner Books, 1985.

Whitfield, C. *Healing the Child Within.* Hollywood, Fla.: Health Communications, 1987.

Woititz, J. *Adult Children of Alcoholics.* Hollywood, Fla.: Health Communications, 1983.

· 13 ·

Sexual Abuse

I still see the shadow in the darkness
of the night from the bed where
warmth and safety should have
been my given right.

INCEST VICTIM

Individual and mass rape have been recorded since biblical times. Yet before the women's movement, the devastating effects of rape were overlooked by mental health professionals. Two common beliefs prevailed: First, that the victim was sexually provocative or was acting out unconscious fantasies of rape; and second, that the trauma was minimal and resulted from exacerbation of preexisting problems. When teenagers were raped, these same attitudes prevailed. But when we learned that very young children of both sexes were being sexually abused, we could no longer "blame the victim," and our attitudes changed. By sexual abuse we mean an adult or person five years older than the child who uses the child as an object for sexual satisfaction regardless of the acts performed.

Studies of the symptoms common to women who were victims of forcible rape led to a syndrome named "rape trauma syndrome." Most victims were considered emotionally healthy and to be experiencing a crisis. The acceptable intervention was crisis counseling, issue-oriented and supportive. Symptoms were viewed as normal coping responses to the assault. Long-term counseling was not viewed as necessary and seen as supporting a "blame-the-victim" concept.[1] Yet the trauma of rape can include the threat of death, massive environmental assault, violation of bodily boundaries, activation of unconscious conflicts and fantasies, disruption of important relationships, and loss of feelings of control—all insults unlikely to respond to brief counseling techniques. Follow-up studies of rape victims do not confirm recovery following crisis intervention counseling, as many remained symptomatic and reorganized their personalities around the symptoms, conflicts, and defenses activated by the trauma. Yet rape and child abuse are not synonymous. If the child is a teenager and forcibly raped, the situation may be similar. But what if the child is "raped" over time by her father, a person who is supposed to care for and look after her needs? What if the rapist is the mother's boyfriend upon whom the mother depends for financial and emotional support? And what if rape is not involved, but the child is young and required to fondle her father, an uncle, or someone else known to the child? We are just beginning to learn about the long-term consequences of such abuse upon children.

In general, we know that abuse by a stranger is less traumatic than abuse by a family member, and that those abused over long periods display serious difficulty handling life's challenges. We also know that all children experience events differently so that the actual act committed against the child can be less important than the child's interpretation of the experience. Some children are more upset following fondling than are others following intercourse. Some children are more upset by what happens following their revelation of the abuse than by the abuse itself. Family life is disrupted; some are removed from the home; others are punished, treated with contempt, and forced to recant; interviewing doctors and counselors are viewed as punishers by some; and still others become involved in lengthy court proceedings.

Those studying the effects of abuse classify its occurrence along a number of dimensions, which, taken alone or together, may influence the child's functioning.

1. *Type of abuse*—what activity took place.
2. *Duration*—how long the abuse occurred.
3. *Age at onset*—the age when the abuse began.
4. *Frequency*—how often the abusive contact took place.
5. *Identity of the perpetrator*—was the abuser a stranger, famil-

iar person, trusted person, distant relative, close relative, or step- or quasi-relative (i.e., mother's or father's lover)?

6. *Consensual or nonconsensual*—whether the child initiated, freely participated, was coerced or submitted to the activities (most agree that contact is never consensual in cross-generational incest because of the power and authority of the adult over the child).

7. *Use of force*—includes threats made to the child as well as physical assault.

Experiences that are of long duration, involve frequent contact, occur with a parent, are nonconsensual, and involve use of force are believed to cause the most severe psychological aftereffects. Nevertheless, evidence suggests that the child's response to abuse is more often related to a whole host of other factors than it is to any of the seven variables listed above. For example, the attention a young girl receives from her abusing father may compensate in part for a strained relationship with her mother who she may be "parenting" herself. Yet the need for secrecy may result in the family's isolation from outsiders. The insulation of the family can result in the father's becoming even more dominating. He may monitor phone calls and come to control all communications between the family and the community. The daughter, angered by her father's limitations, reports the abuse in retaliation. She does so in spite of her past feelings of favoritism.

Contrast this with the child who receives little attention at home and who seeks out the affectionate pedophile on a regular basis, often bringing friends along when he visits. Both these children may develop long-standing problems related more to the reasons they were abused than to the abuse itself. Children with poor impulse control and those whose parents disagree over the child's expression of sexuality are more prone to be sexually abused.[2] Such children fail to develop a consistent and stable conscience that will prohibit the expression of sexual impulses.

Consider the girl whose mother, jealous of her daughter's developing attractiveness and experiencing her own sexual difficulties, continually refers to her daughter as "a little flirt," or the father, defending himself against his own incestuous desires in an unrewarding relationship with his wife, refers to his daughter as "a little slut." Both girls are higher risks to become sexually abused than are other children. This fact is emphasized, not to cast blame on the child, but to caution the counselor to study thoroughly the backgrounds of abuse victims or victims of suspected abuse. To imply that children are simply the passive victims of abuse and that the trauma of the abuse is what has caused their problems is a naive viewpoint. Many abused children have had significant problems prior to the abuse.

Children will behave seductively for many reasons. For example, when they feel jealous and left out; when they are angry at one parent; they may even cause themselves to be abused to win a parent's sympathy. Frequently, children fantasize sexual activity with an adult. If such activity actually takes place they feel responsible for its occurrence. If the sexual activity occurs with the father or stepfather, the girl may fear her mother's retributions or feel guilty because she has stolen her mother's partner. She also fears discovery because discovery could mean that her mother would lose her husband, or her mother, faced with the choice of rejecting her or her husband, may reject her. "I would end up with no parents."

Remember, however, that children do not fantasize sexual acts that they do not know about. Children, particularly preschoolers, often are accused of having fantasized their contact with the offender. This is rarely the case. The preschooler who reports "the touch felt tingly, it was nice but then he hurt my hiney" is reporting an actual event, not a fantasy.

We must also remember that the child can enjoy sex play and harbor no ill feelings toward the abuser. In addition, some parents who feel guilty about failing to prevent abuse may become overly permissive with their child in an effort to "make up" for the abuse. This attitude can result in the child's experiencing difficulty in mastering developmental tasks, with the parent wrongly attributing the failure to the past abuse, aggravating parental guilt, and furthering parental mismanagement. All these factors need to be considered when counseling abused children. Otherwise, true understanding of the child's difficulties will not occur.

When some gratification results from the experience, the youngster feels both guilt and anxiety that the experience will recur. Typically these feelings are dealt with by dissociating oneself from reflections about and memories of the event. The molested child feels overwhelmed both by the physical overstimulation experienced and by the distortion and confusion of being in the wrong role at the wrong time in relation to the wrong person. If the child is young, the development of self-awareness, self-regulation, and identity formation is impaired. If the child is older, the experience jeopardizes the recasting of these earlier developing structures; such recasting occurs during adolescent separation from parents when ego ideal and identity are consolidated.

If the very parent who abuses, and is experienced as bad, must be turned to for relief of the distress the parent has caused, then the child must, out of desperate need, register the parent—delusionally—as good and himself or herself as bad. In order to survive, the child must keep in some compartment of his or her mind the delusion of good parents and the delusive promise that all terror and pain someday will be transformed into love. The establishment of isolated divisions of the mind results in contradictory images of the self and of the parents. Feeling and trusting are compromised, registration of what has happened and what is happening is compartmentalized. George Orwell describes a similar process in *1984* where brainwashing is used to enforce the delusion of the good "Big Brother." At various times all of us brainwash ourselves, wanting to believe that a situation is better than it really is, that our girlfriend's recent interest in another man is not what it seems to be, or that things will get better simply because we want them to. Why should we be surprised by children who act similarly?

The offender typically behaves as if nothing has happened, consoling himself with the thought that the child is only a child and will forget it all. Since the child cannot understand what has been done to her, her mind is unable to deal with and to work over what is not understood. Enormous confusion accompanies the recovery from each attack. The child feels split—innocent and culpable at the same time—unable to believe what her senses tell her.

If the offender is the father, the following thoughts can run through a victim's mind. What has happened? Who is to blame? Is father bad? Is she herself bad? Mother does not seem to care! Father, so confident of his greatness and rightness, must be good. But how can that be? In one compartment the father is good and right and the child bad and wrong. Yet alongside, in another compartment, is some registration that the father is bad. These mental compartments are walled off and the child is prevented from bringing the contradictory pictures together by the danger that the anger felt will be overwhelming and obliterate the good parent image; but the anger is there, covered over by the presenting symptom picture. The counselor's job is to allow the anger to be expressed in tolerable doses and to correct the child's misconceptions about self and others.

Crisis Counseling versus Long-Term Counseling

Many children referred for counseling following disclosure improve during the initial sessions. Disclosure and discussion of the abuse itself appear therapeutic. Grades improve, somatic complaints lessen, and presenting symptoms abate or vanish. Yet, follow-up reveals that for many children nightmares continue, phobias appear, low self-esteem is experienced, and a polarized reaction to the opposite sex develops (i.e., fearful avoidance appears along with hasty, heedless involvements, particularly in the incest victim). Some incest victims develop superficial coping skills and a pseudomaturity that mask serious problems in interpersonal relationships, chronic anxiety, and depression. Adams-Tucker states:

> Sexual victimization is a psychic injury that requires coping throughout the life of the child. His, or more commonly, her ego is constantly rechallenged with trauma as development ensues, even if actual seduction has ended. The events and memories of them must be grappled with in a different way throughout each stage of childhood.[3]

Most sexually abused children display marked increase in daydreaming and fantasizing, supporting Robert Fliess's position in his disagreement with his father's long-time friend Sigmund Freud. Fliess felt that Freud should not have changed his original view that traumatic memories caused neurosis to one favoring fantasy over memory. Fliess said,

> No one is ever made sick by his fantasies. Only traumatic memories in repression can cause the neurosis. . . . Fantasies, in particular compulsive ones, are a symptom of the disease, never its cause.[4]

For those severely abused, there exists a lifelong *dread* of the return of the traumatic state and an *expectation* of it. Both dread and expectation characterize abused children's fantasies, but often in a disguised form (i.e., fear of accidents). This dread can result in a fear of one's emotions, particularly those related to sexuality and the guilt that accompanies sexual feelings. As a result, abused children actively avoid situations where they think strong emotions may be aroused and inhibit such emotions when they do occur. At the same time, they are compelled to reproduce the trauma in order to master it.

Self-injurious behavior occurs in a number of adolescent incest victims, sometimes to blot out feelings of pleasure from the sexual contact. "Please don't make it feel good." "I'm bad, my body is bad." The dynamics thought to trigger self-abuse result from a punitive conscience that overwhelms the adolescent when facing the stress brought about by the cycle of inhibition, repetition, and inhibition. Children also can act in such a manner that others physically abuse them so that "injury" by others serves the same purpose. The sight of the injury (many perform self-inflicted acts in front of a mirror as they report feeling no pain) followed by a calm, frees the child from the intense guilt feelings, and remobilizes defenses against anxiety.

Abused children resist verbalizing their experiences because they fear reactivation of overwhelming dread. Counseling is also difficult because the cycle of abuse, anxiety, surrender to help-lessness, and numbing results in cognitive constriction. Such con-striction, which impairs self-observation, includes a blocking and dissociation from one's past, making it difficult for even older vic-tims to describe what happened to them and how they felt, and even more so for children whose self-observation skill is poorly de-veloped.

Many sexually abused children, particularly incest victims, will need ongoing counseling or periods of counseling when they react inappropriately to the challenges of different developmental stages. Crisis counseling, however, definitely has its place as children pro-vided with such assistance following the report of abuse fare better than do those not given help. But crisis counseling should include helping abused children to realize that help may be needed at different times in their lives and that seeking help is not a sign of weakness.

Marshal Positive Forces

While this chapter is about counseling the child referred for help following disclosure, some counselors may become involved in interviewing children to verify that the child's reports are valid. Counselors performing this role are referred to Hindman[5] and White[6] for guidelines. Other counselors may be involved in preparing a child for court testimony. While some children testify in family court, most children never testify in criminal court, because of plea bargaining and the absence of adequate evidence to win a conviction. In addition, they rarely testify in incest situations because the nonoffending parent often is unable to support the child through the court process. Plea bargaining occurs because the prosecuting attorney is aware that children can make poor witnesses unless properly prepared to testify. In addition, a child's disclosure usually needs corroboration by inclusive medical evidence of abuse, a witness to the abuse, expert testimony, and a confession by the offender. Therefore, even a good witness is not good enough to achieve a conviction in many cases.

While the details of children's testimony are accurate from their viewpoint, they are perceived as inaccurate from an adult's perspective. Juries are still influenced heavily by "real sex" concepts: "Did he put it in?" and by an attitude that the child must have done something to cause it. Juries, made up of individuals like ourselves, are uncomfortable with child abusers in their midst. They would rather believe that the child simply told a "little lie."

Often offenders are respectable members of the community who have worked with children in some caring capacity (scout masters, Big Brothers, teachers, day-care providers), and neighbors and friends just cannot believe they would do such a thing. Testimonial letters are written to the court on the offender's behalf. "Mr. So-and-So would never do such a thing." Stories are also printed about respectable adults whose lives are ruined by such investigations. Defense attorneys can be intimidating, using a line of questioning designed to make the child appear to be a promiscuous seductress leading the abuser into sexual abuse.

Court testimony, in some cases, can be a positive experience for children regardless of what the jury may decide. Court involvement can be particularly beneficial to older latency aged children and adolescents if they are well prepared for cross-examinations. Such involvement reassures them of the strong stand that parents and society take against offenders and appeals to the strong sense of fairness and justice that characterizes their thinking at this stage of development. Certain superego and ego-ideal standards are reinforced by the court process. Court testimony can be quite traumatic for a child when he or she is asked to testify against one parent while the other parent is still in denial. Nevertheless, the district attorney often will decide not to prosecute a case for lack of credible evidence. Such a decision can result in the child's seeing society as not holding the offender responsible for his own acts. This is a crippling experience for a child. Children thus learn that adults are frequently too weak to stand up for victims, that they view the child as the guilty party, or that society's sexual standards are a sham.

While preparing a child for court testimony occurs infrequently, some of the procedures to be described can be employed in counseling to assist children in understanding what has happened to them. Some of these techniques have been used with children who never testified in court but who wished they had. Such opportunities serve to justify and concretize the anger they feel towards the offender. They can put the offender on trial.

Celebrating the Disclosure
The first step to establish a healthy attitude about the court testimony is in celebrating the disclosure. When children are encouraged to feel positive about their disclosure, they feel better and make better witnesses. During the initial period following disclosure, adults can do any or all of the following:

• Use films and books designed for prevention that speak positively about disclosure (Books, *Speak Up, Say No, A Very Touching Book;* Film, *"Who Do You Tell?"*).

• "The Party," a simple gathering of important people in the child's life who want to participate in a small celebration of the disclosure. This can include other children, known to the counselor, who have disclosed.

• Pen Pals. Encourage other children who have disclosed to write letters to the child to communicate their approval of the disclosure. Teachers, ministers, scout masters, and others can also write expressing their approval.

• Teach parents ways to encourage the child to be proud of their disclosure.

Under some conditions, children should be encouraged to believe that they have an obligation to testify. A number of older children want to testify. They are angry at the offender and when denied the opportunity to testify, this anger never gets fully expressed. Children should never be told that the jury's decision results from their testimony. They should know that a celebration for fulfilling their obligations to testify begins immediately after their own testimony. Children can begin preparing for the celebrations rather than struggling with thoughts about upcoming court procedures.

When the offender is a parent, however, the issue is more complicated, because some mothers threaten to disown their children if they testify against their partner.

Preparing for Testimony

The counselor should prepare children for testimony by familiarizing them with the physical court setting, acquainting them with the prosecuting attorney, and assisting them with their specific testimony. Visits should be made to the courtroom with the supporting parent and hopefully with a peer who has participated in a courtroom experience. These visits should include one when the court is in session for some other purpose. The roles of the judge, attorneys, jurors, bailiff, and others can be explained to the child and the child can role-play their varied responsibilities. The child should also be aware that the offender will be present and a "stuffed doll" can be used in role play to represent this person. The child should also be familiar with the courthouse, learning about hallways and restrooms. A room should be located where the child can wait for the court appearance, to prepare for the celebration, and to return to after giving testimony. The child should collect play materials and toys that can occupy the child while waiting to testify. A pillow and blanket should be available as considerable "waiting time" typically occurs in courts. The child should also be prepared for adjournments and educated to the fact that such postponements are typical of court proceedings.

The child should be acquainted with the prosecuting attorney and his or her role. The counselor informs the child that the attorney likes children and wants to help children who tell the truth about "touching troubles." The children need to understand that they are not "in trouble" and that the prosecutor is concerned about crimes committed against children. Peers who have had experience with the prosecutor can be used to help the child. During the first visit with the prosecutor, the child should bring a drawing, toy, etc., that can be left with the attorney. If you, as counselor, have found certain questions to be helpful in eliciting information from the child, you should share those questions with the attorney.

The child should be given many opportunities to tell about the sexual abuse prior to the hearing or trial. He or she should explain what is remembered in his or her own way. The aim is for the child to feel positive about talking, rather than being coached as to what to say. Children typically reveal their "coaching" in court and their testimony is not accepted. Leading questions are never asked, such as "Did Uncle Bob touch you here?" Such questions cannot be used in court nor should they be used by the counselor. As in any counseling, sessions should not be interrogative. Recantation often occurs when children are repeatedly forced to testify. Counselors' questions can be viewed as pressure to talk. Active listening and carefully chosen questions are critical.

The first step often is to tell the child what has been heard.

ADULT: Children who come to see me are those who have worries and troubles that bother them. Some of these children are those who have been touched in private places and worry about what they feel. But they may not want to get anybody in trouble. They may have been hurt by the touching and been angry and worry that it will happen again. Your grandmother told me that your father touched you with his wiener (a word the child uses for penis).

CHILD: (Silence)

ADULT: It must be hard for you to talk about it, particularly when you don't know me, but it's important for me to know more about it. We can play for a while and when you know me better you can help me with some of the questions I need to ask. One of my jobs is to try and protect children and to prevent such touching from happening again.

CHILD: (Silence)

ADULT: Why don't you draw what happened?

CHILD: (Remains immobile)

ADULT: I'll tell you what—I'll draw a picture of the touching trouble that happened to you and you tell me what to put into the picture.

ADULT: (after a time) I'm so glad you told me about the touching trouble. Could you tell me more so that I know all about it? I would like to make a list of what you tell me because I have a hard time remembering.

Allow the children to use their own words for sexual parts or sexual events and encourage the children to teach you the words they use. Make mistakes so they can correct you, thereby clearly establishing the terms they employ. If the child has no words for parts, teach the correct terminology, but never change the child's terminology. Because others around the child often pressure the child to recant, the child sometimes alters the story to make it sound more believable. This alteration convinces others that the accusations are untrue. Counseling can help prevent such an occurrence. With older children the counselor may say something like:

ADULT: Relationships between fathers and daughters can be close and sometimes this closeness can cause confused feelings. I remember having mixed feelings about my mother, when I was little, wanting to marry her when I grew up. But I get the feeling that—and you can stop me if I'm wrong—that something happened between you and your dad that caused you considerable worry.

Children should also be prepared for the competency phase of the hearing. They can practice answering questions about their home, neighborhood, and school. Children also need to understand the importance of telling the truth, or "what really happened." They can practice describing the difference between the truth, or "what really happened," and a lie, or "what did not happen." Examples from the child's past can be used so that the child can verbalize the difference between past fabrications and past truths.

The meaning of the oath, or a "promise" to tell the truth, also needs to be understood. Children should practice in their own words, conveying their understanding of the meaning of the swearing-in process. In addition, the child should be helped to say, "I don't know," or "I don't understand." Questions can be asked that you know the child cannot answer, followed by instruction in how to put limits on what is known. Children can appear to be lying when they do not understand these limitations.

Keep in mind, however, that an offender has used a variety of techniques to keep the child silent. It is a giant step for the child to tell and one usually taken anxiously. In addition, children often report abuse at a time when they are going through other crises in their lives, and these crises may preoccupy their thoughts more than the abuse.

Consequently, counseling sessions to help the child prepare for court rarely proceed smoothly. Often only a part of a session can be devoted to this topic. Some children's guilt, emotional constriction, fear, concern about their own involvement, and repression prevent active participation in the process. These issues need to be addressed first. An example of such counselor activity appears below. The boy began the session by undressing the adult and child male dolls and positioning them so that the adult was sodomizing the child. Yet he would not talk directly about this experience as having happened to him.

CHILD: There he is, sticking his dick in his butt.

ADULT: I wonder how the boy doll feels about that.

CHILD: He's bad.

ADULT: The man doll is bad or the boy doll is bad?

CHILD: The boy doll.

ADULT: I know some little boys who thought they were bad when that happened to them.

CHILD: They were bad, my mommy said so.

ADULT: So did their mommies, but their mommies meant they were bad if they did this to another boy. They didn't mean they were bad if a grown-up did it to them. They wished they had known how to stop the man, but they didn't. So the boys changed their minds and decided they weren't bad.

CHILD: (Repositions the dolls)

ADULT: These boys kept showing me what happened—how he stuck his dick in their butt and how it hurt, and how they didn't know how to stop him.

CHILD: (Silence)

ADULT: I told the boys that the man who did that was not like other men and that the boys weren't able to stop such a man. This didn't mean that they were bad.

CHILD: Let's play guns.

ADULT: Yeah, let's shoot the man who hurts little boys.

Following a decrease in the boy's presenting symptoms, he was willing to describe the events that led up to his abuse and what the man had said to keep him from revealing the abuse.

Counseling Techniques

The counseling process, whether crisis-oriented or long-term, involves restoring a sense of trust, emotional repair through discussion of the abuse or reenactment via symbolic play, correction of cognitive distortions, an educational component involving making children aware of their own behavior, and developing self-protective behaviors and coping strategies. Other issues include addressing children's expectations that the counselor will not believe them, role boundary confusion, counterphobic seductive behavior, patterns of self-protective compliance, desire to rescue the offender, and the hope that the counselor will protect them from future abuse.

In crisis counseling, effort is directed at marshaling positive forces such as improving the child's relationships and affirming relationships with important caretakers; supporting defenses and mature coping efforts; and encouraging verbalization. Often children cannot verbalize their experience until positive forces have been marshaled and defenses restored.

The counselor must also remember that a child may have resolved problems related to the abuse experience. Consequently, pressures on the child to deal with feelings that are no longer meaningful confuse the child. In other instances, particularly with adolescent girls, encouragement to discuss their abuse can perpetuate a deviant self-image. Often girls who spontaneously talk of their sexual experiences do so to avoid legitimate responsibilities or to provoke shock or rejection. Redirecting them into conversations about more constructive interests and activities can be helpful.

Other counselors, particularly those from deprived backgrounds, want to make up for the pain they believe the child experiences. Overly patronizing attempts to "rescue" children communicate a message that they are helpless and increase their sense of vulnerability. Remember, active effort to persuade a child to accept help can be experienced as "assaultive."

Making Children Aware of Their Own Behavior

The counselor also needs to appreciate the child's need for power and control in most stressful situations. Counselors are cautioned not to attempt to relieve the children's sense of guilt immediately by trying to convince them that they are blameless because they had little power to influence the offender. Actively listen to the child first and you will find that children believe that they played a part in the interaction and that they made some choices and had some power. They do not always feel like victims simply because we would feel like victims in similar circumstances. It has always been poor counseling practice to say to a client, "You shouldn't (didn't need to, don't have to) feel. . . ." The client does not feel understood and resentment builds up. "But I do feel guilty." Children are no exception.

Counselors should take care not to convey victim status to abused children and thereby diminish their feelings of power, feelings that will be important to them in the future. Saying, "It's not your fault," does not address the sense of power and control that some children often feel in addition to their guilt. They feel that they made some choices, no matter how small, that led to a continuation of the abuse. Unfortunately, the children's choices had little positive effect. Secrecy itself is a choice. Some attempt to avoid the abuser rather than tell.

Children will also show their power by attempting to manipulate the counselor. Implicit in such behavior is the expectation that their acts will have an effect on adults. Children need to learn that their acts will have different effects on different adults. They need to learn that some of their choices showed poor judgment not because they were bad but because they had not learned enough to make the best choice in certain situations. The counselor can then help the child to assess which adults in the child's life can offer support and which actions would be beneficial should threatening situations recur. Another example follows:

CHILD: (Dances suggestively around the playroom)

ADULT: Some grown-ups would think you were trying to get them to touch your body when you dance like that.

CHILD: (Dances more vigorously)

ADULT: But others, like myself, would think you were trying to be friendly and would tell you that it's more friendly for you to ask to play a game with them.

Recall the interview with the boy who was sodomized. The counselor did not state that the boy was not to blame for the man's actions but that he was not able to avoid such men. He also did not himself say that the man was bad because abused children often attempt to perform similar acts with other children.

The tendency of children to attempt to master the abuse by abusing others should be explored. This is true for preschoolers on up. For example, adolescent girls should be asked in a tactful and supportive manner if they ever have thoughts about touching or hurting other children, maybe those for whom they baby-sit.

Counseling Magic Years Children

During the magic years, children move through three chief developmental stages. From early positive experiences of caring, infants form an impression of a secure, trustworthy world. Toddlers discover their own bodies and how to control them. When they succeed in doing things for themselves, they gain a sense of self-confidence and self-control. Preschoolers explore beyond themselves and discover how the world works. They also give up longing for the opposite sex parent and identify with the same sex parent. If their explorations, projects, activities, and identifications are generally affective, they gain a strong sense of initiative. Sexual exploitation, particularly if prolonged, can result in problems in any or all of the three stages.

Parents who have been intimately involved in child rearing have loving attachments that diffuse the sexual attraction towards their child. Parents who sexually abuse their child often are those who have been less involved in their care and are less bonded to them.

Prior to the child's victimization, older magic years children may have longed for a close relationship with the distant opposite-sexed parent and this longing remained an unfulfilled wish. When this distant parent, usually the father, turns to the child, the child can eagerly greet such attention. The incestuous activity often begins with massages followed by fondling and progresses to more genitally focused activities. Young children often are simply enticed and coaxed into playing a new and interesting game and are told that all parents play such games with their children. Attention received from the abusing parent can compensate for deprivations experienced from the other parent. Because such children wished for the distant parent's affection, their egocentricity can result in their feeling responsible for the attention that followed.

ADULT: Daddy never played with you much before you and daddy played touching games.

CHILD: (Closely engaged in playing with the dollhouse furniture)

ADULT: I know lots of children who wished their daddies would play with them more. Some of these children also played touching games with their daddies. They also thought that their wishes made daddy play these touching games.

The situation can be quite different, however, with infants and many preschoolers. Often such children are the victims of the sadistic offender who does not differentiate by sex. Male and female preschoolers are equally represented in clinics serving abused children and many are sibling pairs. Such children can develop serious difficulties because neither parent is attached to the child.

Because abusing parents place their needs before their child's, the child experiences them as untrustworthy and generalizes these feelings to others. Such beliefs can be more detrimental to the child's growth than the actual abuse.

Development of self-control can be hampered either by the child's being overstimulated sexually or by the excessive anxiety experienced by those repeatedly abused. Bowel and bladder control may be disrupted and the child can be castigated by both parents for being messy. As a result the child feels shame and self-doubt.

During this stage of development the father's role is to help the child separate from mother by exposing the child to exciting opportunities away from mother's protective arms. If the father is the abuser, then the "exciting opportunities" are conflictual and development is interrupted.

The development of initiative may be delayed if the child feels criticized or is "punished" for regressed behavior following abuse. Frequently, the offender is angered by feeling guilty and remorseful and becomes overly moralistic, to "save the child." The offender then behaves harshly to save the child's soul. The child becomes confused by the harsh manner in which she is treated outside of the sexual situation.

At this state of development, girls become very attached to their fathers, often become rivals of mother for father's attention. If dad is the offender, the child has won the rivalry and identification with mother may not take place. Further hampering identification is the child's belief (often supported by mother's behavior) that mom is mad at her. This failure to identify with mother has long-lasting effects on a young girl's life.

Many offenders against young children bribe the child with attention, affection, or candy and made the situation gamelike. Consequently, the emotional damage may not be substantial when the abuse is by someone outside the immediate family. Counseling should explore whether the child feels bad for getting the offender in trouble. If the sex play proceeds over a long period, however, the child can become excited by sex play and may relate to others in a sexualized manner. This makes the child more vulnerable to abuse by others. Being sexually preoccupied makes concentration difficult and interferes with task mastery. Counselors should focus on educating them about their behavior.

Young children do not understand the meaning of sexual approaches nor are they able to comprehend the sexual nature of the experience, "Daddy peed on me." In early childhood, notions of sexuality have an oral and anal flavor. While many young children believe that babies always existed or are manufactured,[7] some believe that "you get a baby by eating" or that "babies come out like poopies." Even older children hold such beliefs. For example, a seven-year-old Australian girl explained, "The father mixes the seed in the cocoa at night and mom swallows it."[8] Consequently, they interpret their experience in light of these conceptions. If the child has orally stimulated the offender, the child can develop oral fantasies including the fear of being pregnant. Such children can display tremendous excitement at meals and experience eating difficulties.

Fortunately, young children tend to blame others for their misbehavior and are, therefore, less likely to belive the offender's insistence that they are to blame for the abuse. Young children's use of denial, repression, projection, and displacement prevent them from feeling self-accusatory. Perhaps this is why some studies show less emotional difficulties in young abused children.[9]

If children have been forced into sexual activities that hurt them, then they react to the pain inflicted and fear its return. "It hurt my peepee, that makes me mad." Many children are physically injured by abuse.[10,11] Physically injured children display sleep disturbances, nightmares, bodily complaints, restlessness, speech and motor discharge, increased urination, and constant sighing, all signs of heightened anxiety and characteristic of stress reactions. Because young children take things literally, they are more likely to believe and to fear the offender's threats of harm.

Reaffirming Positive Relationships

Since young children hold their parents responsible for any distress they feel, they react to pain with hatred and hostile wishes towards their parents. But because they also love their parents, they experience conflict over expressing their anger.

ADULT: Children I know who have been hurt like you can get mad at their mommies for letting it happen.

CHILD: (Continues to destroy dollhouse in which mommy doll lives)

ADULT: But it's hard to get mad at mommy because mommy also feeds you good food when you're hungry. But I'll bet you'd like to say, "Mommy I hate you because you didn't protect me from that mean man!"

CHILD: (Continues to rebuild house, puts mommy doll aside and destroys house but with less vigor. Child then spanks mommy doll.)

ADULT: Bad mommy for not keeping me safe.

ADULT: (In another session following decreasing signs of anger towards mom) What does your mommy do when you get cut or have a booboo?

CHILD: Puts a Band-Aid on it.

ADULT: Why didn't mommy put a Band-Aid on your weewee when it hurt?

CHILD: (Silence)

ADULT: She might have but she didn't know it hurt until you told her and then she sent you to a doctor to fix it. Mommy can't know you're hurt unless you tell her.

Young children make unique connections between events and may attribute their abuse to something they did or to an unusual happening prior to the abuse. They also can view their abuse as a punishment for something they did, felt, or wished, particularly if warned not to do something by their parents. "Don't talk to strangers." If the child became involved with a stranger as a rebellion against parental demands, self-recrimination can occur.

When the preschool child exhibits little or no manifest distress, repeated probing into the details of the sexual experience should be avoided. Because of their limited understanding of sexual matters, efforts at correcting their misconceptions are futile. Trying to explain to the child that Daddy didn't "pee on" her but ejaculated will fall on deaf ears. Instead, counseling should focus on developing an understanding of when an adult's approaches are inappropriate and when protection should be sought from a responsible adult. When parents perceive themselves as failures (failing to protect the child or to raise the child to avoid such situations), they often respond poorly to their child's needs. Parents should be helped to respond appropriately to the child as their own anxiety may prevent them from providing the calm reassurance the child needs to master the experience. Counselors can refer such parents to a support or treatment group specifically designed to address such concerns.

Education about Their Behavior

When young children show marked changes in behavior following abuse, then structured sessions should be provided where they can play out their concerns. Keep in mind, however, that such children have probably been abused for some time and factors other than the abuse itself will contribute to the child's difficulties. These children are often sexually provocative, climbing on the counselor's lap and attempting to touch the counselor's body. They also experi-

ence the counselor's attempts to instruct them in appropriate behavior as rejections.

CHILD: You don't like me, do you?

ADULT: I like you very much but I don't like it when you touch
my private parts. It's all right to give me a hug but not to touch
me there.

CHILD: Why, my father loves me and he touches me there.

ADULT: And you think I don't like you because I don't want you
to touch my privates?

CHILD: Yes.

ADULT: This touching makes me uncomfortable and makes me
feel that I need to protect my body. It doesn't mean I don't like
you.

Encouraging Verbalization

For less disturbed children, providing appropriate play materials
allows them to work through feelings about the abuse during counseling sessions. One child became so preoccupied playing with an
anatomically correct male doll's penis that she started undressing.
When she became aware of what she was doing she became embarrassed. The counselor responded with "I'm glad you showed me
what happens so that I could learn how scared and excited you
must have been when you were made to do this."

With magic years children, and even with immature middle years
children, the counselor must watch for play behaviors often associated with sexual feelings. Painting, water, sand, and other messy
play can be signs of anal and urethral preoccupations. The building
of tunnels or subway lines can be signs of bodily concerns. Heavily
loaded vehicles can be an expression of pregnancy concerns. Preoccupation with broken toys and missing parts from toys can be
signs of concerns about bodily damage. The more the counselor
knows about the veiled nonverbal communications of children the
easier it is to transform play actions into verbalizations.

CHILD: (Picks up from among the toys a stuffed monkey with a
torn tail and demands that the counselor fix it)

ADULT: I can't fix it now because it needs sewing, but I'll take it
home and sew it. Is there something on your body that might
need fixing also? Some kids think things are wrong with their
penises when they have been touched there a lot.

Emotional Repair

Young children, typically frightened by their experience, use play counseling sessions not only to reenact abuse scenes, but also to regress to an infantile position. They suck on baby bottles, demand to be fed or read to, and become aggressive, requiring the counselor to set limits on their behavior. This behavior represents their simultaneous need to express their anger at not being protected and adequately cared for and to reassure themselves that such care is available. They will display similar behavior at home and their parents will need to understand the reasons for their behavior and how to respond to it.

Group Counseling

Some counselors have employed psychodramatic group play counseling sessions with preschool children, as they feel that the play behavior of one child can serve to stimulate such behavior in another child. Group play thereby facilitates the working-through process that occurs when children master anxiety by playing out experiences. Children reluctant to play out conflict are stimulated to do so by other children's modeling such behavior. Group counseling also helps to affirm and validate the child's experiences.

Middle Years Children

Because middle years children are capable of conceptual thought and are more attuned to their own feelings and to those of others, they can experience internal conflicts. The middle years is a time when one's sense of self is enriched by the development of numerous skills and competences. Comparison with peers is important and a negative evaluation of oneself in comparison to others is particularly damaging at this time. Unlike younger children, middle years youngsters can respond to abuse with internalized anxieties. The anxieties lead to behavioral symptoms such as poor school work or destructive outbursts. Often provocative or seductive behavior is displayed towards male counselors and ongoing belligerent behavior with seductive overtones is displayed towards female counselors. The anger towards females reflects their desire to test the female's strengths—"Can she protect me like my mother couldn't?" The seductive behavior turns to anger and anxiety followed by a need to be taken care of and protected. Unlike younger children, however, they are more conflicted about their dependency needs.

Middle years children jump to conclusions from false premises, displaying concerns such as, "I'd be better off as a boy, and then this couldn't have happened," "Am I still a virgin?" "Have I committed adultery?"

Middle years children also expect happy endings, and since reports of abuse place pronounced stress upon their family, they are disillusioned by the painful realities and family disruption following the report. Because the child reported the abuse, she blames herself for the events that follow. In many families, the blame is reinforced by other family members. "It's your fault daddy's in jail." "It's your fault that Jane and I have to be in this foster home; Daddy never touched us!" Mothers have been known to force their child to visit Daddy in jail to emphasize their blame in Daddy's mistreatment. This often happens in families where the father is the sole wage earner. "I wouldn't have to go to work if Daddy was home." Mother's employment deprives the child of mother's time, and both parents are now unavailable to the child.

If the abuse is by a parent on whom the child depends, the child often takes responsibility for the adult in order to maintain an image of the parent as loving and good. Some do this by convincing themselves that the actions in which they engage are normal. Middle years children also dread that emotions aroused will be endlessly unbearable and self-destructive. They cannot bare the overwhelming anxieties that accompany continued abuse and they take action to ward off the anxiety caused by their reflections about the experience. In an effort to assimilate the experience, they reexperience the act in thought and sometimes reenact the experience with another child. This compulsive repetition alternates with denial—"This can't be happening to me." Eventually this repetition leads to tolerable doses of thought and affect. Crisis counseling can assist the child in this process.

But if the anxiety is too strong, the child has no chance but to repress the experience and numb all feelings. Middle years children, like adolescents, have strong emotions connected to the memory of specific acts, but unlike adolescents they rarely verbalize them.

Other children, particularly those approaching adolescence, may tolerate abuse by a parent in an effort to remain close enough to attempt by love, manipulation, or magic to "cure" the parent. This attempt also enables them to disassociate themselves from the victim position. "I did that," says their memory. "I could not have done that," says their pride, and eventually their memory yields and the experience is repressed. Memory also yields because to admit being abused also is to admit to feeling vulnerable and to the possibility of the abuse's repetition. The counselor will need to verbalize possible feelings the child may have in an effort to get the child to remember the details so that the emotions can be expressed.

ADULT: Most kids I know who were treated like you are mad at themselves for allowing the touching trouble to happen to them.

CHILD: I got mad at myself for not running away.

ADULT: Tell me more about that.

The counselor will need to empathize with the mortification and disillusionment the child feels at being betrayed and seduced. The counselor should express anger if he or she feels it. Experiencing that someone else is mad about what happened to them is helpful to some children.

When counseling middle years children, pay careful attention to veiled communication. For example:

CHILD: Can I put your hair in a bun?

ADULT: You can put it in a ponytail if you want. Who fixes your hair at home? Who washes it?

CHILD: I wash it myself. No one touches my body, just my mother.

ADULT: And your mother can touch it anywhere she wants to?

CHILD: Sometimes, she spanks me on my butt, but not in front of my brother.

What started out as a request to put the counselor's hair in a bun ended up in a discussion of touching, which eventually resulted in revelation of sex play with the brother. Counselors need to keep continually alert for meaning in nonverbal communications and attempt to make them verbal. Sometimes even a child's banging on a table is a message that she has been banged-on and not just a sign of anger.

Middle years children who are incest victims often come to see themselves as damaged and as having the right to demand special attention. These children sometimes employ sickness and help-lessness to solicit sympathy, a symbolic way of receiving the grati-fication they used to receive for feeling special. In some cases, crisis counseling will need to be followed by long-term counseling.

Group Counseling

Group play counseling is useful with middle years children be-cause it helps them to learn that sexual molestation occurs in other families, and that the molestation itself can be an experience that is shared rather than repressed. Seeing others express their feelings can free children to express themselves more fully.

ADULT: In this group you can talk about what happened with your fathers and how you feel about it.

The children selected typically sit in a circle and begin by telling what each thinks the group will be like and something about his or her family. The children can draw pictures of themselves and their families and discuss their drawings. Toys for regressive dependent play should be available as they will often play baby and ask to be rocked, hugged, fed, and cuddled. Role playing of counseling and court sessions is encouraged. A ritualized ending of each session with a circle of held hands or round-robin back rubs is helpful to allow for physical nurturance in nonthreatening, nonsexual ways.[12] Some children, however, should be allowed to sit out from such exercises if they do not want any touch.

Adolescence

In chapter 3, we described adolescents as self-preoccupied, self-critical, sensitive to shame, fearful of social ridicule, unsure of themselves, and dissatisfied with their physical appearance. They can reorganize possibilities as well as actualities and as a result become idealists. They judge their own behavior in terms of sexual normalcy and abnormalcy. The adolescent seeks basic values and attitudes that cut across the various roles they are called upon to play and that can be integrated into a consistent identity. In late adolescence, the chief task is to establish intimacy with others without fear of losing one's own identity. Sexual abuse not only seriously interferes with this task but also contributes to a sense of disillusionment and alienation.

Because of their newly found cognitive skills, adolescents look back at themselves as children and perceive themselves as having the same cognitive, emotional, and physical abilities they have in the present. If the abuse occurred when they were younger, and particularly if it was ongoing, they often berate themselves for not having stopped it. They hate themselves for giving in. "I should have thrown him out of my room," "I should have put a lock on my door," "I should have called the police," "I should not have worn that nightgown."

ADOLESCENT: I hate myself for letting him take me into the basement—I should have stopped him.

ADULT: You might have stopped him had you been as big as you are now.

Adolescents subject to incest are angry at mother who should have known what was going on, should have protected them, and should have had better sex with dad. They may feel guilty because mother is jealous of their special relationship with father. Frequently, the adolescent girl has taken on aspects of mother's role and resents mother for burdening her with these responsibilities. "She made me into daddy's partner."

Adolescents with no sexual experiences prior to the abuse are violently forced to confront sexual feelings without adequate emotional preparation. Because of discomfort and shame, mixed with sexuality, the girl can develop doubts about her own sexuality. In addition, inhibition of sexual arousal is the way most girls handle the incestual situation. "I took my body out of the experience." "I wasn't really there." Nevertheless, strong incest imagery and sexuality are associated. "I keep seeing my father doing that." When sexual feelings occur in the context of heterosexual relationships, these strong images interfere with the girl's responsiveness. Practiced at cutting off feelings, feelings are cut off when it is not appropriate to do so, causing girls to doubt their own sexuality. Added to these doubts is self-hate and disgust for allowing themselves to be abused. "I felt tarnished and dirty—I get depressed just talking about it." "Feeling you have no control over your body is humiliating." "I feel disgusting, so I must look disgusting." "I'll never have a normal life." "What if my boyfriend finds out?"

Adolescents abused over long periods cannot describe themselves objectively and resist looking at themselves in mirrors or photographs. Many of these youngsters display reaction formations against sexual excitement. They lock themselves in their rooms or yell that others are looking at them.

Other girls display a pseudomaturity, superimposed over child-like wishes and fantasies. "Even when I'm thirty-four and he gets out of jail, he's taking me to Disney Land!" The pseudomaturity results from a desire to grow up fast, in order to avoid the helplessness associated with the ongoing abuse. When adolescents finally reveal long-standing abuse, their report often results from new sexual stirrings and preoccupations characteristic of this stage.

Adolescent victims are more in touch with their own sexuality and can have very conflicted feelings about their bodies being sexually responsive and enjoying the touch. This should be pointed out to them early in counseling.

ADULT: A lot of girls are afraid to talk about any part of the touching that may have felt good. When they do tell me this I always say, "That's great, it means your body is working the way it's supposed to," and I tell them they will probably have a lot of confused feelings about this once we begin to discuss it.

Adolescents are more likely to identify with the offender because of their awareness that such people are "sick" and need help. This identity prevents them from fully expressing their anger at the offender. They also are prone to flashbacks and pseudohallucinations, sometimes hearing the offender condemn them for sending him to prison. They experience recurrent obsessive ideas, repetitive dreams, place themselves in degrading situations out of shame for what they feel they did, or attempt suicide.

The incest victim who denigrates and abuses herself or attempts suicide is more likely to use denial and introjection (taking on another's belief) as defense against the anxiety resulting from the abuse. She will take longer to report the ongoing abuse because she values family loyalty, believes that what dad did was OK, and blames herself for the abuse.

Careful Encouragement of Verbalization

Counseling abused adolescents is difficult for several reasons. Adolescents frequently experience the mildest discussions of sex as seductive, sometimes even when the counselor is female. Because they strongly experience feelings, they more actively resist resurrection of the feelings felt during their abuse. Their denials serve to ward off overwhelming feelings and are therefore healthy defenses. Denial allows the adolescent to control strong emotions. The counselor's job is to induce thoughts that are not overwhelming so that the adolescent can discuss aspects of the experience under tolerable doses of stress. The counselor will need to dampen rapid expression of feeling as it can result in a retreat from counseling.

> ADULT: These things are of great importance and in time they will be fully discussed, but for the moment I think it is best to talk more about things that bother you at school, or perhaps you can tell me more about what you like to do.

Emotional expression is therapeutic only when it is integrated and understood; if it leads to disorganization, the counselor must help the adolescent to control such expression. The counselor can help by frequent subject changes and by bringing up material the adolescent already uses defensively. For example, if you note that when strong emotions are aroused the adolescent changes the topic to a consuming interest, the counselor can spontaneously switch to this topic when the adolescent is about to lose control over her feelings. Adolescents also have strong emotions tied up in specific memories of specific acts, but they can verbalize them better than can younger children.

> ADOLESCENT: I hated it when father paraded me in front of his poker buddies and they all patted my rear and pinched my chin and said "gichi-goo!"
>
> ADULT: You felt so helpless—I'll bet you wished you could have killed them all.

Reinforcing Defenses

Remember that crisis counselors should conceive of defensive behaviors as adaptive efforts. Pseudomature behavior should be interpreted as providing strength to endure, denial of parental wrongdoing conceived of as an effort to protect the parents, self-hurt viewed as making up for hurts they feel they caused others, and the responsibility toward the offender seen as a positive quality that can be expressed constructively. Help the adolescent to develop a more positive self-image through encouragement to undertake activities of an altruistic nature. Showing concern for others often resolves guilt better than endless discussions. Those dressing provocatively can be directed into more normal exhibitionistic activities, such as modern dance or school plays.

Group counseling can be employed with adolescents and can be the crisis treatment of choice for many. Since kind words and touching are associated with some sexual assaults, individual counseling sessions can be fearful. Group counseling provides a setting where the adolescent is not constantly the focus of attention and where emotional support and physical contact are not threatening.

Suggested Reading for Children

Adams, L., Fay, J., and Loren-Martin, J. *No Is Not Enough.* Palto Alto, Calif.: Impact Publishers, 1984. (adolescents—avoiding acquaintance rape, peer pressure)

Bassett, K. *My Own Very Special Body Book.* Redding, Calif.: Hawthorne Press, 1983. (preschool children)

Brady, K. *Father's Days.* New York: Dell Publishing, 1979. (adolescents)

Gill, E. *Outgrowing the Pain.* San Francisco: Launch Press, 1983. (adolescents)

Hindman, J. *A Touching Book.* Durke, Oreg.: McClure-Hindman Books, 1983. (latency age)

Krause, E. *For Pete's Sake Tell.* Oregon City, Oreg.: Krause House, 1983. (latency-age males)

Krause, E. *Speak Up, Say No!* Oregon City, Oreg.: Krause House, 1983. (latency-age females)

Mackey, G., and Swan, H. *Dear Elizabeth.* Leawood, Kans.: Children's Institute of Kansas City, n.d. (adolescents)

Terkel, S., and Rench, J. E. *Feeling Safe, Feeling Strong.* Minneapolis, Minn.: Lerner Publications, 1984. (latency age)

Wachter, O. *No More Secrets for Me.* Boston: Little, Brown and Company, 1983. (latency age)

· 14 ·

Love, and Do
What You Will

We conclude *Crisis Counseling with Children and Adolescents* by suggesting that you work in the spirit of our approach, and regard our recommendations not as a collection of ironclad procedures and techniques, but rather as ways to develop, affirm, and refine your own natural style of being empathic. We gave practical approaches, but have probably left out other outlooks. Generally speaking, caring, spontaneous responses to troubled children will be the most effective.

Be open. Learn more about children and the ways to work with them. Many adults resist further training—"I *care* about Bobby. That's what counts." Caring is essential, but caring without reflection or continuing education and training may meet the adult's needs more than the child's. Similarly, proven practical approaches, swiftly and mechanically applied without a sensitive human touch, will do little good.

"Love, and do what you will." The words of St. Augustine. If you love, you can make a heartfelt response and will be driven in your concern to keep trying. Genuine love is humble and giving and holds the best interest of the other first. If you truly love, you will seldom go wrong. You will be led in the right direction to seek advice, to be flexible, to approach the child with a problem from different angles until you finally find a way to help.

John was constantly badgered by the school bully. He would push John around in the halls, insult him in class, pester him on the playground, and in general make life miserable for John. This treatment was highly unfair to John, who is personable, a good student, and a helper to classmates and teachers. John suffered the bully's torments stoically. Although it was a great burden, he never complained, until one day the ultimate indignity occurred: the bully followed John into the washroom and shoved his head in the toilet.

John cried to his father that evening. Should his father call the principal and demand disciplinary action? Should a firm stand be taken, once and for all, against the bully's intolerable behavior? Should John's older brother beat up the bully?

John's father surprised everyone: he invited the bully to John's birthday party the next week. He explained to John that bullies usually have no friends and don't know how to make them. Said John's father, "And they try to make friends in the wrong way. Soon nobody likes them. Then they act worse. Our job is to help this bully learn how to make friends the right way." He was right. The bully soon became friends with John, and there was no need to administer punishment.

Once, in a day treatment center, an angry six-year-old whose mother had stormed in the previous day and threatened the staff, demanded to call her mother. She refused to respond to questioning and insisted on calling. The adult replied that there was a pay phone across the street where she could call her mother and that he'd give her a dime. The angry child looked on as the adult searched his pockets for a dime. Coming up empty, he said, "I'm sorry, Janie, I don't have a dime." The child stormed back to class saying angrily, "I can't call my mother; Dr. Frank doesn't have a dime." Only God knows why that worked.

Floyd Patterson, former world heavyweight champion, grew up in poverty and later attended a residential school for defiant youngsters. His life was headed in the wrong direction. Every Friday in school his teacher held a contest: Students who could answer certain questions would win a prize. On the toughest question, for the best prize, Floyd Patterson knew the answer. But he didn't raise his hand. He was afraid that if he was wrong, the class would taunt him, and he couldn't take that risk.

Nobody in the class knew the answer, and the prize went unclaimed. Furious at himself, young Floyd stormed out of the class, slamming the door. His teacher caught up with him, and calmly said, "Floyd, I know you knew the answer. Here's the prize—you've won it." Looking back, Floyd Patterson felt this occasion changed his life. It was the first time he had experienced such care and trust. His teacher had realized that teaching is more than strategy, content, and limit setting; she was open to an opportunity to reach Floyd and seized the moment when it arrived. No book or consultant could have suggested how she should act.

When working with children, there's always a surprise—some unexpected way in which adults can show their love, and that makes an enormous difference. Love, and do what you will.

NOTES

Chapter One

1. C. Winnicott, "Face to Face with Children," *Social Work Today* 8 (1977): 7–11.
2. J. Isherwood, K. S. Adams, A. R. Hornblow, and A. R. Lifte, "Life Event Stress, Psychological Factors, Suicide Attempt, and Auto-Accident Proclivity," *Journal of Psychosomatic Research* 26 (1982): 371–83.
3. S. H. Ackerman, S. Manaker, and M. Cohen, "Recent Separation and the Onset of Peptic Ulcer Disease in Older Children and Adolescents," *Psychosomatic Medicine* 43 (1981): 305–10.
4. M. E. Seligman, *Helplessness* (San Francisco: W. H. Freeman, 1975).
5. W. Ehrhardt, EST training workshops.
6. S. Fraiberg, "Some Aspects of Casework with Children. I: Understanding the Child Client," *Social Casework* 33 (1952).
7. A. Buchanan and A. Webster, "Bedtime without Battles," *British Journal of Social Work* 12 (1982): 197–204.
8. J. Mordock and D. Phillips, "The Behavior Therapist in the Schools," *Psychotherapy: Theory, Research, and Practice* 8 (1971): 231–35; and D. Phillips and J. Mordock, "Behavior Therapy with Children: Some General Guidelines and Specific Suggestions," paper presented at the annual convention of the American Association of Psychiatric Services for Children, Philadelphia, November 1970.

Chapter Two

1. S. Fraiberg, *The Magic Years—Understanding and Handling the Problems of Early Childhood* (New York: Charles Scribners, 1959).
2. H. Ginsberg and S. Opper, *Piaget's Theory of Intellectual Development,* 2nd ed. (Englewood Cliffs, New Jersey: Prentice-Hall, 1979).
3. Ibid.
4. W. Labov, *Language in the Inner City* (Philadelphia: University of Pennsylvania Press, 1972).
5. H. Ginsberg and S. Opper, op. cit.
6. R. P. Hobson, "The Question of Childhood Egocentrism: The Coordination of Perspectives in Relation to Operational Thinking," *Journal of Child Psychology and Psychiatry* 23 (1982): 43–60.
7. A. N. Applebee, *The Child's Conception of Story* (Chicago: University of Chicago Press, 1978).

8. E. J. Robinson, "Conversational Tactics and the Advancement of the Child's Under-standing about Referential Communication," in *Communication in Development*, W. P. Robinson, ed., European Monographs in Social Psychology 14 (London: Academic Press).
9. C. Sarnoff, *Latency* (New York: Jason Aronson, 1976), p. 3.
10. Ibid., p. 153.
11. E. Markman, "Realizing That You Don't Understand: Elementary School Children's Awareness of Inconsistencies," *Child Development* 50 (1979): 645–46.

Chapter Three

1. B. Elkind, "Egocentrism and Adolescence," *Child Development* 38 (1965): 1025–34.
2. A. Frazier and L. Lisbondee, "Adolescent Concerns with Physique," *School Review* 58 (1950): 397–405.
3. J. H. Bamberg, "Adolescent Marginality—A Further Study," *Genetic Psychology Monographs* 88 (1973): 3–21.
4. J. Kitwood, *Disclosures to a Stranger: Adolescent Values in an Advanced Industrial Society* (London: Routledge and Kegan Paul, 1980).
5. R. A. Gardner, *Psychotherapeutic Approaches to the Resistant Child* (New York: Jason Aronson, 1975).
6. Ibid., p. 62.
7. For an excellent treatment on appropriate self-disclosure, see G. Egan, *The Skilled Helper* (Monterey, Calif.: Brooks/Cole, 1975).
8. T. J. Tuzil, "Writing: A Problem-Solving Process," *Social Work* 23 (1978): 63–70.
9. R. R. Ross and H. B. McKay, *Self-Mutilation* (Lexington, Mass.: Lexington Books, 1979).
10. Ibid.

Chapter Four

1. C. Rogers, *A Way of Being* (Boston: Houghton-Mifflin, 1980).
2. Ibid.
3. Ibid., p. 151.
4. D. Aspy and F. Roebuck, "From Humane Ideas to Humane Technology and Back Again, Many Times," *Education* 95 (1974): 163–171.
5. N. Raskin, "Studies on Psychotherapeutic Orientation: Ideology in Practice," *AAP Psychotherapy Monographs* (Orlando, Fla.: American Academy of Psychotherapists, 1974).
6. T. Gordon, *Parent Effectiveness Training* (New York: Peter Wyden, 1970), p. 53.
7. Ibid.
8. Ibid.
9. J. Piaget, *Judgment and Reasoning in the Child* (New York: Harcourt Brace, 1928), p. 8.
10. B. Bandler, "The Concept of Ego-Supportive Psychotherapy," in H. J. Parad and R. Muller, eds., *Ego-Oriented Case Work: Problems and Perceptions* (New York: Family Service Association of America, 1963).
11. C. Donnelly, "Active Development of the Positive Introject in Severely Disturbed Patients," *British Journal of Medical Psychology* 53 (1980): 307–12.

Chapter Five

1. S. Ramos, "Learning about Death: The Hardest Lesson of All," *New York Times Magazine,* 10 December 1972.
2. C. Rosenblum, "What to Say When a Parent Dies," *New York Daily News,* 14 November 1976.

3. S. Ramos, op. cit.
4. C. Rosenblum, op. cit.
5. Ibid.
6. D. Gross, "Child Care Worker's Response to the Death of a Child," *Child Care Quarterly* 8 (1979): 59–66.
7. Ibid.
8. E. Lindemann, "Symptomatology and Management of Acute Grief," *American Journal of Psychiatry* 101 (1944): 141–48.
9. E. Kübler-Ross, "The Searching Mind," *Today's Education* 61 (1972): 31.
10. J. M. Lewis, "Dying with Friends: Implications for the Psychotherapist," *American Journal of Psychiatry* 139 (1982): 261–66.
11. E. Kübler-Ross, *Living with Death and Dying* (New York: Macmillan, 1981).
12. Ibid., p. 43.
13. G. P. Koocher, "Why Isn't the Gerbil Moving Anymore? Discussing Death in the Classroom and at Home," *Children Today* (1975): 18–21.
14. S. Ramos, op. cit.
15. G. P. Koocher, op. cit.
16. J. R. Hawkinson, "Teaching About Death," *Today's Education* 65 (1976): 41–42.
17. D. Gross, op. cit.

Chapter Six

1. J. S. Wallerstein and J. B. Kelly, *Surviving the Breakup: How Children and Parents Cope with Divorce* (New York: Basic Books, 1980).
2. Ibid.
3. Ibid.
4. Ibid.
5. Ibid.
6. J. S. Wallerstein and J. B. Kelly, "The Effects of Parental Divorce: The Adolescent Experience," in E. J. Anthony and C. Koupernik, eds., *The Child in His Family: Children at Psychiatric Risk* (New York: John Wiley & Sons, 1974).
7. Ibid.
8. Ibid.
9. P. Skeen and P. McKenry, "The Teacher's Role in Facilitating a Child's Adjustment to Divorce," *Young Children* 35 (1980): 3–12.
10. R. D. Allers, "Helping Children Understand Divorce," *Today's Education* 69 (1980): 26–29.
11. P. Skeen and P. McKenry, op. cit.

Chapter Seven

1. M. A. Sarvis, "Psychiatric Implications of Temporal Lobe Damage," *Psychoanalytic Study of the Child* 11 (1960): 352–80 in R. S. Eissler et. al, eds., *Physical Illness and Handicaps in Childhood* (New Haven: Yale University Press, 1977), p. 258.
2. C. Pochedly, "Sickle Cell Anemia: Recognition and Management," *American Journal of Nursing* 71 (1971): 1948–51.
3. J. D. Watkins, D. E. Roberts, T. F. Williams, D. A. Martin, and V. Cole, "Observations of Medical Errors Made by Diabetic Patients in the Home," *Diabetes* 16 (1967): 882–85.
4. R. H. Haslam and P. J. Vallantutti, eds., *Medical Problems in the Classroom* (Baltimore: University Park Press, 1975).
5. G. L. Freeman and S. Johnson, "Allergic Diseases in Adolescence. II, Changes in Allergic Manifestations During Adolescence," *American Journal of Diseases in Children* 107 (1964): 560–66.
6. K. Reif, "A Heart Makes You Live," *American Journal of Nursing* 72 (1972): 1085.

7. C. A. Neill, "The Cardiac Child and His Family," in M. Debuskey and R. Dombro, *The Chronically Ill Child and His Family* (Springfield, Ill.: Charles C. Thomas, 1970) pp. 33–52.
8. *Help Yourself: Tips for Teenagers with Cancer* (Office of Cancer Communications, National Cancer Institute, in conjunction with Adria Laboratories, Columbus, Ohio, 1982).
9. J. D. Nilsen, "Nursing Care in Childhood Cancer: Adolescence," *American Journal of Nursing* 82 (1982): 436–39.
10. Ibid.
11. Anton Chekhov in *The Cook's Wedding and Other Stories,* quoted in N. J. Long, W. C. Morse, and R. Newman, *Conflict in the Classroom: The Education of Children with Problems* (Belmont, Calif.: Wadsworth, 1976), p. 9.
12. J. Robertson, *Young Children in Hospitals,* 2nd ed. (London: Tavistock, 1970).
13. E. H. Waechter, "Children's Awareness of Fatal Illness," *American Journal of Nursing* 71 (1971): 1168–72.
14. Ibid.
15. Ibid.
16. A. T. Sigler, "The Leukemic Child and His Family: An Emotional Challenge," in M. Debuskey and R. Dombro, *The Chronically Ill Child,* pp. 53–60.
17. The discussion of defense mechanisms in hospitalized adolescents is based on A. Hoffman, R. Becker, and H. Gabriel, *The Hospitalized Adolescent* (New York: The Free Press, 1976).
18. Ibid.

Chapter Eight

1. W. Somerset Maugham in *Of Human Bondage,* quoted in N. J. Long, W. C. Morse, and R. Newman, *Conflict in the Classroom: The Education of Children with Problems* (Belmont, Calif.: Wadsworth, 1976), p. 30.
2. From personal communication with David Shaw, social worker, Children's Rehabilitation Center, Kingston, New York.
3. N. J. Long et al., op. cit.
4. *Inside Education* (Albany: New York State Education Department, 1981).
5. For further discussion see S. Fraiberg, "The Origins of Identity," *Smith College Studies in Social Work* 38 (1968): 79–101; and J. B. Mordock, "The Separation-Individuation Process and Developmental Disabilities," *Exceptional Children* 46 (1979): 176–85.
6. H. Viscard, Jr., *A Man's Stature* (New York: John Day, 1952).
7. K. Ohnsted, *The World at My Fingertips* (New York: Dobbs-Merrill, 1942).
8. R. Goldman, *Even the Night* (New York: Macmillan, 1947).
9. B. A. Wright, *Physical Disability and Psychological Approach* (New York: Harper & Row, 1960).
10. Ibid.
11. D. Elkind, "Egocentrism and Adolescence," *Child Development* 38 (1965): 1026–34.
12. S. Gordon, *Living Fully: A Guide for Young People with a Handicap, Their Parents, Their Families, and Professionals* (New York: John Jay, 1975).
13. Ibid.
14. B. A. Wright, op. cit., p. 249.
15. M. Killilea, *Karen* (Englewood Cliffs, N.J.: Prentice-Hall, 1952), p. 111.

Chapter Nine

1. K. C. Faller, M. Ziefert, and C. Jones, "Treatment Planning, Process, and Progress," in K. C. Faller, ed., *Social Work with Abused and Neglected Children: A Manual of Interdisciplinary Practice* (New York: The Free Press, 1981).

2. G. J. Williams and J. Money, eds., *Traumatic Abuse and Neglect of Children at Home* (Baltimore: Johns Hopkins University Press, 1980).
3. R. Geiser, *The Illusion of Caring; Children in Foster Care* (Boston: Beacon-Press, 1973).
4. R. E. Helfer and C. H. Kempe, *The Battered Child* (Chicago: University of Chicago Press, 1968).
5. M. J. Paulson and A. Chaleff, "Parent Surrogate Roles: A Dynamic Concept in Understanding and Treating Abusive Parents," *Journal of Child Clinical Psychology* 2 (1973): 38–40.
6. J. Reed, "Working with Abusive Parents: A Parent's View. An interview with Jolly K," *Children Today* 4 (1975): 6–9.

Chapter Ten

1. R. L. Geiser, *The Illusion of Caring: Children in Foster Care* (Boston: Beacon Press, 1973).
2. Ibid., p. 39.
3. Ibid., p. 35.
4. Ibid.
5. Ibid.
6. Ibid., p. 42.
7. Ibid.
8. Ibid., pp. 79–80.
9. Ibid., p. 76.

Chapter Eleven

1. C. H. King, "Countertransference and Counterexperience in the Treatment of Violence-Prone Youth," *American Journal of Orthopsychiatry* 46 (1976): 43–52.
2. T. Gordon, *Parent Effectiveness Training* (New York: Peter Wyden, 1970).
3. K. A. Dodge, "Social Cognition and Children's Aggressive Behavior," *Child Development* 51 (1980): 162–70.
4. L. Berkowitz, "Is Criminal Violence Normative Behavior? Hostile and Instrumental Aggression in Violent Incidents," *The Journal of Research in Crime and Delinquency* 15 (1978).
5. From interview with Ellie Isaac, assistant supervisor of child care, The Astor Home for Children, Rhinebeck, New York.
6. S. Sheehan, *Is There No Place on Earth for Me?* (New York: Houghton Mifflin, 1982).
7. C. H. King, op. cit.
8. The Crisis Prevention Institute, 3575 North Oakland Avenue, Milwaukee, Wisconsin 53211, offers excellent training programs in "Nonviolent Management of Disruptive, Assaultive, or Out of Control Behavior."
9. P. Bakker, *Ciske, the Rat,* quoted in N. J. Long, W. C. Morse, and R. Newman, eds., *Conflict in the Classroom: The Education of Children with Problems* (Belmont, Calif.: Wadsworth, 1971), pp. 77–83.

Chapter Twelve

1. Timmon Cermak, *A Time to Heal* (New York: St. Martin's Press, 1988).
2. National Council on Alcoholism, "Facts on Alcoholism and Alcohol-related Problems" (Washington, DC: US Government Printing Office, 1985).
3. Ibid.
4. Ibid.
5. This is taken from Alateen, "Hope for Children of Alcoholics" (New York: Al-Anon Family Group Headquarters, Inc., 1973).

Chapter Thirteen

1. A. W. Burgess and L. L. Holstrom, "Victims of Sexual Assault," In A Lazare, ed., *Outpatient Psychiatry, Diagnosis, and Treatment* (Baltimore: Williams and Wilkins, 1979).
2. J. Weiss, R. Estelle, M. Darwin, and C. E. Dutton, "A Study of Girl Sex Victims," *Psychiatric Quarterly* 29 (1955): 1–27.
3. C. Adams-Tucker, "Defensive Mechanism Used by Sexually Abused Children," *Children Today* 14 (1985): pp. 9–12, p. 34.
4. R. Fliess, *Symbol, Dream, and Psychosis* (New York: International Universities Press, 1973), p. 212.
5. J. Hindman, *Step by Step: Sixteen Steps Toward Legally Sound Abuse Investigations* (Ontario, Oreg.: Alexandria Associates, 1987).
6. S. White, G. Strom, and G. Santilli, "A Protocol for Interviewing Preschoolers with the Sexually Anatomically Correct Dolls," Unpublished manuscript, Case Western Reserve University School of Medicine, Cleveland, Ohio (1985).
7. A. C. Berstein, "How Children Learn about Sex and Birth," *Psychology Today* 10 (1976): pp. 31–35, p. 66.
8. R. Goldman and J. Goldman, *Children's Sexual Thinking* (London: Routledge and Kegan Paul, 1982).
9. A. Brown and D. Finkelhor, "Impact of Child Sexual Abuse: A Review of the Research," *Psychological Bulletin* 99 (1986): pp. 66–77.
10. N. S. Ellerstein and W. Canavan, "Sexual Abuse of Boys," *American Journal of Diseases of Children* 134 (1980): 255–57.
11. B. A. Woodling, "Sexual Abuse and the Child," *Emergency Medical Services* 15 (1986): pp. 17–25.
12. N. Delson and M. Clark, "Group Therapy with Sexually Molested Children," *Child Welfare* 60 (1981): pp. 175–82.